CUCHAMA

and Sacred Mountains

G. Warrington Bass
'56

CUCHAMA

and Sacred Mountains

W. Y. Evans-Wentz

Edited by Frank Waters
and Charles L. Adams

SWALLOW PRESS
Chicago

Other Books by W. Y. Evans-Wentz

The Fairy Faith in Celtic Countries
The Tibetan Book of the Dead
Tibet's Great Yogi Milarepa
Tibetan Yoga and Secret Doctrines
The Tibetan Book of the Great Liberation

Library of Congress Cataloging in Publication Data

Evans, Wentz, W. Y. (Walter Yeeling), 1878-1965
  Cuchama and sacred mountains

  Bibliography: p.
  Includes index.
  1. Indians of North America—Religion and
mythology. 2. Tecate Peak (Calif.) 3. Indians of North America—California—
Religion and mythology
4. Mountains (in religion, folk-lore, etc.)
I. Waters, Frank, 1902-   . II. Adams, Charles L.
III. Title.
E98.R3E77 1981   299'.7   81-8749
ISBN 0-8040-0411-0   AACR2

Swallow Press Books
are published by
Ohio University Press
Athens, Ohio

Dedicated
to
the Children of
the Great Mystery
throughout all the Americas
who are nurtured by
Father Sun and Mother Earth
and taught by
The Shining Beings

CONTENTS

PART III

THE MARTYRDOM AND RELIGION OF THE RED MEN 85

PART IV

ADDENDA

PREFACE

It is an interesting phenomenon of our utilitarian age that more and more scientists, as well as laymen, have become interested in, and sometimes hypnotically fascinated by, the world's high mountains, most of which are sacred mountains. As evidence of this accelerated interest, new books about mountains are continually appearing.

And this is heartening, symbolizing, as it does, man's eternal quest. There is more to climbing a "celestial" mountain than conquering perpendicular footage. Upon returning, men report having found a true peace of mind on Sacred High Places, sometimes akin to that of a spiritual initiation.

There is, in fact, an ever-growing cult of Sacred Mountains. Young men visiting Japan have always yearned to climb Mt. Fujiyama as on a sort of personal pilgrimage, and they bring back more than the stout notched stick, souvenir of the mountain climber. A modern pilgrim might well girdle the earth on a sacred-mountain quest. Such a seeker would be rewarded with a spiritual exaltation that would alter his material destiny.

It is not commonly known that throughout our own Americas there are a number of sacred mountains with a spiritual history apparently as ancient as that of the continent's primordial inhabitants.

When a young man, I was something of a pilgrim myself, sojourning in India and Tibet, and especially in Sikkim, where, guided by my guru, the Lama Kazi Dawa-Samdup, I assisted in the translation of various Tibetan texts, including the *Bardo Thodol,* or *Tibetan Book of the Dead.*

After visiting many of the sacred mountain regions of Asia, and researching others of our planet, I present herein, for comparative study, an ethnic and psychic account of our Sacred Mountain Cuchama in San Diego County, California, on the Mexican border, an easily accessible "retreat." Known on the map as Mt. Tecate, its Indian name is Cuchama (pronounced Coo-cha-ma), and its inspiring tradition is worth perpetuating. Long known as a true Sacred Mountain, and used as a center of restorative pilgrimage by our American Red Men, Cuchama is destined to become once more a spiritual shrine of a renascent America in the century that lies ahead.

Anthropology has shown that the understanding of one race of mankind, no matter how isolated geographically, is dependent upon a comparative study of many races. Accordingly, in order to understand Cuchama rightly, it is necessary to understand the cultural and psychological significance of High Places in lands far apart and among various peoples.

In my research towards this purpose, I am particularly indebted, among scientists, to Dr. John P. Harrington, of the Bureau of American Ethnology, Washington, D.C., who aided me in problems of ethnology and philology; and also to Mr. Alan J. Stover, formerly Professor of Botany in Theosophical University, Covina, California, who accompanied me to Mt. Cuchama and explained its remarkable geological and botanical history.

As to the shaping of the text, the assistance of Dr. John R. Theobald, Professor of English, in the San Diego State College, and author of *The Earthquake And Other Poems* and *Introducing Poetry,* has been of paramount importance. I am similarly indebted to John and Winifred Davidson, our San Diego historians, for having critically and constructively read this book.

Mr. G. Warrington Bass, artist and painter of religious and mystical subjects, of Los Angeles, who has done much archaeological research in Yucatan, is to be credited with the designing of the frontispiece and of the very appropriate emblems which appear on the cover of this volume, and also for preparing the map showing the geographical position of Cuchama.

I am under grateful obligation to Mr. Frank Waters, not only for the invaluable assistance of his *Masked Gods,* but also for his having obtained from the Museum of Navajo Ceremonial Art in Santa Fe, New Mexico, a photographic copy of each of the two sand-painting designs of the sacred mountains of the Navajos, and for his aid in preparing the explanation of the designs herein set forth. To the curator of the Museum, Mr. Lloyd Moylan, credit is due for permission to reproduce and publish the designs.

To Mr. Charles M. Russell, the illustrious depictor of American Indian life, I am indebted for permission to reproduce herein his painting entitled "The Medicine-Man."

To Dr. Framroze A. Bode, high priest of the Parsi community of Bombay, India, I am indebted for the little-known matter from original source set forth in Section IX of Part II, entitled "Sacred Mountains of Zoroastrianism." To Lic. Mario Somohano Flores, adviser in international law, Tijuana, Mexico, formerly a member of the faculty of the Yucatan State University, I am indebted for assistance touching philological and ethnological problems relating chiefly to Baja California.

I am especially grateful both to Lama Anagarika Govinda, for the very appropriate Foreword, and to the Maha Bodhi Society of India, for permission to publish herein copious extracts from the notable article entitled "The Mystic *Mandala* of Kailas and Its Sacred Lakes," by the Lama A. Govinda, in the Tibet and Sikkim Number of *The Maha-Bodhi,* Calcutta, July, 1951. To Lama Govinda, the Himalayas, especially Mt. Kailas, where he has been on pilgrimage, have been for many years a source of unceasing inspiration. To him and to Li Gotami, his companion in cultural research, I am additionally indebted for the two photographic reproductions of their paintings of Mt. Kailas upon which the illustrations herein are based.

To Mrs. Ruth Verrill (Wah-nona), of Tuscarora and Wabenaki lineage, member of the League of North American Indians, and recipient, in 1954, of the League's highest award, the Eagle Merit Award, whose critical reading of this study led to its improvement, I am much indebted, as I also am to the writings of her husband, Mr. A. Hyatt Verrill.

Among others who have assisted, with books and suggestions, in the making of this volume, I am debtor especially to Mr. Theodor Reich of San Francisco, to Mrs. Dorothy A. Friend of San Diego, and to Mr. Louis Blevins of the Self-Realization Fellowship, Encinitas, California. And finally to Helen Eva Yates, author of *Bali, Enchanted Isle,* and other books on Asian subjects, for editorial suggestions.

May this volume, dedicated to the Children of the Great Mystery, like the four volumes setting forth the results of my Tibetan studies, serve as one more bond of Right Understanding between East and West. May it help to show that the Red Men of our Americas are also co-sharers in the High Culture of which Asia, since immemorial time, has been the chief custodian.

W. Y. Evans-Wentz
San Diego, California

DESCRIPTION OF ILLUSTRATIONS

Made on the second day of the Shooting-Chant: Male Branch Ceremony *(Nahtohe Baka)*. The Medicine-Man, or Singer, was Lukai Yazhi, or "Blue Eyes." The sand-painting was copied by Mrs. F. L. Newcomb, of the old Newcomb Trading Post, at Newcomb, New Mexico, sometime before the year 1933. The sand-painting shows a circle of Central Water surrounded by four ovals (the Four Sacred Mountains in directional colors) in the form of a lotus, with dragonflies resting upon the ovals. At the four cardinal points stand four Holy People. Between them are four buffalo with their paths, the paths being shown by lines leading to the Central Water. Their breath of life is shown by lines leading from their hearts and out through their mouths. Medicine-wands, or feathered prayer-sticks, are implanted in their hearts. A mist-rainbow with feathers attached to it surrounds the symbolic design, and each of its two entrances is guarded by a buffalo.

Sand-Painting of the Four Sacred Directional Mountains of the Navahos   p.76

Made on the second day of the Shooting-Chant: Big-House Form *(Nahtohe Kin-Be-Hatral)*. Again, the Singer was "Blue Eyes." It was copied by Mrs. Newcomb in the year 1932. The sand-painting depicts four buffalo, with masked heads, each carrying, suspended from a cord, a small swastika-shaped circle, symbolical of their magical means of swift travelling. In the center is the Central Water with dragonflies resting on the lotus-shaped four oval symbols of the Four Sacred Directional Mountains, between which radiate the four holy plants growing from the Central Water. Surrounding the whole is a feathered mist-rainbow, with a buffalo guardian at each of the two entrances on the East.

Frank Waters, to whom the writer is indebted for the photographs of these sand-paintings, explains that all such sand-paintings are "owned" by the Singer or medicine-man who conducts the "sings," or ceremonies for which the sand-paintings are prepared. "The sand-paintings are committed to memory, never recorded, and are handed down only to initiates who are in training to become Singers themselves. The sand-paintings are destroyed the same day they are made, immediately after they have served their purpose. Although one may be allowed at times to observe or to participate in the ceremony, rarely is one allowed to copy the sand-paintings."

DESCRIPTION OF EMBLEMS

The Sun above a pyramid (which symbolizes the Exalted High Place), on the spine of the book. The four rays from the four cardinal directions symbolize the American Sacred Number Four.

Four-rayed Suns with the Swastika, sacred to the Americas as to Asia, at the center, on the front of the book. Both emblems were designed by G. Warrington Bass.

MAP

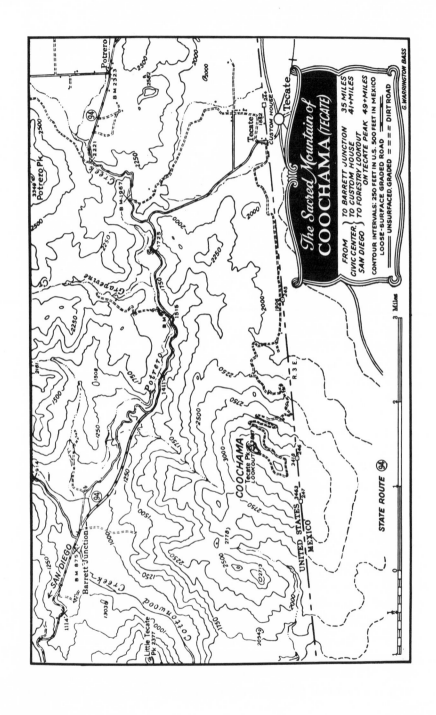

INTRODUCTION by Frank Waters

The present book, so different in subject from the familiar volumes we associate with the name of W. Y. Evans-Wentz, seems to me to complete a psychic and geographic circle rounding his life and work.

Dr. Evans-Wentz was born in Trenton, New Jersey, in 1878, and lived his early years in La Mesa, California, just east of San Diego. Studying at Stanford University, he received a B.A. in 1906, and an M.A. degree in 1907. He then went to Oxford University where he took a B.Sc. degree in 1910. For four years he did psychic research among the Celtic peoples of Ireland, Wales, Cornwall, Scotland, and Brittany, who believed in the existence of those otherworld beings they called fairies. The University of Rennes in Brittany awarded him a doctorate for his resulting thesis, which was published in 1911 as *The Fairy Faith in Celtic Countries.*

Shortly thereafter he sailed for the East to continue his investigations of the psychic and spiritual realm. In Egypt he spent three years of research in the ancient funeral rites described in the *Egyptian Book of the Dead,* followed in 1917 by five years of travel through Ceylon, India, and Tibet. This led him into an intensive study of Tibetan Buddhism. On this he became a world authority, with the eventual publication under his name of those now well-known, ancient treatises which he edited and annotated: *The Tibetan Book of the Dead, Tibet's Great Yogi Milarepa, Tibetan Yoga and Secret Doctrines,* and *The Tibetan Book of the Great Liberation.* In recognition of his work on the first two volumes, Oxford University conferred upon him, in 1931, the degree of Doctor of Science in Comparative Religion, a rare distinction. Dr. Evans-Wentz himself embraced the faith of Mahayana Buddhism and settled in India, buying property in Almora, Kumaon Province. Here he lived in an *ashram* on the Hill of Kasar Devi, hoping to develop it into a research center in Eastern religious philosophies. The outbreak of the Second World War put an end to his efforts. He returned to the United States, settling in San Diego.

He had inherited a great ranch of more than 5,000 acres, some twenty-five miles southeast of San Diego, lying astride the international border of California and Baja California. It embraced Mount Tecate, known to the Cochimis, Yumas, and other Indian tribes as the Sacred Mountain of Cuchama, the "exalted high place" on whose summit young men had undergone initiation into the mystic rites of their people. Dr. Evans-Wentz became interested in the traditions concerning it and in the religion of the American Indians. So, now in his later years, and back home in his native land after studying for three decades in Great Britain, Egypt, India, and Tibet, he resumed his research into the meaning of the Red Man's Shining Beings, those otherworld spiritual beings known to the Celts as fairies and to the Hindus as devas. The compilation of the present book occupied him until his death in 1965. Its great underlying theme, as we shall see, is the psychic unity of the East and West.

At his death, Dr. Evans-Wentz left his property in India and $3,000 to the Maha Bodhi Society to establish a Buddhist educational and religious center in Kasar Devi village. Most of his property in California was placed in trust at a San Diego bank. The net income from it, and the mineral rights to his 5,000-acre ranch were left to Stanford University for the purpose of providing a professorship and scholarships in Oriental philosophies and religions. According to his will, 2,261 acres of his large ranch, including the sacred mountain of Cuchama, were deeded to the State of California with the request that Cuchama itself be made a public property to be "maintained forever as a mighty monument to symbolize goodwill and fraternity between the races and faiths of the Occident and the Orient across the wide ocean of peace over which it looms."

Stanford University received his bequest of a large collection of Oriental manuscripts and private papers. These included the manuscript of the present book. I have reluctantly undertaken, along with Dr. Charles L. Adams of the University of Nevada, Las Vegas, the task of editing and annotating this last work of such a devout and eminent scholar only because of my long friendship with him and the great help his books have given me. Yet, it is a great pleasure to know that the treasures of this book will now be made accessible to others.

My correspondence with Dr. Evans-Wentz began in 1947. I had discovered in the first volumes of his Tibetan series, at that time not popularly known, many Tibetan parallels to the esoteric beliefs and rituals of the Pueblos and Navajos which I was recounting in my own writings. Dr. Evans-Wentz, upon reading my book *The Man Who Killed the Deer,* wrote me that he found it "quite unlike any other book in as much as it interprets the inner meaning of life to the Red Man in a quite unique manner, and I appreciate its esoteric character." He was then completing the fourth and last of his Tibetan series, and planned to return to India when it was published.

Publication of *The Tibetan Book of the Great Liberation* was postponed until 1954, and his advancing age prevented him from leaving America. Meanwhile, he had developed an interest in the American Indians. As he wrote me after reading my *Masked Gods: Navaho and Pueblo Ceremonialism,* "You have gone deeply into the esotericism; and the parallels which you point out with Oriental religions are well founded. The more I delve into the lore of the Red Man, the more I am astonished with its fundamental similarity with the lore of the Hindus and Tibetans."

His growing interest focused on Cuchama, sacred to the Cochimis, Yumas, and other Indian tribes. He began to collect the traditions about it from surviving members of the tribes. As a result, he wrote me in 1953, that he was undertaking a book on Coochama,* incorporating accounts of other sacred mountains

---

*The spelling was changed to Cuchama seven years later.

xxii | *Cuchama and Sacred Mountains*

throughout the world such as Kailas in Tibet, Omei in China, and Arunachala in India. There were other sacred mountains in America with which he was not familiar, and he asked for any information I could give him. Our correspondence increased as I sent him material, and I visited him in San Diego.

As befitting a Pilgrim on the Noble Eight-Fold Path, he was living in a cheap downtown hotel. Although in his seventies, he looked twenty years younger—a tall, slimly built man with clear blue eyes. He was reticent of manner, but warm in character. Although I was not a Buddhist, he had often addressed me in his letters as "Fellow Pilgrim," "Friend of the Path," and "Brother Waters." He now made no mention of his faith and gave me freely of his vast experience and mystical insights.

Through him I met in Los Angeles his close friend George W. Bass, who had served in a British army detachment in India, and later studied pre-Columbian ruins and mythology in Yucatan. At this time he was preparing illustrations for Dr. Evans-Wentz' book, and Dr. Evans-Wentz relied greatly upon his advice. Correspondence among the three of us increased as Dr. Evans-Wentz sent us material to appraise.

At about this time he also arranged a trip to Cuchama for Mr. Bass and his wife; Eddie, his young nephew, who was a psychic; and myself. The chaparral-covered mountain rose above the Mexican village of Tecate. A fire lookout station had been built on the summit and the road was opened for us.

For several hours we wandered over the irregular summit, looking at unusual rock formations. Young Eddie received the psychic impression that a certain level area had been the rocky floor of a great cave long before a catastrophe had lowered Cuchama to its present height. He picked up two small stones which he believed had been part of the ancient floor. Dr. Evans-Wentz found a small artifact from which he received the sensation of fire and smoke, which he drew in with his *prana.* We then offered prayers dedicating this "exalted high place" to the good of all mankind in the centuries to come.

When the Bass family and I returned to Los Angeles, Mr. Bass took the two small stones and the artifact to Charles F. Smith, a psychometrist, for a reading. One of the stones, thin and flat, he too believed had once been part of the floor of an immense cave.

The other stone was slightly curved, showing ancient water marks. From both of them the psychometrist received impressions of smells, heat, and the sound of dripping water. Cuchama, he said, had been occupied during three culture periods. The first human beings were remnants of a migrating race already extinct in their original homeland. They were of gigantic size with short legs and arms, but with enormous torsos developed from drawing in the vital forces of nature. Where they came from, and how long ago, he did not venture to say, save that when they arrived Cuchama was a lofty beacon peak visible from far out in the Pacific. The artifact found by Dr. Evans-Wentz evoked for him the picture of a tall woman with a tight headband. The large piece it had broken from evidently had been a cooking tool or utensil used in comparatively recent times. This confirmed Dr. Evans-Wentz' sensation of fire and smoke.

It is interesting to note that these psychic impressions and psychometry readings generally correspond with the geological, anthropological, and mythological data on Cuchama which Dr. Evans-Wentz included in his present text.*

During the years that Dr. Evans-Wentz' book took shape, he sent Mr. Bass and me portions and drafts of the manuscript for review and whatever help we could give him. Before it was completed, Mr. Bass died in Prescott, Arizona, in 1961, having written me a note on the day of his death. In 1963, Dr. Evans-Wentz wrote me from Mexico City, where he was ill and discouraged. His book was finished, and he hoped to go to England to submit it to Oxford University Press. He had made no later efforts to find a publisher. Two years later, on July 17, 1965, he died in Encinitas, north of San Diego.

It seems fitting that I take the opportunity of expressing here my gratitude for the long friendship, help, and encouragement of these two men. Their passing is a great loss to us all. For it is

---

*For a more detailed description of Cuchama, the reader is referred to the account of an overnight pilgrimage twenty years later, in 1975, made by Philip S. Staniford, Associate Professor of Anthropology at San Diego State University, and five companions. Their psychic impressions and detailed descriptions, together with sketch maps outlining the shape of the mountain and drawings of its unusual rock formations, Professor Staniford records in an article published in the Summer, 1977 issue of *Phoenix* magazine.

through such devout Pilgrims that the underlying unity of the West and the East will finally be recognized.

****

And now a note about the book itself.

It kept growing and being revised through Dr. Evans-Wentz' habitually thorough research. This was particularly true of the last half, as he became involved in the religion of the Red Man, not familiar to him at the start, and in the tragic conquest of Indian America and its psychic consequences to its White conquerors today.

He was meticulous in his writing and in all personal contacts. After having sent me a copy of his manuscript for review, he insisted on reimbursing me the 54 cents return postage on it. His utter lack of egotism—contrary to most writers of his eminence —was unusual. He solicited comments and criticisms from many persons to whom he sent copies of his manuscript for review. Two of these persons were Theodor Reich in San Francisco and Hazel Dreis in Pacific Grove. One weekend, Mr. Reich and I met with Ms. Dreis in her home to discuss her opinion of the manuscript.

Hazel Dreis was an accomplished book-maker of fine and rare books. She had directed for the Rydal Press in Santa Fe, New Mexico, the design and printing of the *Navajo Creation Myth* recorded by Mary C. Wheelwright and published in 1942 for the Museum of Navajo Ceremonial Art. The book is now a collectors' item, as are so many others of hers. Her appraisal of Dr. Evans-Wentz' manuscript, which she confirmed by letter to him, was from the viewpoint of a book-maker concerned with the problems of publication and distribution which related to sales. Her honest criticisms were largely negative:

(1) The manuscript embodied four books in one: Cuchama, Sacred Mountains of the World, Martyrdom of the Red Man, and the influence of Indian Religion upon American Religion. This resulted in the manuscript's lack of unity. . . . (2) The manuscript was entitled *Cuchama,* but this subject received the least emphasis. She suggested that another title be chosen, representing the subject which offered the widest appeal. . . . (3) Very few sacred mountains outside of those in Asia were described. Others in

Africa, South America, Mexico, and in the United States especially, should be covered. . . . And finally, (4) she recommended more copious annotations to explain Eastern beliefs and terms not familiar to general readers.

These criticisms are recounted here since they may be similar to the first reaction of some casual readers to the published book, for Ms. Dreis' criticisms do have some validity from her point of view. Also they suggest the problems posed to Dr. Adams and myself in editing the manuscript.

We have rearranged its structural organization, but have made no major editorial changes in content. The author, of course, was never concerned with its possible exploitation as a popular book with wide sales appeal. He prepared it on a level higher than the *sangsaric* plane, our material world of appearances. The entire book reflects his more comprehensive perspective. All four parts, disparate in subject as they might first appear, are unified by one interpenetrating theme, Dr. Evans-Wentz' conviction of the spiritual unity of all peoples and faiths throughout the Occident and the Orient.

Cuchama and Sacred Mountains is not an encyclopedia of all sacred mountains throughout the world; nor would this have been possible had the author so intended. The book, however, deals primarily with those in the Himalayas, with which he was familiar. To further emphasize his premise that the meanings and functions of sacred mountains everywhere are the same, the editorial annotations have included reference to a few others with striking parallels in the ritual practices observed upon them.

We have not thought it advisable to add a plethora of annotations explaining Hindu and Tibetan terms and the tenets of Mahayana Buddhism beyond those incorporated in the text. Most Western readers are generally familiar with them through the recent influx of Eastern metaphysical writings and teachings. Those who desire further information are referred to the Tibetan series which largely opened Western doors to Eastern metaphysics fifty years ago.

The principal subject of the book is not as new to us today as it might have been when it was written. Unlike most peoples throughout the world, we have never recognized the role of sacred mountains. Nor have we Euro-Americans regarded the earth itself as a living entity, our Mother Earth, as have the Native Americans, the Indians. From our first arrival, and throughout our westward course of empire, we viewed the living land as no more than a continental expanse of inanimate nature existing solely to be exploited for our material gain. No conquest of all nature—mountains, forests, grasslands, rivers and lakes, the very air itself —has been so ruthless, so swift, and so complete.

Our continuing onslaughts against nature have made us today the richest and most materialistic nation in history. Yet under our national ethic of economic progress at any price, we have bought the physical energy derived from the land at the expense of its psychic energy so necessary for our survival as a spiritually healthy commonwealth. All the living entities of the mineral, plant, animal, and human kingdoms comprise one integrated life-system. Each part must help to maintain the life of the whole. When we do violence to any part, we injure our inner-selves. We have yet to fully realize that the physical and psychical realms are two aspects of one transcendental unity. It is from this viewpoint that Dr. Evans-Wentz regards sacred mountains as centers or repositories of psychic energy upon which mankind may draw.

Just how far the reader can accept his belief in the Shining Beings, and other spirit-forms mentioned throughout his text, raises another question. Western psychology holds that all such otherworld beings are projections of our own minds. "Psychology accordingly," writes Dr. C. G. Jung in his Psychological Commentary to *The Tibetan Book of the Great Liberation* [xxix], "treats all metaphysical claims and assertions as mental phenomena and regards them as statements about the mind and its structure that derive ultimately from certain unconscious dispositions." And more specifically, he states [1], "The gods are archetypal thought-forms. . . . Their peaceful and wrathful aspects, which play a great role in the meditations of *The Tibetan Book of the Dead,* symbolize the opposites."

Dr. Evans-Wentz himself, in his Introduction to the latter book [66], asserts, "In reality there are no such beings anywhere as gods, or demons, or spirits, or sentient creatures—all alike being phenomena dependent upon a cause. . . . All phenomena are transitory, are illusionary, are unreal, and non-existent save in the *sangsaric* mind perceiving them."

One must look at these two statements more closely. For behind their apparent agreement lies a basic disagreement on what constitutes mind and phenomena. The two viewpoints are well expressed in Dr. Jung's Psychological Commentary and Dr. Evans-Wentz' Introduction to *The Tibetan Book of the Great Liberation.* Western psychology, according to Jung, knows the mind as the mental functioning of an individual [xxxiii], and does not assume that the mind is a metaphysical entity or that there is any connection between an individual mind and a hypothetical Universal Mind [xxix].

The basis of Eastern metaphysics, on the contrary, is the premise of one Universal Mind, which embraces all gods, spirits, and entities, including our own selves. Dr. Evans-Wentz quotes the 8th century Great Guru, Padma-Sambhava, to this effect: "The whole *Sangsara* (the phenomenal Universe of appearances) and *Nirvana* (the Unmanifested or noumenal state), as an inseparable unity, are in one's mind (in its natural or unmodified primordial state of Voidness)" [2].

This noumenal source of the cosmic whole, the Universal Mind, Body, and Essence which pervades all forms of life even to the atom and the cell—"the Primordial, Unmodified, Formless, Eternally Self-Existing Essentiality of Divine Beingness" [3]—is known to Mahayana Buddhists as Dharma-Kaya, the essence of Buddhahood. Recognition of it by those who thereby realize their own true nature through yogic disciplines constitutes Enlightenment.

To Jung, "The One Mind is the Unconscious, since it is characterized as 'eternal, unknown, not visible, not recognized' " [li]. Thus, he considered the Dharma-Kaya, or Universal Mind, to be the Eastern equivalent of Western psychology's concept of the collective unconscious [lvii]. Dr. Evans-Wentz simply acknowledged that Dr. Jung's Commentaries served as a "bridge between the best thought of the Occident and the Orient." He, of course, adheres strictly to the viewpoint of the Mahayana in his present narration of the psychic nature of sacred mountains and the guardian spirits surrounding them. They are no less real for being phenomena, once it is accepted that they—and those who perceive them—are alike phenomena in relation to the One Reality.

Marie-Louise von Franz, an eminent Jungian psychologist, records an interesting observation in *Number and Time* (Evanston, 1974): "It is being more and more firmly established that parapsychological phenomena occur mainly in the surroundings of an individual *whom the unconscious wants to take a step in the development of consciousness.* . . . Creative personalities who must fulfill a new creative task intended by the unconscious also attract such phenomena. . . . "

This, I think, might apply to Dr. Evans-Wentz. *Cuchama and Sacred Mountains* is not a treatise. It is an intensely personal narrative expressing in his own way what another great visionary, the late Sioux medicine-man Black Elk, said years ago:

> Then I was standing on the highest mountain of them all, and round about me was the whole hoop of the world. And while I stood there, I saw more than I can tell and I understood more than I saw; for I was seeing in a sacred manner the shapes of all things in the spirit and the shapes of all shapes as they must live together as one being.
>
> And I saw the sacred hoop of my people was one of many hoops that made one circle wide as daylight and as starlight, and in the center grew one mighty tree to shelter one mother and one father. And I saw that it was holy.

In the present book, Dr. Evans-Wentz has helped greatly to advance our progress toward the goal to which he devoted his life and work—our recognition of the spiritual unity of the East and West.

FOREWORD

SACRED MOUNTAINS
by Lama Anagarika Govinda*

There are mountains which are just mountains and there are mountains with personality. The personality of a mountain is dependent upon more than merely a strange shape which makes it different from other mountains—just as a strangely-shaped face or strange actions do not make an individual into a personality. Personality consists in the power to influence others, and this power is due to consistency, harmony, and one-pointedness of character. If these qualities are present in an individual in their highest perfection, he is a fit leader of humanity, be he a ruler, a thinker, or a saint; and we recognize him as a vessel of supramundane power. If these qualities are present in a mountain, we recognize it as a vessel of cosmic power, and we call it a sacred mountain.

The power of such a mountain is so great and yet so subtle that without compulsion pilgrims are drawn to the mountain from near and far, as if by the force of some invisible magnet, and they will undergo untold hardships and privations in their inexplicable urge to approach and to worship the sacred spot. Nobody has

*Author of *Foundations of Tibetan Mysticism, The Psychological Attitude of Early Buddhist Philosophy,* etc.

conferred the title of sacredness upon such a mountain; by virtue of its own magnetic and psychic emanations the mountain is intuitively recognized to be sacred. It needs no defender of its sanctity, nor any organizer of its worship; innately each of its devotees feels the urge to pay it reverence.

This worshipful or religious attitude is not impressed by scientific facts, like figures of altitude, which are foremost in the mind of modern man, nor by the ambition to "conquer" the mountain. Instead of conquering it, the religious-minded man prefers to be conquered by it. He opens his whole being to the potent influences of the mountain and allows them to take possession of him, because only he who is "possessed" partakes of the spirit of the divine. While the modern man makes it a feat of personal prowess, for his own glorification, to climb an outstanding mountain and be the first on top of it, the devotee is more interested in his spiritual elevation than in the physical feat of climbing.

To see the greatness of a mountain, one must be at a distance from it; to understand its form, one must move around it; to experience its moods, one must see it at sunrise and sunset, at noon and at midnight, in sun and in rain, in snow and storm, in summer and winter, and in spring and autumn. He who can see the mountain in this manner comes near to the life of the mountain, which is as intense as that of a human being. Mountains grow and decay, they breathe and pulsate with life. They attract and collect invisible energies from their surroundings: the energies of the air, of the water, of electricity and magnetism; they create winds, clouds, thunder-storms, rains, waterfalls, and rivers. They fill their surroundings with life and give shelter and food to innumerable living things. Such is the greatness of a mountain.

But even among mountains that are sacred, there are some of such outstanding character and position that they have become the spiritual foci of the most ancient civilizations and religions of humanity, milestones of the eternal quest for perfection and ultimate realization, signposts that point beyond our earthly concerns towards the infinity of a Universe from which we have originated and to which we belong.

In the dust-filled valleys and lowlands of our daily existence we have forgotten our connection with stars and suns; and so we need the presence of these mighty milestones and signposts to awaken us from the slumber of self-complacency. There are not many who hear the call or feel the urge under their thick blankets of petty self-interests, of money-getting, and of pleasure seeking. But the few who do form a perennial stream of pilgrims and keep alive throughout the ages the arcane knowledge of these terrestrial sources of divine inspiration.

Cuchama, A Sacred Mountain of the Red Men

PART I

The Religion of the Mountain

We may truly say that the highest religion is the Religion of the Mountain. What is that religion? When we reach the mountain summits, we leave behind us all the things that down below weigh heavily on our body and spirit. We leave behind all sense of weakness and depression; we feel a new freedom, a great exhilaration, an exaltation of the body no less than that of the spirit. We feel a great joy. The Religion of the Mountain is in reality the religion of joy, of the release of the soul from the things that weigh it down and fill it with a sense of weariness, sorrow and defeat.

* * *

The mountains uphold us and the stars beckon to us. The mountains of our lovely land will make a constant appeal to us to live the higher life of joy and freedom.

General Smuts, in *Speech on Table Mountain*

Cuchama, the Sacred High Place. The northwesterly slopes of Cuchama, as seen from the heights on the west above Barrett, San Diego County, California. *Photo by Edwin T. Knutson.*

1

Cuchama,
A Sacred Mountain of the Red Men

I: THE NAME AND THE NATURAL HISTORY

Cuchama, one of the holiest of Earth's mountains, is situated partly in San Diego County, California, about twenty-five miles due east from the Pacific Ocean, and partly in Mexico, the international boundary line so bisecting it along its southern slopes that its summit and the major portion of its granitic mass lie wholly within the United States. The White Man geographer knows this mountain only as Mount Tecate.[1] The Red Men, conscious of the magnetic and psychic influences focussed in the mountain, revered it as a most sacred shrine, specially reared and sanctified by the Great Mystery, whereon man might commune with the gods. And so, since immemorial time, the Red Men called the mountain Cuchama, "The Exalted High Place."[2]

To the geologist and botanist, no less than to the ethnologist and anthropologist, Cuchama offers much of unusual interest. The Mountain is composed largely of Jurassic rocks, which were formed about the middle of the Mesozoic Era. That was many millions of years ago, in the Age of the Great Reptiles; Cuchama was then an island in a tropical sea which covered most of what

[1]Concerning the history and philology of Tecate, see pages 18–24.
[2]Concerning the name Cuchama, see pages 16–18.

5

is now Upper and Lower California. More than once a depression of the land has made Cuchama an island. The last such occasion was in the Pliocene Epoch at the time that the coastal terraces of Southern California were deposited in a series of shelves. Cuchama was venerable when the Himalayas arose; and long antedates the first coming into physical bodies of the race of men.

Until quite recent times, Cuchama was forested. Professor Stover[3] reports that its summit, now denuded, supported a grove of giant cypress which destructive white men cut down for firewood. Its rugged slopes, particularly those on the west favored by the moisture-bearing winds from the Pacific Ocean, and its deep canyons still support a varied and, in some instances, a rare flora. The Mountain is noted especially for its peculiar species of cypress, a few of which still flourish on the Mountain, known as the Tecate Cypress, lately given the Latin name *Cupressus Forbesii* in honor of the botanist who investigated it. Like much else that Nature has evolved and held in reserve for man's enjoyment, the Tecate Cypress is proving to be a boon to horticulturists because of its immunity to cypress canker, which, throughout California, has almost exterminated the cultivated Monterey Cypress. The Tecate Cypress is found only in a few other places, among which are Otay Mountain and Guatay Mountain in San Diego County, parts of Lower California, and Sierra Peak in the Santa Ana Mountains of Orange County, California. Each of these isolated places was also, like Cuchama, once an island during long-past geological ages; and thereon the Tecate species of cypress and other flora of the ancient world established themselves and still survive, while their less fortunate kindred in lower altitudes were drowned out. The Red Men of California themselves tell of a great flood or at least of a time when their whole country, with the exception of certain mountains, was covered with water.[4]

Another of Cuchama's interesting and geologically ancient plants is the mountain-misery, better known to botanists by its Latin name *Chamadbatia foliolosa australis,* an aromatic shrub with delicate fern-like foliage producing beautiful, small white blossoms in clusters followed by small reddish berries. It is a close

[3][Ed. nt.: See p. xii, C. A.]
[4]Cf. H. H. Bancroft, *The Native Races* (San Francisco, 1886), iii, 88.

relative of the mountain-misery covering the high Sierras near Sequoia Park. Claude Scheckler, a pioneer settler on the United States side of the Cuchama country, told me, when one day we were together on the Sacred Mountain, how, years ago, mountain-misery, such as that amidst which we stood, used to be known as "bear-mat" because bears, and most likely other wild animals, too, were habituated to roll in it to rid themselves of vermin. That mountain-misery might very well serve, as obviously the bears had discovered, as an efficient vermin-expellent becomes self-evident when examined closely; for, upon contact, it conveys a sticky, oily substance which is very penetratingly pungent and highly charged with the plant's characteristic aromatic odor. The name "mountain-misery" arose as a result of hunters and prospectors and herdsmen with cattle and sheep traversing areas covered by this plant and finding their clothing and livestock in a miserably sticky and unaccustomed odoriferous condition because of these peculiarities of the plant.

II: AS "THE MOUNTAIN OF CREATION"

In one of the recorded symbolical ground-painting designs of the Diegueño Indians, of San Diego County, California, four sacred places are indicated,[5] and three, perhaps four, of them are

[5]Cf. A. L. Kroeber, *Handbook of the Indians of California* (Berkeley, California, 1953), design e. p. 663. These ground-painting designs of the Diegueño, and also of the Luiseño, are essentially the same as those known as *mandalas* in India and Tibet, especially among Hindu and Buddhist Tantrics. Being for initiations, the ground-painting design was made in the ceremonial enclosure. The Luiseño used it in the *Yunish Metakish,* or death rite for initiates, and called it *torohaish* or *tarohaish* (*ibid.,* p. 662). Among the Tibetans, the *mandala,* quite like the California ground-painting design, is a geometrical diagram outlined with dust or sand, commonly of different colors, either on a floor, if the initiation be in a temple or house, or on the bare rock or earth, if the initiation be in a cave or in the open air. Then the Deities are invoked, usually by intoning their secret name, a special place within the diagram being assigned to each of them. Initiates possessed by clairvoyant vision say that when the invocation is properly performed, by a highly-developed human guru, the Deities appear, each in the place assigned in the *mandala,* and make the Mystic Initiation very real and effective psychically, the neophyte at once obtaining divine insight and ecstatic joy. Thence come the mystic regeneration and the true baptism in the fire of the spirit, and the conferring of the new name which invariably suggests the chief spiritual qualities of the neophyte receiving it. For further details see W. Y. Evans-Wentz, *Tibet's Great Yogi Milarepa,* pp. 132–33.

identifiable. Four having been a sacred, or ceremonial, number among the Diegueño and other tribes comprising the Yumas, as among the Red Men everywhere through the Americas, these four sacred places were, very probably, places where initiations took place.[6] To the northeast is the San Bernardino Mountain (or else the Gorgonio Mountain); to the northwest, the Santa Catalina Island mountain-mass; to the southwest, the partly submerged mountain peaks known as the Coronado Islands; and, to the southeast, "The Mountain of Creation," which may be Cuchama. The only other likely alternative mountain-mass to displace Cuchama would be the Cuyamacas; but inasmuch as Cuchama has the correct geographical correspondence and the outstanding physical prominence to fit the design as well as traditional sanctity, we may be justified in assuming, at least tentatively, or until evidence to the contrary is discovered, that "The Mountain of Creation" is "The Exalted High Place." If this surmise be true, the designation "Mountain of Creation" would seem to indicate the survival of incalculably ancient traditions among the Diegueño suggestive of Cuchama's remarkable geological history and primordial igneous origin.

In the New World, no less than in the Old World, myths of creation, and especially of a deluge, seem to be associated with mountains, whereon the ancestors of primitive races dwelling in the vicinity of such sanctified High Places were believed to have found refuge when continents, now under oceans, were cataclys-

---

[6]Cf. D. G. Brinton, *The Myths of the New World* (Philadelphia, 1905), p. 83ff., wherein it is shown that the number Four is sacred in all American religions and a key to their symbolism. A. L. Kroeber, in *The Handbook of the Indians of California*, p. 717, states that Four was, likewise, the sacred or ceremonial number among the Diegueño and other tribes of the Yuman Nation, as we have found it to be. It occurs twice in the autobiographical narrative by the medicine man, and once in the matter quoted from Big White Owl given below.

[Ed. nt.: The Yuman tribes may be more properly considered a linguistic family rather than a nation such as other well-known federated tribes. The Yumas, although possessing a strong sense of tribal unity and tribal chiefs, had little formal government. They were noted for the importance they gave to dreams, particularly "Great Dreams" that gave power to the dreamers. (*The Indian Heritage of America*, Alvin M. Josephy, Jr., New York, 1968.) This confirms the present text. F.W.]

mically submerged. Sometimes, as among the Araucanians of Chile, the fabulous retreat was a "mountain which had the properties of floating on water," or in other words, an island mountain such as was Cuchama, seemingly afloat on the surrounding waters like a Noah's Ark in a primeval ocean.[7]

Of the Indians of the San Juan Capistrano region, Father Boscano (1776–1831) wrote: "These Indians believe and say that at a remote time the sea began to fill up so that it came in over the valleys, and the water rose over the mountains, and all the people and animals died, except some who went to a very high mountain, and the water did not reach them there."[8]

In the Diegueño ground-painting design, the two northerly sacred places are indicated by two small circles; the southwesterly sacred place is indicated by a small circle within a circle; and the "Mountain of Creation" is indicated by a similar circle within a circle, this inner circle being bisected by a horizontal line. Thus, judging from this more elaborate symbolic representation of it, the "Mountain of Creation" seems to be the most important of the four sacred places.

That the Diegueño ground-painting design is not fanciful, but is definitely geographical and astronomical, Professor A. L. Kroeber makes clear by his careful and detailed description of it: "They [the Diegueño] paint the world indeed; but it is the visible universe. The enclosing circle [of the ground-painting design] is merely the horizon, or the edge of the Earth. The figures within it are a downright map of the mundane surface and the celestial sphere. The Milky Way stretches across the middle as it bisects the heavens. On one side are the summer constellations Aquila and Cygnus; on the other, Orion and the Pleiades of winter—each group identifiable by its form. The sun and moon are too conspicuously visible overhead to be omitted; so they are represented. . . . His [the Diegueño's] mountains, too, are . . . actual named peaks; and the four in figure *e* [containing symbolical representation of the Mountain of Creation] stand in very nearly the relative geo-

---

[7]Cf. D. G. Brinton, *op. cit.,* p. 239.
[8]Cf. John P. Harrington, *A New Original Version of Boscano's Historical Account of the San Juan Capistrano Indians of Southern California* (City of Washington, 1934), Smithsonian Miscellaneous Collections, Vol. 92, no. 4, p. 48.

graphical positions, with Diegueño land as a center, that they occupy in the painting."[9]

III: THE EXTERNAL VISION; AND THE MOUNTAIN'S
MESSAGE

Although Cuchama's altitude of 3,887 feet is small when compared with other California mountains such as those of the Sierra Nevadas, Cuchama is, nevertheless, as the Red Men well knew, the highest mountain of the extreme southwestern part of California between the Pacific Ocean and Imperial Valley. Having been ideally placed, by primeval creative forces, like a mighty sentinel meditatively on guard over that southwesterly region of the North American Continent, midway between Asia and Europe, its summit affords an unimpeded panoramic view of unique grandeur in every direction, limited only by the immense circle of the world's horizon.

Its marvellously gorgeous sunrises are kindled over the lowlying mountains on the rim of the Colorado Desert to the east; its crimson sunset fires fade over the broad expanse of the Ocean of Peace and the Otay (or "Brush-Clad") mountains to the west. When the full moon has risen, the Sacred Mountain becomes enhaloed in an ethereal glory. When there is no moon thus to transmute into translucent silver the Mountain's igneous surfaces in the clear, calm empyrean, the sister planets of our System, together with innumerable distant suns and nebulae and worlds, shine as they move in their majestic and silent procession through the unfathomed depths of cosmic space.

By day, when the air is clear, the Sun reveals, to the southwest, the pulsating Pacific encompassing the Mexican archipelago of Los Coronados, which, in the distance, resemble dark blue sapphires inset in the Ocean's turquoise waters. They are, like Cu-

[9]Cf. A. L. Kroeber, *op. cit.,* p. 664. It should be noted here that the three Indian tribes, the Yuma, the Cochimi, and the Diegueño, to whom reference is made throughout this study, belong to one racial group, designated by ethnologists as the Yuman; and since they are related intimately, both linguistically and culturally, the study of the language, traditions, and customs of any one of them contributes to the anthropological understanding of any of the others.

chama, merely part of the remnants of a continent submerged long ages ago.[10]

Southward from the Holy Mountain are to be seen many well-cultivated small valleys of Lower California. There, too, stands Table Mountain, its flat, grass-grown summit comprising a large segment of the level surface of the Earth's crust uplifted by titanic forces ages ago; and eastwardly from it rise the purple-shadowed peaks of the many-folded Mexican Sierras. Northward lie the Cuyamacas, "The Rain-Holding Mountains," distinguishable by the dark colors of their forests of pine and oak. And beyond them, in winter and sometimes in early summer, may be seen the snows on the summit of Old Baldy in Los Angeles County and on the high peaks of the San Bernardino Range.

All of this wondrous panorama of things external is, in large measure, for many who behold it, chiefly a feast for the eyes; but for those psychically empowered (including, perhaps, more of us than we are apt to admit), like the initiates among the Red Men, it induces an inner awakening in heart and mind.

Whether it be here amidst the mountains of Western America, or amidst the mountains of Asia and Africa and Europe, or of the islands in the seven seas, there is ever perceptible the subtle rhythm of the manifested oneness of all animate and inanimate things. Each of the mountains encircling the Earth is placed, as Cuchama is, like a never-sleeping and silent tutelary deity eagerly but patiently awaiting that far-distant age when mankind shall have grown to the full stature of godhood, here in mankind's divine School of the World.

As do all mountains upon which are hieroglyphically inscribed nature's own historical records, Cuchama tells man of the planet's birth-throes, of the upheavals above the oceans and the submergences, and of the transitoriness of all visible terrestrial forms and of their occult relationship with invisible and immutable forces

---

[10]The fuller and more correct name for these islands, which are four in number, given to them on November 5, 1602 by Sebastian Vizcaino, is Los Cuatro Martires, "The Four Crowned Martyrs," to whom, in the calendar of the Roman Catholic Church, the fifth of November is dedicated. Cabrillo had named them Las Islas Desiertas, "The Desert Islands," in 1542. Other names that have been applied to them are Dead Men's Islands, and the Isles of St. Martin. The largest of the four islands resembles a corpse or mummy lying flat on its back, and very fittingly the Spaniards named it Corpus Cristi, "Body of Christ."

ever active throughout the Universe. The forces of preservation and construction complement those of dissolution and destruction as Vishnu, the Preserver, complements Shiva the Destroyer. Where once fire and molten rock reigned, now the cooling winds move through the canyons and across the summit and give rhythmic movement to glistening shrubs and grasses. Though the foundations of Cuchama are deep-hidden in fiery abysses, its massive outer form stands revealed and serene, supported by its Mother Earth, and it rejoices in the light of the sun and moon and stars.

As men live their little lives, year by year, day by day, hour by hour, minute by minute, and die, triumphed over at the last by the cosmic forces which unceasingly affect their fleshly bodies from the moment of conception, so during the course of myriads of millenniums, Cuchama, too, will die in like manner. The sun's heat, the winds, the rain, the hail and frost and all the other cosmic forces will transform it into a level plain entombed under the great waters. And as men rise from their own levelling and entombment and take bodies again, so will the level plains under the oceans once more rise on high into the ambient air. Responsive thus to the all-embracing rhythmic law, men and mountains alike ever die and are reborn until Earth itself, in its own turn, becomes once more dissolved, in death.

IV: "CELESTIAL" CLIMATE

Lightning, although frequently striking round about Cuchama, has not, as yet, been known to strike Cuchama itself.[11] Appar-

---

[11]This observation has been confirmed by Mr. Lee O. Wyatt, of the California State Forestry Service, now (in the year 1962) in charge of the Mt. Tecate Lookout, as he has been for a number of years. I am also indebted to him for having prepared for me a table of the meteorological records so far compiled at the Tecate Lookout, and for the details of Mr. Baird's radio record.

[Ed. nt.: Subsequent data on this point would be fascinating, but the weather station was discontinued some years ago. However, on February 7, 1978, Dennis Dutton, who lives at the base of Cuchama, wrote me: "On pages 10-11 [of the original manuscript], Wentz . . . says that lightning, although frequently striking ground about Cuchama, has not, as yet, been known to strike Cuchama itself. This holds true by our experience. I don't believe that Wentz mentions *another* lightning effect associated with the mountain—the lightning-ball. More than once, different persons among us have seen a glowing ball of light appear on the peak and other sections of Cuchama. One person saw it suddenly appear on the peak, grow in intensity, and then roll down the ridge in a southerly direction until it passed out of sight into the valley. . . ." C.A.]

ently, as the Red Men would say, the Thunder Gods protect the Exalted High Place. This peculiar immunity of Cuchama may be due to a protective envelope of terrestrial magnetism, or to a psychic force, emanating from the Sacred Mountain, and akin to that associated with Mt. Omei in China and with Mt. Kailas in Tibet.

Owing to its position of climatic balance between the Pacific Ocean on the west and the Colorado Desert on the east, Cuchama enjoys a very equable climate. The weather recordings made at the lookout for the months of January to November 1944 inclusive, the only weather recordings yet made for that length of time in any one year, show an average mean temperature of 68°, Fahrenheit. In June, July, and August, over a period of ten years, 1943 to 1952, the average mean temperature was 76°. The greatest cold recorded was 31°, in March 1944, and the greatest heat, 99°, in August 1944.

In its spring-like winter sunshine, which is made more glorious by the sunlight glistening on the Pacific, the summit of the Exalted High Place is frequented by flocks of migrating birds and butterflies. They seem to bathe most gleefully in the Mountain's magnetism; and, unlike most human creatures, they are, perhaps, consciously responsive to its invisible inspiring influences.

Ordinarily, snowfall on Cuchama is little more than a filmy white veil, which disappears within a few hours. At all seasons, the Mountain's natural shrubbery, as prim and well-ordered as though under the care of an expert landscape gardener, is refreshingly green, especially on the westerly and northerly slopes, in marked contrast with the summer brownness of most California mountains. Not only do the moisture-laden winds from the Pacific help to keep the shrubbery perennially fresh, but hidden within the Mountain itself there is, according to a belief of the Red Men, a lake, which assists in maintaining the Mountain's greenness, and whence issue springs of clear, artesian-like water.

A thermal belt, apparently sharply demarcated, extending north and south above Cuchama's summit, frequently acts as an invisible barrier to fog-banks moving inland from the Pacific Ocean. Thereupon, while the westerly slopes of Cuchama are covered by fog-banks up to the edge of the thermal belt above the summit, the adjacent easterly slopes are reposing in unobscured sunshine.

V. PHILOLOGICAL DATA

I have personally consulted a number of the oldest surviving Indians most competent to contribute relevant historical and philological data on Cuchama. Among these were Jim Chaleco, one of the Yuma, aged ninety-six when I met him in 1937, and Arsenius Chaleco, his son, who, as tribal poet, was well versed, as was his father, in the primitive traditions and initiatory lore of their nation.

During the spring of the following year, I interviewed Feliciano Manteca, born about 1840, and Maria, his second wife, herself about ninety at the time of the interview. These two were outstanding representatives of the once numerous Cochimí nation, Feliciano being the chieftain of his tribe. I found them at home on the tribal land of their ancestors in a secluded valley known as Neji (or Nehhi) Canyon, where Feliciano was happily cultivating his well-irrigated garden of beans and maize. The site is twelve miles inside Lower California by a winding road called the Tanama Road, southeast of the Mexican town of Tecate. Feliciano and Maria Manteca are mentioned in *The Kiliwa Indians of Lower California* (University of California Press, 1939, p. 83, "Appendix: Kiliwa Neighbors"), the author, Mr. Peveril Meigs III, having interviewed them in 1936.

Of these four Indians, Arsenius Chaleco alone knew English. His father and the two Mantecas conversed during the interview chiefly in the tongue of their respective tribes, making, when necessary, explanations in Spanish. Recourse has also been had to such contributory data as are available in published form.

The son, Arsenius Chaleco, was by nature a poet, in whom had been reposed the sacred chants and initiatory teachings of his Yuma tribe. In the compilation of the traditional lore associated with Cuchama, the aid of Arsenius was as invaluable as was that of his aged father. Without their assistance, our biography of the Exalted High Place would have lacked much of its deeper significance and historic content. And to both of them, each reader of the biography owes a debt of gratitude.

Feliciano Manteca, chief of the once numerous Cochimí tribe. A reproduction of a photograph taken when he was well over one-hundred-years old.

Were my researches to be undertaken today, the writing of this book would not be possible, for Jim and Arsenius Chaleco and Feliciano Manteca, who bore faithful witness to the sanctity of Cuchama, are now deceased, and much of the lore for which they were such worthy receptacles has died with them.[12]

1. The Name Cuchama

In our rendering of Cuchama as "Exalted (or Sacred) High Place," Coocha (or *Cuchan*) is taken to mean "Exalted," and *ma* to mean "High," "Place" being understood. Assistance in reaching this interpretation of Cuchama (or *Cuchanma*) was afforded by a letter from Dr. John P. Harrington, of the Bureau of American Ethnology, dated June 9th, 1938, in which he states: "The Yumas told me that *Yuma* is a White Man name given to them and that their old designation is *Ku-tcan*—we use *tc* for English *ch*—and that it means 'Exalted' and, also, 'Sincere.' " And Dr. Harrington takes the *ma* to be translatable as "high." Jim Chaleco, deriving from the *ma* a sense of sanctity, or sacredness, or highness of a religious kind, made an alternative rendering of *Cuchama* to be "Exalted Sacred Place (or Mountain)," "Place (or Mountain)" again being understood.[13] That Cuchama is one of the ancient High Places sacred to the Red Men was affirmed by Feliciano Manteca. Clavigero, in his *History of [lower] California* (Stanford University Press, 1937 edition, page 87), reports that in his day (1731–1787) the Indians inhabiting the northern part of what is now Lower California, which included the region tributary

---

[12][Ed. nt.: In Dr. Evans-Wentz' original manuscript, the following paragraph appears:

"Here is appended, and so placed on record, a letter, photographically reproduced, which is self-explanatory, from Mr. W. Norwood Cox, Assistant to the Superintendent of the Fort Yuma (Indian) Sub-Agency, Yuma, Arizona, concerning Jim Chaleco, the Yuman Indian I interviewed. Unfortunately, no photograph of Jim Chaleco has as yet been found, although one is believed to have existed.

(Letter to be placed here.)"

No copy of this letter has been found, nor one of the photograph. The above paragraph is quoted in order to affirm the value of both letter and photograph should subsequent researchers discover either or both. C.A.]

[13]The sacred hill of the Pueblo Tesuque is known as "the very high hill." So also is a sacred eminence at San Ildefonso and another at San Juan. These three synonymous renderings of the Indian names of sacred hills are in keeping with our rendering of *Cuchama* as "Sacred High Place." Cf. E. L. Hewett, B. P. Dutton, and John P. Harrington, *op. cit.,* pp. 34–36.

to Cuchama, were known as the Cochimí.[14] If Cochimí is taken to be another form of Cuchama (or Coochima), as we suggest that it may be, it would imply that the mountain was of such peculiar significance to the Cochimí as to be honored with their tribal name or, vice versa, that the tribal name was derived from the name of the Mountain. This would fit in with Jim Chaleco's understanding of the religious significance of Cuchama and tend to establish our alternative translation of it. Señor Aurelio de Vivance, referring to the Mountain in his *Baja California Al Dia* (1924, p. 250), gives its name in Spanish as *Cuchama.*[15]

[14]It should be noted here that there is uncertainty as to the exact territorial distribution of the Cochimí and as to whether or not they inhabited, as this study assumes they did, the Cuchama region. From a letter to me of December 31, 1953, by Miss Winona Adams, of National City, who has made research in the American ethnology of San Diego County, I have collected the information that follows, which is of interest and value in this connection:

Surviving Campo-Manzanita Indians consider the Cochimí mentioned by modern authorities as having inhabited northern Baja California to be a division of a Yuman Kumiyai stock. Of this stock, a Paipa, or Pai-pai, dialect division occupied the Tecate valley and thus the Cuchama region. Kumiyai, and not Cochimí, these Indian informants say, was the name for all their people (of similar linguistic basis) extending through what is now Imperial Valley and the Laguna Mountain ridge to the coast at San Diego, including, in addition to the Paipa, the Kiliwi (or Kiliwa), known to the Kumiyai as the Kwiliu, in present-day Baja California.

As Kroeber states (*op. cit.,* p. 709), "At Ensenada, 60 miles south of San Diego, the speech is still close to that of the Diegueño. The Indians through this stretch have no group names for each other, except by directions." In this connection, it should be observed that any tribes of the Cochimí who may have occupied this territory, inclusive of the Cuchama territory, before or at the time of the Spanish conquest, were like the Diegueño, members of, or closely related to the Yuma nation, to whose language group the name Cuchama is taken to be associated.

[Ed. nt.: According to the modern classification of North American language groups by Harold E. Driver in *Indians of North America* (Chicago, 1961), both the Yuma and Cochimí are included in the Hokan linguistic stock, believed to be one of the older ones on the continent. (*The Indian Heritage of America,* Alvin M. Josephy, Jr., New York, 1968.)

The Yuman tribes are said to have occupied the lower valleys of the Colorado and Gila rivers, Imperial Valley, and extreme southern California; and the Cochimís the northern portion of the peninsula of Baja California. (*Handbook of American Indians North of Mexico,* A. L. Kroeber, Vol. 2, New York, 1965.) F.W.]

[15]Record should be made here of a tradition that, in stagecoach days, an Indian bandit, habituated in waylaying and robbing the stagecoaches en route from New

Inasmuch as the summit of Cuchama is sometimes wreathed in clouds or mists, the Mountain is known by some of the present-day inhabitants of the locality as "The Fog-capped" (or "The Fog-bound"), and this appellation, derived from observing a natural phenomenon, appears to have become synonymous in the folk-mind with the locally well-known name Cuchama, the true meaning of which none of them could give.

That *Cuchama* (or, as it may also be written, *Cuchima*) is undoubtedly American is suggested by the name of the Inca chieftain Chall-cuchima, of which, however, we have not as yet ascertained the meaning. Chall-cuchima, like many of the leaders of the Red Men of Peru, died a martyr, having been burned alive by the order of Pizarro, the inhumane conqueror and despoiler of the empire of the Incas.[16]

2. History and Philology of Tecate

Tecate being the name most commonly assigned to Cuchama and to the territory round about Cuchama on the east and south, this history of the Tecate region is also the history of the corresponding Cuchama region.

The first post-Columbian Europeans to enter the Tecate region were undoubtedly Spanish, but there is no known record of who they were. They found there a *ranchería,* or Indian village, to which the name Tecate was already attached.[17] As a place name, Tecate is, therefore, undoubtedly of pre-Columbian origin; and, as is suggested in the third paragraph below, may be Aztec.

Mexico and Arizona to San Diego of their gold bars in transit, made Cuchama his stronghold and was known as "Cuchama." From this it sometimes has been assumed, but erroneously, that the Mountain derived its name from the bandit. My researches have established that the Mountain bore the name of Cuchama before the time of the bandit, as Feliciano Manteco (referred to in the Preface), who recollected the bandit, confirmed, and that it was because of the bandit's close association with the Mountain that he came to be called after it and not conversely.

[16]Cf. W. H. Prescott, *History of the Conquest of Mexico* (New York, n.d.) and *History of the Conquest of Peru* (New York, 1847), p. 983, 989.

[17]Cf. P. T. Hanna, *Dictionary of California Land Names* (Los Angeles, 1951), pp. 325–26.

Various attempts have been made to determine the meaning of Tecate. One writer, evidently erroneously taking the pronunciation of the first syllable to Tecate to be Teek, reports that Tecate is derived "from Teca, teak-wood,"[18] of which the pre-Columbian Red Men are not likely ever to have heard. Another interpretation is that Tecate "may contain the common Mexican name *tecats* for the species of gourd, *cucurbita maxima;* or it may be derived from Mexican *atecate,* which Santamaria interprets as meaning 'water in which the baker moistens her hand while making *tortillas,*' but which one of Robelo's informants translates as *agua turbia,* 'muddy water.' "[19]

The statement of Charles F. Emery, San Diego County pioneer, who arrived in about the year 1870, also has interest. Being interviewed at Tecate by John and Winifred Davidson, of the San Diego Historical Society in 1934, Mr. Emery said, "The Indians tell me that *Tecate,* pronounced Tay-kah-tay, refers to a kind of coarse grass that abounds here. I have never heard any other explanation of the meaning." Lic. Mario Somohano Flores, formerly a member of the faculty of the Yucatan State University, offers the following comment: "There is here philological confusion; for it is not the word *Tecate,* but the word *Zacate* (pronounced Thah-cah-tay), that refers to a kind of coarse grass, namely, couch-grass, or dog's grass, which is cut and made into hay. On the other hand, Professor Martinez's view [set forth below] that the name Tecate is a corruption of the Aztec Indian term *Tolcuate,* appears to be plausible."

On May 18, 1938, when I visited the Government School in Tecate, Mexico, Professor Martinez, then the head master, told me that in his view, the name *Tecate* (or *Tecarte*) is a corruption of the term Tolcuate, appertaining to the Nahuatl language, the language spoken by the Aztecs, and meaning, in Spanish, *"Arbol Caido,"* or, in English, "Fallen Tree." Inasmuch as the Indian tribes who formerly inhabited the Tecate region are believed to have belonged to the same racial stock as the Aztecs, this place-

[18]Cf. H. L. Wells, *California Names* (Los Angeles, 1934), p. 85.
[19]Cf. F. G. Gudde, *California Place Names* (Berkeley and Los Angeles, 1949), p. 354.

name may very well be Aztec; and, if Professor Martinez's view be sound, the name when applied to the Mountain may be of profound anthropological significance, as suggested by the following legendary lore concerning Montezuma, the Aztec emperor of Mexico, and the fallen sacred tree:

> When the name of Quetzalcoatl was no longer heard from the teocalli [or sacred hill] of Cholula, that of Montezuma took its place. From ocean to ocean, and from the river Gila to the Nicaraguan lake, nearly every aboriginal nation still cherishes the memory of Montezuma, not as the last unfortunate ruler of a vanished state, but as the prince of their golden era, their Saturnian age, lord of the winds and waters, and founder of their institutions. When, in the depth of the tropical forests, the antiquary disinters some statue of earnest mien, the natives whisper one to the other, "Montezuma! Montezuma!" In the legends of New Mexico he is the founder of the pueblos, and entrusted to their guardianship the sacred fire. Departing, he planted a tree, and bade them watch it well, for when that tree should fall and the fire die out, then he would return from the far East, and lead his loyal people to victory and power. When the last generation saw their land glide, mile by mile, into the rapacious hands of the Yankees—and when new and strange diseases desolated their homes—finally, when, in 1846, the sacred tree was prostrated, and the guardian of the holy fire was found dead on its cold ashes, then they thought the hour of deliverance had come, and every morning at earliest dawn a watcher mounted to the housetops, and gazed long and anxiously in the lightening east, hoping to descry the noble form of Montezuma advancing through the morning beams at the head of a conquering army.[20]

Accordingly, the Mountain, having been recognized for unknown centuries as a place of initiation and unusual sanctity under the more usual and probably more ancient appellation Cuchama, as our research has discovered, may have come to be, after the

[20]Cf. D. G. Brinton, *op. cit.,* pp. 223–24. A cult of the sacred fire, believed to have been a cultural inheritance from the Mound Builders, who appear to have adopted it through ancient Mayan influences, prevailed in North America, as it did in Mexico, Central and South America, especially among the Natchez, Creeks, Cherokees, Southern Sioux, the Iroquoian peoples, the Winnebagos, and the Algonquin Ottawas. According to the Natchez records, the greatest calamity ever to befall the Natchez nation was extinction of the sacred fire in their temple, due to lack of precaution on the part of one of the two sacred fire's guardians. Cf. P. Radin, *The Story of the American Indian* (New York, 1934), pp. 203–5, 230–31.

advent of the conquering White Men, associated in some mysterious and secret manner with the sacred Fallen Tree and thus called, as it is today, Mount Tecate (or Tecarte). Perhaps it may now be looked upon as destined to play a part in the New Age foretold by the Red Men's seers, when the reincarnation of Montezuma, Avatar of Quetzlcoatl, the Mexican Culture Hero, is destined to appear like a Khalki Avatar and become the American Redeemer.

It should be noted here that Montezuma was not, as Brinton's account implies, the last of the Mexican emperors, who was Cuauhtemoc;[21] Montezuma, or Monteczuma, also known as Montezuma II, or Zocoyotsin, was the last of the Mexican emperors who had known rule in the pre-Spanish era. He was born in 1477 (according to Bernal Diaz, in 1479) and died a martyr to the Conquistadores on June 30, 1530, in Tenochtitlan, now Mexico City. After the Spanish Conquest, the martyred Montezuma became a hero-god among the native people of Mexico and Central America, and his name is still revered as far north as the pueblos of New Mexico and Arizona.[22]

---

[21]Cf. *Historia y Leyendas de Las Calles de Mexico* (Mexico, D.F., 1950) II, 55.

[22][Ed. nt.: The legend of Moctezuma's visit to the pueblos in New Mexico and Arizona bringing the sacred fire is still current in the northernmost of the pueblos, Taos Pueblo, New Mexico. However, there is no mention in Aztec historical records that he traveled so far north, and it is very doubtful that he did so. Nor is there any basis for Brinton's quoted belief that Moctezuma is revered as a hero-god throughout Mesoamerica. He is more generally regarded as a betrayer of his people. The actual facts of his life and death are documented in several Aztec codices and other written narratives of the Spanish conquest of Mexico.

Moctezuma Xocoyotzin (II), grandson of Moctezuma Ilhuicamina (I), was born in either 1479 or 1480 and assumed rulership of the Aztec empire in 1502. He was a weak and sensitive man who believed in the transcendental religion of Quetzalcoatl, the mythical culture-bringer and god of the Toltecs of Teotihuacan who preceded the Aztecs. When Cortés arrived with his Spanish conquistadores in 1519, Moctezuma welcomed him in his capital Tenochtitlan (now Mexico City) without offering resistance, believing Cortés was Quetzalcoatl returning as anciently prophesied. Cortés immediately imprisoned him in the palace and began plundering the city and massacring its inhabitants. Too late, the Aztecs realized the Spaniards were men, not gods, and besieged the palace.

The emperor was forced or induced to speak to the milling crowd from the rooftop, urging his people to stop their revolt and promising that the Spaniards would leave Mexico. His answer was a shower of stones. Whether these killed him, or he was murdered by the Spaniards, is not known. The Spaniards then cast forth his body with that of Itzquauhtzin, one of his nobles whom they had murdered.

The greatness of Montezuma was made manifest as he was dying. When Olmedo, a priest of the Christians, besought Montezuma to embrace a crucifix (a symbol which, by association with the Spaniards, had lost all sacredness in the eyes of Montezuma and of the Aztec nobles who remained faithful to him in death), he coldly repulsed the priest and exclaimed, "I have but a few moments to live; and will not at this hour desert the faith of my fathers."[23]

Unlike the meaning and philology of Tecate the place-name, which we have found to be uncertain but perhaps most reliably evaluated by Professor Martinez, the post-Columbian history of Tecate, the *rancheria* (or Indian village), now a flourishing town at the southerly and easterly approaches of the Mountain, is available in written records from whence has been formulated the greater part of the following summary.

In keeping with the White Man's ways of acquiring property (as is set forth more fully in Section IV which follows), Juan Bandini, a Spaniard born in 1800 in Peru, who came to San Diego as a youth with his father, a Spanish adventurer, was gifted, on July 12, 1834, the Tecate *rancheria,* comprising 4,439 acres of land on both sides of what is now the U.S.A.-Mexico Boundary,[24] which was established in 1847. In the eyes of the Spanish regime who made the gift, the native inhabitants of the Tecate *rancheria* had no right of occupancy therein save as serfs, such as the Red Men

---

According to the *Florentine Codex,* compiled by Aztec spokesmen under the direction of Fray Bernardino de Sahagun soon after the Conquest (Vol. 12, p. 63–64, of the English translation, 1955), the Aztecs gently carried Itzquauhtzin's body to the temple courtyard at Quauhxicalco. Flags were hung, food set before it, and the body burned with great honors. In contrast, the body of Moctezuma was carried to Copulco and laid on a pyre. And "it seemed to lie sizzling, and it smelled foul as it burned. And as it burned, with pure hatred, with little good will, some chid him, and said, 'This evildoer! He terrorized the world! In all the world there was fear and fright before him. . . . And still many who cursed him. . . .' " His tragic death took place in 1520, not in 1530.

The Aztec hero of the Conquest was not Moctezuma, but Cuauhtemoc, the last brief ruler. He tried vainly with his people to resist the Spaniards, but was defeated, tortured, and finally hanged by Cortés in 1525. He is commemorated today by the famous statue erected on the Paseo de la Reforma in Mexico City. F. W.]

[23]Cf. W. H. Prescott, *op. cit.,* p. 435.
[24]Cf. P. T. Hanna, *op. cit.,* pp. 325–26; W. E. Smythe, *History of San Diego* (San Diego, 1907), pp. 112, 164.

generally were in all the Missions and *rancherías* controlled, as the Tecate *ranchería* nominally was, by the Mission Fathers, throughout the whole of what are now Upper and Lower California.

Bandini was operating the Tecate *ranchería* in 1836.[25] But it was unlike most of the ranches of San Diego County, notably the Warner Ranch of hot-spring fame whence, as late as 1902,[26] the Indians, helplessly protesting, were wrongfully removed to the inferior area of Pala; the Tecate Indians took matters into their own hands and drove Bandini out of the Tecate *ranchería* in 1837–38,[27] only about three years after the attempt had been made to wrest it from them, even though they were unquestionably its rightful owners.

Like almost all of the White Men, both north and south of the Rio Grande, Bandini appears to have been aggressively inimical to the Red Men. Governor Alvarado accused Bandini of "claiming the honor of having killed a large number of Indians." Bandini is reported as having said that he had killed "only a few" Indians. How many of these were of the Tecate *ranchería,* as presumably some were, is not stated. There is, however, a complementary report that in a campaign of ten days the Spaniards killed "all they could find" of the Indians.[28]

Despite the Spanish Governor's serious charge against Bandini and Bandini's own admission of having killed "a few" Indians, no criminal action was instituted or, apparently, even contemplated against Bandini or his accomplices. Indeed, throughout the whole length of North and South America, the White Men, with very few exceptions, thought little more of killing a Red Man than of killing a rabbit or a deer.[29]

[25] Cf. H. H. Bancroft, *History of California* (San Francisco, 1886), III 612[n].
[26] The Warner Ranch contained 26,629.88 acres, unjustifiably wrested from the Red Men, who had been in rightful possession of it for unknown centuries and had well-ordered villages thereon.
[27] Cf. *Publications of the Historical Society of Southern California* (Los Angeles, 1898), IV, 243.
[28] Cf. H. H. Bancroft, *History of California,* iv, 68, 69[n].
[29] In Bandini's time, many of the Red Men inhabiting what is now San Diego County, having been despoiled of their food-producing lands and of their game preserves and grazing lands, were faced with the dire choice of starving or of raiding the ranches which the White Men had stolen from them. There being then no paternal government to place them on reservations or to feed them, they,

The writer recalls having seen the eroded and much rusted remains of a cache of old-time muskets found in a small cave on the easterly slope of Mt. Tecate by members of the Austin Spurlock family who then lived nearby on their ranch (probably a part of the Bandini grant). The muskets were recognized as being souvenirs of the days when adventurers of Anglo-Saxon rather than of Spanish lineage sought to possess not only the Tecate region, as Bandini had, but Baja California as a whole.

Feliciano Manteco remembered how the Tecate Red Men had wars with the Tijuana[30] Red Men; and that when the wars were in progress the Tecate Red Men were accustomed to make Mt. Tecate their stronghold. Undoubtedly, long before the advent of the White Men, there were numerous, purely Red Men wars of like character in which the Tecate Red Men took part. Therefore, the latter must have been quite competent not only to recover from Bandini their stolen Tecate *ranchería,* but to look after their own worldly affairs independently of the Mission Fathers. Due to this independence, the Tecate *ranchería* is quite unlike most California *rancherías* in never having been lost to the control of its rightful owners.

---

quite naturally, chose raiding; and one after another of their famished bands of raiders suffered merciless massacre.

The White Men having initiated raiding, by raids against the Red Men, the latter, originally friendly and peaceable, began, in their reprisals, to emulate the White Men by making raiding profitable, through stealing, in addition to bread stuff, cattle, and horses. Although the historical records are far from complete and often lack clarity, there appears to be reason for suspecting that the White Men's raid-killings which ensued, like those in other parts of the Americas, were sometimes, if not commonly, conducted—apart from the covetousness for loot —as a sport like fox-hunting. The Red Men had relatively little defense against the firearms and superior accoutrements of the White Men, but they fought with such bitter desperation that the White Men were not always the victors. That Bandini was well acquainted with these Indian-killing practices of his compatriots and participated in them, as he admitted having done in killing "only a few" Indians, is emphasized by his own report of how in one of the "campaigns," as the Indian-killing expeditions were euphemistically called, the Spaniards were defeated. (Cf. H. H. Bancroft, *History of California,* iv, 69[n].)

[30] *Tiwana,* a Red Man place-name, probably meaning "by the sea," was corrupted, through resemblance in sound, into *Tia Juana,* Spanish for "Aunt Jane." Cf. N. Van de Grift Sanchez, *Spanish and Indian Place Names of California* (San Francisco, 1914), p. 47.

VI. NATURE'S OWN TEMPLE; THE SECRET INITIATORY
CAVERN; AND A RACE OF GIANTS

The Red Men to whom Cuchama was sacred reared no material shrine upon it. Like the Druids of Europe, who worshipped in oak groves, the Cuchama Red Men revered the Sun, the Moon, and the Stars, and Nature's phenomena. They needed no lesser temple such as man might build. So there are no ancient ruins on the Sacred High Place awaiting exploration. Earthen pots in fragments, arrowheads, and other objects of these Red Men's fashioning have been found there, and they testify to the now vanished race that once possessed Cuchama.[31]

According to tradition, there is, however, within the Mountain a temple-like cavern, which is said to have been known to the Red Men of the past—and probably, too, to a primeval race of men that preceded the Red Men—and to have been used by them as a place for secret initiatory rites. According to early Spanish missionaries to Lower California, there was such a primeval race. And as indicated by skeletons found there by these missionaries, and by petrographs still well-preserved in various caves of Lower California, the race was a race of giants.[32]

---

[31]One of the most artistic of the arrowheads, made of white quartz, triangular in shape, and 1–¼ inches long, was found on the summit of Cuchama in the year 1955 by Mr. Raymond C. Hirsch of El Cajon, California, and is now in the writer's custody.

[32]Cf. F. J. Clavigero, *The History of [Lower] California* (Stanford University, 1937), pp. 84–86; A. W. North, *Camp and Camino in Lower California* (New York, 1910), pp. 65–71, concerning petrographs of a pre-historic race there, and his *Mother of California* (New York, 1908), pp. 124–26; *University of California Publications in American Archaeology and Ethnology*, Vol. XXIV, no. 2, pp. 47–238; and H. H. Bancroft, *op. cit.,* Vol. IV, p. 695, Vol. V, pp. 49–50, 197–99. Tradition also tells of a family of giants who inhabited a cave in the Black Mesa, the most conspicuous geographical feature of the Tewa Valley, between San Ildefonso and Santa Clara. The Indians called Black Mesa, "large, flat, high place," cf. E. L. Hewett, B. P. Button, and John P. Harrington, *The Pueblo Indian World* (University of New Mexico Press, 1945), pp. 37–38.

According to apparently trustworthy reports, Mr. Paxton Hayes, about the year 1947, discovered in Sonora, Mexico, about ninety miles south of Alamos, in the region of the Rio del Fuerte, north of San Blas near the border of Sinaloa, in a mountain cavern, at an altitude of about 7,000 feet, a lost city of beehive-shaped huts wherein were found mummies of giants eight to nine feet in height wrapped in saffron-colored robes. On the robes there were blue pyramid-like emblems upon which were series of white dots said to be correlatable with the

It is traditionally believed that parts of this now lost cavern in the Sacred Mountain were shaped by man, and that on the cavern's granite walls there are hieroglyphic-like inscriptions.

VII. THE VISION OF GUIDANCE

Among the early Californian races inhabiting the territories round about Cuchama, long before the coming of the European invaders, the subtle power of the Sacred Mountain to awaken the Superior Man had become so widely recognized that the Mountain was a spiritual sanctuary of paramount importance. As the young men of the tribes tributary to Cuchama approached manhood, after having undergone the preliminary initiation of earlier boyhood, singly and solitarily, one by one in turn, when the tribal elders had prepared them, they went on pilgrimage to the summit of "The Exalted High Place" to choose their lot in life.[33]

Invocation having been made to the Great Mystery and to the guardian deities of the Mountain, the suppliant, when the Sun had set and the stars were lit, lay down there in the solitude on the summit and slept throughout the hours of darkness. In the mystic dream which was vouchsafed to him, he was, for a moment, empowered to recollect how, in past aeons, before entering the door of the womb on Earth for the first time, he had dwelt with

---

Mayan time-cycle of 25,000 years. The Yaqui Indians, who guided Mr. Hayes to this lost city of giants, and the Seri Indians of Tiburon Island told him that the giant race originated in a land now submerged. Dr. I. J. Bush met an Indian who knew of a cave in the Arroyo de Los Yglesias of the Tarahumara Indian country, Chihuahua, which contained two mummies eight feet tall. Cf. I. J. Bush, *Gringo Doctor* (Caldewell, Idaho, 1935), p. 115.

[Ed. nt.: The alleged discovery by Mr. Hayes has not been substantiated. F. W.]
[33]In this connection, it is interesting to observe, on the authority of Mr. Malcolm Rogers, lately Scientific Director of the Museum of Man, San Diego, that the Toluache Cult (based upon sacramental drinking of a decoction made of the jimson-weed, *datura stramonium,* by youths undergoing puberty initiation), which was widespread among the Red Men of what is now Los Angeles County and northern San Diego County at the time of the Spanish Conquest, seems never to have been adopted by the Yumas who inhabited the territory round about Cuchama. Similarly, Mr. Peveril Meigs III, who studied the Kiliwa, a tribe of the Cochimí, during the years 1928 and 1929, reports (*op. cit.,* pp. 49, 64) that the use of jimson-weed was not associated with any of their initiatory or other religious ceremonies. See, also, A. L. Kroeber, *op. cit.,* p. 661.

the Divine Progenitor of the tribe and possessed spiritual understanding. Then there came to him, in the vision, the Shining Beings, clothed in the radiance of the Sun; and he beheld in
the dazzling splendor the various lots in life from which men
may choose. Guided by his own innate tendencies inherited from
past lives, he had no difficulty or hesitancy in making the right
choice.[34]   And so long as his present incarnation should en-

---

[34]Various beliefs and initiatory teachings relating to pre-existence and reincarnation prevailed generally among the aboriginal races throughout the Americas, as
they did among the Yumas, one of whose medicine-men and myth narrators
stated, "Before I was born, I would sometimes steal out of my mother's womb
while she was sleeping. . . . Every good doctor [*kwasidhe,* almost synonymous
with *sumach,* 'dreamer'] begins to understand before he is born. When a little
boy, I took a trip to Avikwame Mountain and slept at its base. I felt of my body
with my two hands, but found it was not there. It took me four days and nights
to go there. Later, I became able to approach even the top of the mountain." It
was on the mountain, presumably all alone, like the one on Cuchama, that this
Indian youth met Kumastamho, the chief invisible spiritual guardian of the tribe.
The youth, most likely, was secretly undergoing psychic training to fit him to
become, as he did become, a medicine-man and narrator of the tribe's legendary
history. Continuing the narrative about these remarkable experiences of his
boyhood, the medicine-man added, "I now have power to go to Kumastamho
any time. . . . It takes four days to tell [all the old stories I there was taught] about
Kwikumat [another of the non-human teachers] and Kumastamho. I was present
from the very beginning [that these old stories reveal]; and saw and heard all [in
my dreams]. I dreamed a little of it at a time." The Mohave, too, "insist that
they possess all this knowledge through dreams; and, like the Yuma, every
narrator is convinced that he was present at the ancient events he tells of," and
each of their medicine-men "insists that he himself received his powers from
Mastamho [the Mohave's divine progenitor and teacher] at the beginning of the
world." Cf. A. L. Kroeber, *op. cit.,* pp. 754, 783–84. See, also, *Ibid.,* p. 852, as
to pre-existence. Ohiyesa, in *The Soul of the Indian,* p. 167, testifies that "Many
of the Indians believed that one may be born more than once; and there were
some who claimed to have full knowledge of a former incarnation."

Essentially the same belief which is here presented and which the Indians
throughout the Americas generally held, that men in choosing their lots in life
are governed by innate tendencies transmitted from past lives, appears to have
been widespread even among the Greek philosophers. Plato, in the tenth book
of the *Republic,* in telling of the vision of Er, wherein Greek heroes, preparatory
to taking rebirth, were seen choosing lots in their life about to dawn, says—as
the sages of the Red Men would likewise say—"the choice of the souls was in
most cases based on their own experiences of a previous life." An interpretation
of the symbolic character of the lives chosen by these Greek heroes is set forth
on pages 49–53 of *The Tibetan Book of the Dead,* and on pages 190–93 of that
Tibetan treatise on the art of dying and of being reborn there is expounded the
psychic technique of wisely choosing one's lot in a new life when one is about
to reincarnate.

dure, the lot which he had thus chosen and no other was to be his.

When the vision had faded and he awoke, the dawn was beginning to fill the eastern sky. He watched and waited for the coming forth of the Sun; and, then, as its first rays fell upon him, he made obeisance of thanksgiving and praise to it and, descending from the Holy Mountain, returned to his people.

The joyfulness of step and the radiance of countenance of the "new-born one" could be seen from afar by the elders of the tribe who were awaiting him; and glad were the songs of his homecoming. They bathed him to signify his purification of body and clearness of vision, and to confirm him in his spiritual rebirth. Then for four days he entered into meditative retreat, sparingly partaking of only the simplest and purest food, all fatty and fleshy food being prohibited. And he was encouraged to avoid, for as long a time thereafter as possible, the eating of flesh lest his newly-won psychic equilibrium be disturbed.[35]

[35]Of the Luiseño tribe, northern neighbors of the Diegueño, Professor A. L. Kroeber, in his *Handbook of the Indians of California,* page 670, states that when undergoing initiation "the boys are forbidden meat for several months, and are then encouraged to refrain from it, or at least to eat it sparingly, for as much longer as possible." Even among the few surviving Kiliwa, who live about one hundred miles southeast of Cuchama, the same taboo against the eating of flesh food by boys undergoing initiation is still observed. (Cf. Peveril Meigs III, *op. cit.,* p. 49.)

Among many primitive races throughout the world, and also among highly cultured races like the ancient Greeks and Romans, the partaking of flesh food was prohibited to initiates, either permanently, as among the Pythagoreans and Essenes, or for such a time as was deemed sufficient to establish unshakably the spirituality newly acquired by initiation. The Greeks encouraged professional wrestlers and warriors to eat raw flesh and to drink warm blood in order thereby to acquire ferociousness, as tigers do; but philosophers were not to partake of such nutrition because of its passion-producing effects. It was held by most people of antiquity that elemental beings, known then as daemons, to whom animal sacrifice was made, nourished themselves by the impalpable, subtle essence of the blood spilled on the sacrificial altars. A similar belief appears to have been common among the Aztecs, whose nationally-maintained priesthood regularly made human sacrifices. According to oriental sages, the blood in flesh food —as on fields of battle—attracts invisible beings inimical to man's spiritual progress. These entities parasitically attach themselves to flesh-eaters, human and sub-human and, by their incessant and insatiable craving for blood, maintain their victims' carnivorousness. For these and other reasons of an occult nature, neophytes and initiates, especially among Hindus, scrupulously avoid the eating, the touching, and even the vicinity of slaughtered animals. Some such philosophy seems to underlie the Red Men's advice to their own initiates with respect to the eating of flesh, particularly to those in whom the psyche has just been awakened.

Thus he passed from the state of irresponsible youthfulness into that of responsible manhood; and, soon afterward entering the married state, was pledged to assist in the propagation of his tribe and in the transmission of the initiatory esoteric teachings. Even as the elders had guided him on the secret pathway, so would he, in his turn, guide the young men of the coming generation.

VIII. THE LOTS IN LIFE

For the youth of the Red Men, the lots in life were not numerous like those of the youth of the White Men. A favorite choice of one athletically inclined was to be endowed with fleetness of foot and become a runner and scout in the service of the tribe. More ordinary was the choice of prowess in hunting and in warfare. But few chose, or were fitted to choose, the lot of the priestly medicine-man. Success in games of chance was a possible choice, for some of the Red Men were as fond of gaming as are some of their white brethren. Although the accumulation of private wealth, such as that based upon owning oak trees which produced edible acorns, was permissible, it seems never to have been encouraged or to have been an initiatory choice. As one of the wisest of the Mission Indians once explained, the lot of a rich man was never popular among his people before the advent of the White Man. For, at that time, no member of a tribe lacked food or shelter. There was no unemployment and no need for social security. There was joy in living. There was length of life; and the destroying diseases and "fire-water" brought by the White Men were unknown.

What a college or university is to the youth of the White Man of today, the Exalted High Place, and many other holy mountains and places of initiation throughout the Americas were to the youth of the Red Men. For the Red Men, learning was not to be acquired by such external means as books and written languages. Illiteracy was universal among them; and yet they were as a race more truly educated than are most of the literate sons of the White Men who have succeeded them.

"Knowledge is not a thing to be learned, the Mohave declare, but to be acquired by each man according to his dreams."[36] This

---

[36]A. L. Kroeber, *op. cit.,* p. 754.

was also the conviction of the Yuma tribes, to whose cultural life our present study is initially devoted. It is for the purpose of establishing conscious contact with the content of the unconscious that the Red Men underwent—as have most ancient peoples, civilized and primitive—the discipline of initiation, and that the youth of the tribes who reverenced Cuchama sought the Vision of Guidance.[37]

A. L. Kroeber states: "The direct basis of all religion—tradition, ritual song, and shamanistic power—is individual dreaming, in the opinion of the Yuma. They hold to this belief as thoroughly and consistently as do the Mohave."[38] But not until the conscious contact with the content of the unconscious has been established by the initiatory awakening of the psyche is the Red Man capable of psychically-controlled and correct dreaming, in virtue of which he attains right guidance and becomes rightly educated.

That the Red Man's psychic education was not dependent upon the individual's idiosyncrasies, but was quite systematized, and consistent with the hereditary tribal culture, generation by generation, is clearly indicated by the following account by the same Yuma medicine-man and myth narrator quoted above.

After having told how he attained knowledge of the cultural lore of his tribe by going to Kumastamho in dreams, he said, "I would then tell it [the lore] to my friends. The old men would say: 'That is right! I was there and heard it myself.' Or [if the lore be incorrectly reported] they would say, 'You have dreamed badly. That is not right.' And they would tell me right. So, at last, I learned the whole of it right."[39]

Thus the Red Men had good reason to maintain, as did the most illustrious of the Greeks and as do the sages of modern India and Tibet, that all real knowledge lies hidden within man, and that real

[37]Mental concentration upon a mountain believed to be imbued with sacred qualities seems to call forth, or by practice develop, extra-sensory perception in the neophyte, and thus enables him to become really enlightened psychically.
[38]A. L. Kroeber, *op. cit.*, p. 783. When dreaming, as the neo-Platonists likewise believed, man is closer to the divine. The practice of sleeping in a sacred place and appealing to the deities for guidance through dreams was as widespread throughout the ancient world, especially in Egypt, Assyria, Babylon, Greece and Rome, as it was among the pre-Columbian peoples of the Americas. And the practice was more or less adopted by the early Christians in their temple-resorts.
[39]*Ibid.*, p. 784.

education consists in the awakening of this hidden knowledge. Some European and American psychologists, too, influenced by Dr. Jung's concept of the collective unconscious, appear to be tending towards the same view; for, as a result of their own researches, they postulate that innate within the unconscious lies the immeasurably greater part of Man the Unknown.

IX. THE COMPARATIVE CULTURAL PSYCHOLOGY

In this way, the social life of the Yuma, the Mohave, and other tribes originally inhabiting California, Arizona, New Mexico, and parts of Northern Mexico, was shaped much more by psychic than by physical experience. Whereas the European races, in contrast, are more commonly governed in their everyday life by external appearances and, as a direct result, are habituated to ignore, if not to deny, the reality of that inner guidance which each of the Founders of the world's prevailing faiths experienced and proclaimed as being essential to the health of society, the American races were, before their corruption by the White Man, unattached to what the eye beholds in the transitory and non-eternal world. Therefore, the American races were better able to understand the non-transitory and the abiding.

The Red Man, being, as we have seen, introspective, seeks truth spiritually; the White Man, being extrospective, seeks truth materially. Instinctively aspiring for attunement with the cosmic processes, the Red Man gladly surrenders himself to them; but the White Man sets himself individually apart from them and, in a more or less hostile manner and by purely external means, seeks to subjugate them to his own materialistic ends. Accordingly, the Red Man's psychically-based culture, although rudimentary, as we have examined it in connection with Cuchama, is, much more than the White Man's utilitarianly-based culture, in harmony even with such very highly evolved cultures (also psychically-based) as those of Hindustan and China. As was the Red Man's culture, the great oriental cultures were born of man's yogic at-one-ment with Nature. They were derived directly from the jungle schools of the Rishis of the *Upanishads,* from the Buddha's Enlightenment won in the rural solitude under the Bodhi-tree, or from the meditation-halls of Bodhidharma and the tranquil mountain retreats of the Teachers of Tao.

To this day, however, most of the surviving Red Men are very wise in preferring the simple life of their pueblos and reservations (both within the United States and throughout Mexico and Central and South America) to the extreme commercialized utilitarianism and rampant technology of their Caucasian brethren, who, enamored of the artificiality and softening comfort of life in cities and, thereby, cut off from Nature's saving beneficence, have become psychically impotent.

Not without reason do many of these conservative and silent Red Men believe, as their seers foretold, that they as a people need but be patient, that only for a brief season will the White Man possess the land. Were they able to express themselves in the White Man's sophisticated manner, very well might they urge the White Man to return to the salvation of naturalness and simplicity and self-knowledge, and to consider, before it be too late, how the proud Romans, the Greeks, the Egyptians, the Babylonians, also trod the age-old and ever-tempting path of excessive urbanization and luxurious comfortableness—and are no more.

Big White Owl (Jasper Hill), today the leading living representative of the Delawares, is well-fitted to voice and to summarize, as he does, the Red Men's view:

> We who live in this period of ever-changing panorama cannot fully comprehend the mystery and the sublimity of "Kitche Manitou's" great plan, we can only wait, patiently and quietly, for we know that "Kishe-lamo-k'wang" (the Creator) works in a strange and mysterious way His wonders to perform.
>
> Today, as I look out over the vastness of this land, I can see upon the ruins and ashes of our once peaceful villages and ancient council-fires, that a nation of pale-faced people have built a new kind of civilization which seems to be emblazoned with four terrifying and all-consuming monsters: Greed, Prejudice, Hate, Fear. And I find, to my great sorrow, that this new civilization is dissolving into itself, ruthlessly and destructively, all the silent restful places of the land. It seems to have found some sort of romance in converting and diverting the powers of Nature into implements of devastation and destruction. This new way of life is mutilating and destroying and robbing the fertility of our precious soil! Must we of the Lenni Lenape forever sit back and watch this chaos with impassive eyes?

Down through all the painful centuries we have been taught by our wise ones to regard ourselves as mediators and arbitrators. It was our duty to lead the fighting and wayward Indian nations into the ways of peace and brotherhood. We were the sentinels and scouts. We were the trail-blazers and the peace-makers. We were the official keepers of the sacred fire of peace, which was handed to our "Fire Builders" from an altar beyond the horizon of time. . . . Brothers and friends, let us, in this troubled period, once more hold high the torch of liberty and peace! . . . Let us save America! . . . I have spoken![40]

X. THE RETURN TO NATURALNESS

Although the work of the Teachers must needs be chiefly with dwellers in towns and cities, they ever seek, as all mankind should, solitude for meditation and a restoration of physical and psychical energies in the aura of the High Places. Hypnotically entranced by the glamour of their own ephemeral creations, multitudes of unenlightened mankind are fettered to the treadmill of incarnate existence in the great metropolises of the world, where they are born and live and die and exultantly compete to barter away their bodily strength and health and length of days for the things that pass away.

In this epoch, perhaps more than in any past epoch, the city-dwelling multitudes need that spiritual rebirth which is bestowed by Earth's sacred mountains. If our civilization is to endure, it must break its urban fetters and live in attunement with the Great Mother. It must know, as do the Teachers, the music of the silences, the companionship of the solitudes, the inspiration of the High Places.

Let the Christian ponder what St. Matthew has written concerning the Christos, the Perfected Man of the Gnosis, Who, although accustomed to the busy marts of men, felt at times, as have all Sages, a need of that psychic rejuvenation which comes only from a return to naturalness: "When He had sent the multi-

[40]Cf. Big White Owl (Jasper Hill) in "Let Us Save America," in *Indians at Work* (U.S. Department of the Interior, Office of Indian Affairs, Washington, D.C., Jan., 1941), pp.30–31.

tudes away, He went up into a mountain to pray; and, when the evening was come, He was there alone."[41]

XI. THE GREATNESS OF THE RED MEN

No other race of men has been more misunderstood than the race that possessed the New World prior to the arrival of Columbus. The evaluations by which their European brethren have judged them have not been right evaluations. Now, when only a small minority of them remain uncorrupted and are able to bear witness of their ancestral heritage, Science, unmoved by social and religious prejudices, is discovering that their hallowed lore constitutes a uniquely original contribution to the advancement of learning, perhaps as great as any conveyed by written records.

Filled with this rightful understanding, may all who shall hereafter make the pilgrimage to the summit of the Exalted High Place do so with fitting reverence for those of past generations of our human kind that sanctified it by their Vision of Guidance and by their salutation to the Sun reborn at dawn.

Thereby may Cuchama continue to be revered as one of Earth's holiest of temples built without hands. And may it become to the successors of the Children of the Great Mystery, as it was during the long epochs of America's unrecorded past, a place whereon to attain inner guidance and communion with the Invisible, the Formless, the Uncreated.

[41] *St. Matthew*, 17:23.

Other Sacred Mountains Throughout the World

PART II

Hymn to Mt. Blanc at Dawn*

O dread and silent Mount! I gazed upon thee,
Till thou, still present to the bodily sense,
Didst vanish from my thought: entranced in prayer,
I worshipped the invisible alone.

* * * * *

Thou too again, stupendous Mountain! thou,
That as I raise my head, awhile bowed low
In adoration, upward from thy base
Slow travelling with dim eyes suffused with tears,
Solemnly seemest, like a vapoury cloud,
To rise before me.—Rise, O ever rise,
Rise like a cloud of incense from the Earth!
Thou kingly Spirit throned among the hills,
Thou dread ambassador from Earth to Heaven,
Great Hierarch! tell thou the silent sky,
And tell the stars, and tell yon rising Sun,
Earth, with her thousand voices, praises God.

Samuel Taylor Coleridge

*[Ed. nt.: From "Hymn Before Sunrise, in the Vale of Chamouni"]

Mt. Kailas, as seen from Diraphug, Tibet. Reproduction of a painting by Li Gotami.

2

Other Sacred Mountains Throughout the World

In the scriptures of mankind, certain mountains are considered sacred; and they are referred to as being sources of inspiration and revelation to prophets, saints, and sages. Mountains rising on high and merging into the invisible depths of space come to be looked upon as being the abodes of heavenly beings, the repositories of wisdom, and the founts of spiritual illumination. High mountains are ever awe-inspiring, and devotees when immersed in their solitude and stillness attain attunement with the Infinite.

Among the many sacred mountains throughout the world, there are, as Lama Govinda aptly states in the Foreword, "some of such outstanding character and position that they have become the spiritual foci of the most ancient civilizations and religions of humanity." And it is chiefly of these that this part treats, in such manner as to emphasize their cultural relationship with Cuchama and the underlying at-one-ment of the cult of sacred mountains everywhere.

On Olympus, the sacred mountain of Greece, dwelt Zeus.[1] On Sinai Moses received the Tables of the law. On a mountain, Elijah

[1]L. A. Heuzey, in *Le Mont Olympe et L'Arcananio* (Paris, 1860), reports survivals of a worship of Olympus among the Greek peasants who dwell near it, and that they tell of secret or invisible abodes on Olympus, and of magic virtues which emanate from it and subsist in its surrounding atmosphere.

communed with God, and Jacob offered up sacrifice. On the Mount, Jesus delivered the greatest of His sermons; and on a mountain He was transfigured before Peter, James, and John, so that "His face did shine as the Sun, and His raiment was white as the light"; and, there in the vision, He spake with Moses and Elias.[2] In like manner did the great initiates among the Red Men behold and speak with their radiance-robed law-givers, the Shining Beings.

It was on a mountain that the twelve disciples were chosen, where Jesus "continued all night in prayer."[3] While Mohammed sat wrapped in solitude, entranced on the sacred mountain of Arabia, Mt. Hera, near Mecca, the Angel Gabriel appeared and transmitted to him the verses of the *Koran,* just as on Cuchama the neophyte was vouchsafed the Vision of Guidance and was taught the hereditary wisdom of his tribe.

The singers of the *Vedas* ever glorify the deities of the High Places. Shiva, the Lord of the World, still dwells on the Himalayan heights of Kailas, and on other mountains of the Snowy Ranges of Hindustan and Tibet dwell the Great Ones who guard humanity. The Peak of the Vultures, in Central India, was the Buddha's favorite retreat, where He expounded the Dharma to His disciples. The Five-Peaked Mountain and the mysterious Mt. Omei are the most sacred in China. Fujiyama in Japan, Popocatepetl in Mexico, and Chimborazo in Ecuador, are each alike sacred. Adam's Peak in Ceylon is a High Place of pilgrimage for Buddhists, Hindus, Moslems, and Christians. The Kings of Ireland dwelt with their Druids on the Hill of Tara; and the Irish of this generation, faithful to their ancient ancestral customs, still make pilgrimages to the top of the Holy Mountain, now dedicated

---

[2] *St. Matthew,* 17:1–3. A parallel but fuller account of the appearance, on a holy mountain, of Moses and Elias as shining beings is contained in the *Apocalypse of Peter;* and the account is remarkably in keeping with that of the appearance of the Shining Beings of the Red Men on their sacred High Places!

"And my Lord Jesus Christ our king said unto me: 'Let us go unto the holy mountain.' And his disciples went with him, praying. And behold there were two men there, and we could not look upon their faces, for a light came from them, shining more than the sun, and their raiment also was shining, and cannot be described, and nothing is sufficient to be compared unto them in this world." Cf. M. R. James, *The Apocryphal New Testament,* (Oxford, 1924), pp. 518–19.

[3] *St. Luke,* 6:12–13.

by triumphant Christianity to St. Patrick, as their Bythronic brethren of Wales do to the summit of sacred Mt. Snowdon, their national Inspirer and Protector. On all the continents there are hills and mountains which have been sacred since prehistoric times. Amidst vast plains and deserts where hills or mountains are few or lacking, men have reared towers and pyramids that through initiation therein they might be lifted up and joined to the Brotherhood of the Conquerors of Life and Death and become partakers of their divine illumination.

So long as mankind inhabits this planet, its holy mountains will continue to be symbolical of human regeneration and triumph and of spiritual elevation to the altruistic heights of Freedom, above the lowly valleys of worldliness wherein men dwell self-enfettered to the idols of their own making. Inspired by these High Places, as the Red Men also were, the Hebrew psalmist, in gladness of heart, sang:

> I will lift up mine eyes unto the hills,
> From whence cometh my help.
>
> * * * * *
>
> I cried unto the Lord with my voice,
> And he heard me out of his high hill.
>
> * * * * *
>
> Why leap ye, ye high hills:
> This is the hill which God desireth to dwell in;
> Yea, the Lord will dwell in it for ever.[4]

I. MT. OMEI, CHINA[5]

Mt. Omei, on the southwestern frontier of the Land of Shu, Szechwan Province, is considered to be the most beautiful of China's many sacred mountains. From its base to its summit, almost ten thousand feet in altitude, there are more than seventy

---

[4] *St. Matthew,* 17:23.
[5] This account of Mt. Omei is based upon the English translation of a new edition of *The Omei Illustrated Guide Book,* the *O Shan T'u Shuo* in Chinese, by Dryden Linsley Phelps, Ph.D., F.R.G.S., of the West China University, published in Chengtu, Szechwan, in 1936. The new edition of the *O Shan T'u Shuo* was prepared and published by Huang Shou-fu and T'an Chung-yo in 1887 to 1891.

monasteries, in all of which the Bodhisattva Samantabhadra, who made Mt. Omei his place of meditation, is worshipped.

Phenomena of most unusual character are associated with this Sacred Mountain, and at least some of them may merit a more than purely mundane explanation. The monks and pilgrims who frequent Mt. Omei believe these phenomena to be self-evident proof of its sanctity.

Where the ancient Rishis long dwelt, in the Himalayan Holy Land of the Hindus, the physical environment became so attuned to their psychic radiations that to this day it still emits potent, uplifting spiritual influences, just as a place which has been made radioactive by the presence of radium or by the explosion of an atomic bomb emits radiant energy of a destructive character. Similarly, Mt. Omei is a more than ordinary focus of terrestrial magnetism as Cuchama is in a lesser degree; and both mountains seem to be radionically and psychically potent.

The learned and pious monk, Sheng Ch'in, abbot of Chieh Yin Tien, one of the monasteries on Mt. Omei, went into hermitage on the mountain and passed several summers and winters there subduing his passions and destroying desire, and in a Foreword to the translation he testifies concerning his experiences then, as follows:

> Suddenly, I became aware that the Bodhisattva [Samantabha-dra] had bequeathed his manifestation to this human world, dis-playing many varieties of visible appearances. Perhaps it is a matter of foreordained causation. The singular wonder is that every time, when winds and clouds change suddenly and fantastically, there appears unexpectedly a huge, round, bright circle, floating across the mountain, full of strange colors, gathering into splendor. At that moment, peaks, ridges, grass, and trees are all fresh, gleaming, and magnificent. Even when the clouds and mists have already dispersed, this bright sphere still remains illuminated all by itself. Certainly, this is the universally-shining "Buddha's Glory,"[6] amidst which appears a world of encircling cottony clouds. A further wonder is that before this colorful circle appears, clouds and mists must first come into sight. Just at that moment two

[6]The following explanatory annotation is here attached to the Foreword: "*Fu Kuang* [Chinese for 'Buddha's Glory'], a corona of rainbow colors, lying on the cloud-floor below the cliff [whence the 'Buddha's Glory' is usually viewed], in which the spectator's shadow is cast."

strange birds soar and glide to and fro, singing together, "Buddha's Glory is appearing!" . . . Directly following the singing, this view [of the "Buddha's Glory"] becomes visible before one's eyes. Again, this is another verification that the Bodhisattvas make suggestive revelations to all living beings.

Furthermore, when the setting sun sinks westward and the dark night grows heavy, among the cliffs and ravines there appear myriad flitting [lights like] lamp-lights,[7] flying in the emptiness, [like] bright stars, come to pay homage to Samantabhadra.

This explains why the Basic Unity finds countless different expressions due to the spiritual influences of the Bodhisattvas.

There is also a poem about the "Buddha's Glory," translated from the Chinese by Dr. Phelps:

> Something not cloud nor yet mist is rising
> through layers of space,
> Unearthly iridescence and mysterious lights
> curve in strange patterns.
> Will you not try standing on the high level
> of the Stone Terrace, and look out?
> For everyone is within the Glory of the Buddha.

Attached to this poem is an annotation: "Below the terrace is a precipice with careening walls, whence no human eye can fathom the depths. Below the precipice there rises a silken embroidered fabric of clouds lying motionless. In the afternoon, at [about] two o'clock, there appears in the clouds the sphere of 'Buddha's Glory,' more than ten feet in size [or diameter], circled with five colors,—in all seven concentric circles. When one's figure is reflected in the 'Buddha's Glory,' one's eyes and eyebrows can be seen very clearly. One can see only one's own reflection. The monks say that one cannot behold it [i.e., the 'Buddha's Glory'] unless he possess foreordained good luck. It is called 'Buddha's

---

[7]Here, again, there is an explanatory annotation: "Usually called [in Chinese] the *Sheng Teng,* the extraordinary phenomenon of luminous spheres bobbing up and down in the ravines below the cliff." These luminous spheres are suggestive of, although they may not be, will-o'-the-wisps, or *ignis fatuus,* which are phosphorescent. Among the cliffs and ravines where they appear, the magnetic aura of the mountain may be concentrated, or more potent than elsewhere and, thereby, may stimulate their appearance if it does not cause them directly. However explicable, they are, as the text states, extraordinary.

Glory.' I claim that it is the precious glow of the cosmic spirit of the mountain."

Another of the many Chinese poems about Mt. Omei tells of the strange birds of the mountain that make salutation in song to the rising Sun:

> At the Golden Temple the glory of dawn suddenly
> bursts into day:
> From the distance comes the birds' repeated
> calling: "Buddha appears!"
> Strange are the fairy birds, far surpassing
> the birds we know;
> Straight upward they fly, carolling, to Omei's
> very summit.

Since the coming of Buddhism to China, and probably for many millenniums before, Mt. Omei has been a goal of pilgrimage, as Cuchama was before the European invasion of the New World. Our *Omei Illustrated Guide Book* refers to a tradition that as long ago as 2697 B.C., one of China's Emperors, Hsuan Yuan the Yellow Emperor, visited Mt. Omei to enquire concerning the Way. And in every dynasty throughout China's long history, China's poets have made the Omei pilgrimage, and, inspired by Omei's magnificent scenery and conscious of the magnetic and psychic emanations of the mountain, have sung its praises. A select few of these poems, as translated by Dr. Phelps, are here recorded; for they may, very fittingly, be made applicable to Cuchama, which is, as Omei is, the "Cloud Enhaloed," the way to the ethereal emptiness, the source of crystal waters, and a right place of hermitage and meditation.

> In spite of the famous mountain towering
> thousands of feet above,
> I ascend the ethereal emptiness and enter
> the Portals of Heaven.
> * * * * *
> The sun hangs close above me, the sky is just
> overhead; the serried mountains are
> ranged round about.
> I draw near the summit; one glance of the eye
> takes in the eight-sided wilderness
> of space.
> * * * * *

Truly the perilous cliff treasures the spirit
  of ages;
Time after time it has known the blowing of winds
  and the beating of rains.
Though I imitate the emerald and copy the azure,
  my feelings are too deep for expression;
And so I offer a petal of my heart's fragrance—
  incense of sweet perfume.

* * * * *

I have heard that the Crystal Waters give rise to
  holy men;
And so by the dusty world these waters are
  undefiled.
Why comes the sudden western [or autumn] winds
  blowing the trees till the leaves fall down?
The depths of myriad mountains awaken within me
  the primal source of my being.

* * * * *

There is a new heaven in this quiet, cool hermitage
  of meditation;
Unexpectedly coming upon the Pure Land, one here
  finds true contemplation.

The following lines are an adaptation of the concluding poem of the Omei series. They should prove to be applicable to the Cuchama Pilgrimage, especially when, in the near future, the proposed Shrine[8] shall have been built, on that part of the summit where the initiates of the Red Men once meditated, which is a mesa about half a mile southward of the small conical northerly peak which is now occupied by a California State Forestry Lookout.

When the shrine upon the summit is attained,
Let every Pilgrim seek the Silence there,
And then enquire concerning immortality.

II. MT. WU-T'AI, CHINA

Yet more famous as a place of pilgrimage is the sacred five-peaked Mt. Wu-t'ai in the Shansi Province of China. Even as pilgrims seek the enlightening grace of the great Bodhisattva

---

[8][Ed. nt.: An announcement in *Phoenix* I, 1, (Summer, 1977), p. 44, requests contact from "interested individuals" to bring about the memorial. C.A.]

Samantabhadra on Mt. Omei, so on Mt. Wu-t'ai they seek that of the great Bodhisattva Manjushri, the divine personification of Wisdom. Manjushri is said to have been born of a lotus blossom, without father and mother, on Mt. Wu-t'ai, holding in his right hand the Sword of Wisdom. (See W. Y. Evans-Wentz, *The Tibetan Book of the Great Liberation,* pp. 134–36.) There are associated with Mt. Wu-t'ai, as with Mt. Omei, many accounts of supernormal phenomena, and both mountains alike are credited with having been the awakeners of saintliness during many millenniums. The Japanese monk, Ennin, who went on pilgrimage to China in search of the Law of the Buddha, visited Mt. Wu-t'ai in the year 840 A.D., and tells of it in his *Diary* as being one of the places where the psychic influences of great saints are made manifest and where illustrious Chinese patriarchs have attained enlightenment. (Cf. E. O. Reischauer, *Ennin's Diary* [New York, 1955], pp. 149, 186.)

In addition to Mt. Wu-t'ai and Mt. Omei, there are two more Chinese mountains which are held to be of peculiar sanctity, especially by Buddhists; namely, Mt. P'ut'o, a rocky, sea-girt eminence off the coast of Chekiang, sacred to the All-Compassionate Bodhisattva Avalokiteshvara, and Mt. Chiuhua, in Anhui, sacred to the Bodhisattva Kshitigarbha. Each of these four is associated with one of the primary elements of nature: Mt. Omei with the element fire, Mt. Wu-t'ai with the element air, Mt. P'ut'o with the element water, and Mt. Chiuhua with the element earth. (Cf. J. Blofeld, *The Jewel in the Lotus* [London, 1948], p. 49; and pp. 103–4 describing the mysterious "Wenshu lights" which are sometimes seen, like the Aurora Borealis, over Mt. Wu-t'ai and comparable to the probably magnetically-produced, luminous spheres associated with Mt. Omei.)[9]

[9][Ed. nt.: The four sacred mountains in China, as described, were held to be of particular sanctity by the Buddhists, who began to enter China in the second century. But long before this the Taoists designated five other mountains as preeminently sacred. They too were oriented to the cardinal directions: T'ai-shan in Shantung Province, the Mountain of the East; Heng-shan in Shansi, the Mountain of the North; Nan-yuah, the Mountain of the South, in Hunan; Hua-shan, or Flower Mountain of the West, in Shansi. And Sung-shan or Chung-yuah, at the center, in Hunan Province. Hence, to these nine sacred mountains pilgrims came from all over China to climb their steep, narrow trails, praying and depositing offerings at their temples and many shrines. (Cf. *The Nine Sacred Mountains of China,* Mary Augusta Mullikin and Anna M. Hotchkis, Hong Kong, China, 1973) F.W.]

III. FUJIYAMA, JAPAN[10]

The name Fujiyama is a corruption of the Japanese *Fuji-no-yama,* "the Mountain of Fuji." The peasants who live near it speak of it simply as O Yama, "The Honorable Mountain," or merely as "The Mountain." This simplicity of naming compares with that of the Red Men with respect to Cuchama, "The Exalted High Place." *Fuji* may possibly be a corrupted form of *Huchi,* or *Fuche,* the name by which the Ainu, or primitive inhabitants of Japan, knew their Goddess of Fire, presumably the deity anciently presiding over Fuji's volcanic fires.

Geologists believe that during the Glacial Epoch, at the beginning of the Quaternary Period, about 600,000 years ago, two mountains appeared, one after the other, where Mt. Fuji stands now. About 300,000 years later a great eruption of lava enveloped the two mountains, which, so encrusted, gave being to Mt. Fuji in its present symmetrical form. Because Mt. Fuji is thus geologically a young volcano, it still exhibits an almost unbroken regularity of shapeliness. Although it has been inactive for more than two hundred years, previously it was active, often very destructively active. Eighteen of its eruptions are recorded, the worst of these occurring in the years 800, 864, and 1707 A.D. According to Japanese tradition, Mt. Fuji came forth out of the Earth in one single night, about 300 B.C.

Since very ancient times, Mt. Fuji, 12,397[11] feet in altitude, has been revered by the Japanese. It is the highest of the long chain of volcanic peaks extending from the Mariana Islands in the South Seas to Cahima Island and the Ize Peninsula of Japan. Only one other of the world's conical volcanos, namely, sacred Mt. Cotapaxi, 19,498 feet in altitude, in the Ecuadorian Andes, rivals Mt. Fuji in beauty. It is when the huge base of Fuji is hidden in mists and Fuji's snowcapped summit and main mass are alone visible

[10]In preparing this brief account of Mt. Fuji, much assistance was derived from B. H. Chamberlain's *Things Japanese* (London, 1905), pp. 191–95, 370, and from *Japan, The Official Guide* (Tokyo, 1952), pp. 383–97.

[11]There being as yet no agreement among scientists as to the exact altitude of the world's higher mountains, the altitudes given herein will in some instances be found to differ by a few or many feet from those given in other publications. Dr. F. C. Lane, in *The Story of Mountains,* page 111, states that there are several figures quoted for Fujiyama's altitude, the most popular being 12,365 feet; 12 for the months and 365 for the days of the year.

that the Mountain appears to be magically suspended in the firmament; the traveller then approaching Yokohama by sea beholds one of this world's most wondrous visions. Mt. Fuji's divine guardian is known as Ko-no-hana-saku-ya-hime, "the Princess Who Maketh the Blossoms of the Trees to Flower." She is also known as Sangen (or Asama), the name attached to her shrine on the summit. It is said that as the Mountain is ardent with fire, so is the veneration of its devotees for the goddess. Many stories are told of how devotees, impatient to attain the felicity of the divine companionship of the goddess, have voluntarily departed from the realm of men by plunging into the terrestrial fires burning deep in the crater. The crater, opening on the Mountain's summit, is almost circular and has a diameter of 590 yards. The devotees call it Naiin, meaning "Sanctuary," and hold it in special reverence.

The people of Japan visualize Mt. Fuji as being an inverted fan, and they fondly think of the Mountain as radiating a divinely protective influence over Japan. The name *Fuji* has also been interpreted as meaning "not dying," or "deathless"; and, in keeping with this interpretation, there is a legend that the elixir of life was carried to the summit of Fuji. Followers of Shinto, the national religion of Japan, particularly those of the Mountain sects, believe that by ascending Fujiyama the devotee attains purification both of body and of mind, and is, thereby, aided in the Ultimate Quest for union of the human and the Divine.

Like Adam's Peak in Ceylon, Mt. Fuji also casts a remarkable shadow at sunrise on the sea of mists and clouds far below. This shadow is known as Kage-Fuji, "Shadow-Fuji." More than 100,000 pilgrims climb to Mt. Fuji's summit annually. It is believed that the volcanic ashes which fall from the pilgrims' feet and clothing as they descend are spontaneously restored to the very places where they were picked up on the Mountain's sacred heights.

Japanese pilgrims going to Mt. Fuji, Mt. Ontake, and other sacred mountains of Japan, especially those who are of the peasantry, usually wear white garments and very broad and sloping straw hats. While ascending, they often tinkle small hand-bells at frequent intervals, and, as Red Men on a similar pilgrimage would, they chant an invocation to the deities and nature-spirits. The chant of the Mt. Fuji pilgrims is translatable as, "May our six senses (sight, hearing, smelling, tasting, feeling, and spiritual insight) be pure and the weather on this Honorable Mountain be fair."

In the springtime, the base of Mt. Fuji is surrounded by blossoming cherry trees and azaleas, which are reflected in the five sacred lakes there, against the pure white of the Mountain's crown of snow.

Although today pilgrims ascend Mt. Fuji in all seasons, midsummer, when the writer made the pilgrimage in 1920, is the ideal season for ascending through the sanctified ashes of death to the Sangen Shrine of the elixir of life to make obeisance to the Goddess Who Giveth Birth to the Blossoms of the Trees.

Not only is Fuji Japan's supreme sacred High Place but, in this new age of world-wide awakenment, it is, little by little, becoming sacred to all the peoples of the One Human Family. A Japanese poet who lived before the time of King Alfred of England has glorified Fujiyama very fittingly:

> Great Fujiyama, towering to the sky,
> A treasure art thou, given to mortal man,
> A god Protector watching o'er Japan:
> On thee forever let me feast mine eye.

IV: MT. HIEI AND MT. KOYA, JAPAN[12]

Another of Japan's sacred High Places is Mt. Hiei, situated northeast of Kyoto in Honshu. Long prior to the advent of Buddhism in Japan—after which Mt. Hiei became the great monastic center of Japanese learning and culture of the Tendai (or *Lotus Sutra*) School, one of the two chief Esoteric Schools of Buddhism —the mountain appears to have been recognized as having peculiar sanctity, for on it there was already an ancient shrine to the Mountain King, a deity whom the Tendai monks made the tutelary of their Mt. Hiei headquarters. It was in A.D. 788 that Mt.

---

[12]For most of the essence matter of this section, the author is indebted to the excellent compilation of *Sources of Japanese Tradition* by R. Tsunoda, W. T. de Bary and D. Keene, in no. LIV of *Records of Civilization* (Columbia University Press, New York, 1958). Cf. pp. 116 ff., 139, 156 ff., 270 n.6, 314–16 and *passim*.

Hiei was taken over by Buddhism, when Saichō (762–822) founded on its summit a small Buddhist temple. By the year 1571, there were 3,000 temple buildings with 30,000 inmates on the mountain and twenty-one shrines to the Mountain King. During that year, by order of an impetuous military leader inimical to Buddhism, all the buildings were razed by fire, and many of the 30,000 inmates perished in the flames.

On Mt. Koya, a similar High Place in Honshu, the Shingon, the other of the two chief schools of Esoteric Buddhism, established its own monastic headquarters, under the leadership of the monk Kūkai (774–835). That was in A.D. 816, twenty-eight years after Saichō had made Mt. Hiei the Tendai center. Mt. Koya, like Mt. Hiei, had been since immemorial time a recognized abode of various deities, of whom the chief was the goddess Tango.

The Mountain King, otherwise known as Sanno, the spiritual guardian of Mt. Hiei, and the Goddess Tango, the spiritual guardian of Mt. Koya, being Shinto deities of pre-Buddhistic Japan, with histories going back, as Shinto does, to primeval times, indicate, even as does Fujiyama, likewise associated with Shinto, that the cult of sacred mountains is as ancient in Japan as it is throughout Asia, Europe, and the Americas.

In psychic attunement with Mt. Hiei, like the Indian youth in psychic attunement with Cuchama, the monk Saichō, with overflowing joyfulness, was moved to prayerful song, and, extemporaneously, he sang as he dedicated to the Enlightened Ones his little hut-like temple on the Mountain's summit:

O Buddhas,
Of unexcelled complete enlightenment,
Bestow your invisible aid
Upon this hut I open
On the mountain top.

In like spirit may a shrine to all the Great Teachers be dedicated to the Summit of Initiation of Cuchama.

Such invisible aid as was prayed for by the monk Saichō was, indeed, vouchsafed to him and his brother monks on Mt. Hiei, as it also was to the monks on Mt. Omei in China, and to the vision-seeking youths of the Red Men on the sacred High Places throughout the New World.[13]

V: MT. KASSAYA PARBAT, INDIA

It was on the thrice-holy Mt. Kassaya Parbat, 6,300 feet in altitude, overshadowed by the higher Himalayas, the "Abodes of the Snows," near the town of Almora, in Kumaon, that the writer lived and had research headquarters in India. For the benefit of those who revere this world's High Places, a brief descriptive account of Mt. Kassaya Parbat is here added.

In the *Skhanda Purana* (Kumaon version), Kassaya Parbat is referred to as having been sanctified by Sages of the past, who made their abode upon it and achieved self-conquest. Rama, too, and his faithful Hanuman are said to have done penance there.[14]

[13][Ed. nt.: It is interesting to learn from a recent publication that 354 mountains in Japan were worshipped in ancient times. Early in the seventh century there developed *Shugendō*—the "Way" by which human beings could attain the spiritual powers inherent within them by pilgrimages and rituals, or by mountain retreats. The meaning and purpose of *Shugendō* are made clear from the derivation of its name: *Shu*—beginning enlightenment of a pilgrim's inherently divine nature; *gen*—his innate realization; and *do*—his attainment of what Buddhists call *nirvāna* and the Japanese *nehan.*

Of the 134 sacred mountains of the *Shugendō* sect, Mount Haguro with 33 main temples was the most important. On it, formalities were observed in each of the four seasons, or "Four Peaks," during which pilgrims were considered to be "entering the mountain," leaving this world for the "other world." The procession up the mountain and the many rituals symbolized the union of the mythical pair which created the human race, the five stages of gestation within the womb, and the spiritual rebirth from the mountain. This also reflected the Japanese belief that the spirits of the dead return to the mountains and are reborn from them.

Shugendō became infused with ritual elements of Buddhism, Taoism, and Shintoism, and new sites were later established. It was officially proscribed in 1872, but after 1945 new sects were formed on the long-rooted tradition. (Cf. *A Religious Study of the Mount Haguro Sect of Shugendō,* H. Byron Earhart, Tokyo, Japan, 1970.) F.W.]

[14]Rama is the Divine Hero of the *Ramayana,* one of the two great epics of India. As a Champion of Righteousness, or *Dharma,* Rama is comparable to King Arthur, the Protector of Chivalry and Knightly Honour, of the Arthurian Legend. Hanuman, Rama's faithful servitor and follower, represented as being King of the Monkeys, symbolizes the pre-Aryan races of South India who aided Rama in his invasion of Ceylon to rescue Sita, Rama's wife, symbol of the womanly woman, from Ceylon's pre-Aryan King, the Demon Ravana. This invasion of Ceylon is the central theme of the *Ramayana,* or "Path of Rama," a lengthy and semi-historical epic poem, replete with India's philosophical and mystical lore.

According to tradition, Kassaya Parbat was venerated as long ago as the Krita Yuga, or "Age of Gold," which according to Brahmanical chronology began 3,893,056 years ago, reckoning from February 18, 1955.

On the mountain's crest stands a small lingam temple to Shiva, the Patron of Yogins, and on the slope below it, to the southeast, a rock-cave sanctuary of Kawar (or, more correctly, Kassaya) Devi, a Kali goddess, by whose name the mountain is now popularly known. There are ancient rock-inscriptions on the precipitous southerly side, and caves believed to have been occupied by Arhants.

On the horizon northerly from Kassaya Parbat, like mighty castles built by Titans, rise the glaciered peaks protecting the invisible and mysterious abodes of the Great Ones who keep watch over the planet Earth, while the present Kali Yuga, or "Age of Iron," runs its long course, and mankind awaits the Great Awakenment. There, also, are the goals of the greater pilgrimages to Kedarnath, Badrinath, Gangotri, and Jumnotri, amidst the everlasting snows, whence issue India's holiest rivers, the Ganges and Jumna.

Over this Hindu Holy Land, guarded by the "Abodes of the Snows," as over Nepal and Tibet, that form with it one harmonious whole, dwells the brooding presence of an ineffable greatness. It was there, during the course of millenniums, that the purifying thoughts and psychic radiations of unnumbered generations of Rishis and Yogins have been poured forth, so that even until now these regions of the Earth are really holy, their rivers and lakes sacred, and the atmosphere enveloping them emanates a secret radiance. And whosoever can attain attunement with this sacred radiance becomes transfigured.

Beauty and holiness, and the halo of an antiquity far more splendid and cultural than that of Egypt, or Greece, or Rome, or of the modern world, thus glorify Kassaya Parbat and make it today, as written records indicate that it has been since immemorial times, a place of true pilgrimage. There the pilgrim may find peace transcendent and understanding of the imperishable at-one-ment underlying all the multitudinous manifestations of life.

VI: MT. KAILAS, INDIA[15]

The fame of Kailas, or "Paradisaic Abode," above that of all
sacred mountains of the world, has spread and inspired millions
of human beings during thousands of years. There is no other
mountain comparable to it in sanctity, because it has become the
spiritual heart of the world's two most important ancient civilizations, whose traditions have remained intact up to the present day;
namely, the civilizations of India and China. To hundreds of
millions of Hindus and Buddhists, Kailas is central to all parts of
the Universe. It is called Meru, or Sumera, in the Sanskrit texts
and is regarded as being not only the physical but the metaphysical center of the Universe.[16] Because man's psycho-physical organism is a microcosmic replica of the Universe, Meru is
represented by the spinal cord in man's nervous system. Furthermore, just as man's various centers of consciousness are supported
by and connected with the spinal cord, whence they branch out
like many-petalled lotus blossoms, Mt. Meru supports and con-
nects the various strata of the invisible supramundane worlds.
And as the psycho-physical microcosm of man is crowned by the
highest center of consciousness, the thousand-petalled lotus of the
mind, known in Sanskrit as the *Sahasrara Padma* (or *Chakra*),
likewise is Meru, or Kailas, surmounted by the secret temple of
the highest transcendent powers, which to each devotee appears
in the form that to him symbolizes the supreme reality. Thus, to

[15]This account of Mt. Kailas which follows has been compiled from that set forth
by Lama Anagarika Govinda in the article entitled "The Mystic *Mandala* of
Kailas and Its Sacred Lakes," published in *The Maha-Bodhi* (Calcutta, July,
1951). Kailas, over 22,000 feet in altitude, the highest of the Gangri Mountains
of Tibet, is situated near the frontier of India between the sources of the Indus
and Brahmaputra. Pilgrims do Kailas homage by circumambulating at its base,
traversing snow and glaciers, the circumambulation usually requiring about
three weeks. Over-zealous devotees sometimes perform the circumambulation,
in part or as a whole, by measuring the distance with the length of their body.
[16][Ed. nt.: The physical Mt. Kailas and the metaphysical Mt. Meru are not
synonymous, even though metaphysical attributes are projected on Mt. Kailas.
Mt. Kailas is a physical mountain; Mt. Meru is solely metaphysical. Although
the Hindus and Buddhists regard Kailas as manifesting Meru's metaphysical
attributes, a differentiation is necessary.

For further discussion of Mt. Meru, see Part II, 1, "Holy Mountains of the
Navajos." F.W.]

Thunderstorm over Mt. Kailas, as seen from Nyandi Gompa, Tibet. Reproduction of a painting by Lama Anagarika Govinda.

Hindus, Kailas is the throne of Shiva. To Buddhists, it represents a gigantic *mandala,* or divine conclave, of Dhyani Buddhas, who are celestial, or supramundane, Buddhas, realizable only in profound meditation.

Why or how was it that of all the mighty mountains of the Himalayan and trans-Himalayan regions this very peak should have been honoured and by common consent recognized as the center of the world? A glance at any map showing the relationship of Kailas and the river-systems of the Indo-Tibetan region will at once supply the answer. Kailas forms the spire of the "roof of the world," as the Tibetan plateau is called, and radiating from it, like spokes from the hub of a wheel, a number of mighty rivers take their course toward the east, the west, the northwest, and the south. These rivers are the Brahmaputra, the Indus, the Sutlej, and the Karnali; and all of them have their sources in the Kailas-Manasarovar region, which forms a plateau upon the greater plateau of Tibet.

Only he who has contemplated the divine in its most awe-inspiring form, who has dared to look into the unveiled face of truth without being overwhelmed or frightened, will be able to bear the powerful silence and solitude of Kailas and its sacred lakes, and endure the dangers and hardships which are the price one must pay for being admitted into the mystic *mandala* on the holiest spot on the planet Earth. But those who have given up comfort and security, and the care for their own life, are rewarded by an indescribable feeling of bliss, of supreme happiness. Their mental faculties seem to be heightened, their receptivity infinitely increased, so that many see wonderful visions, and hear strange voices, and fall into a trance-like state wherein instantaneously, as in a flash of lightning, which suddenly illuminates what before had been shrouded in darkness, their impediments and difficulties disappear. It is as though their individual consciousnesses, which had obscured or distorted their views or conceptions of the world, were receding and giving place to comprehensive cosmic consciousness.

VII: OTHER HIMALAYAN PEAKS

It is much more than mere coincidence that Asia should be the foci both of mankind's spiritual unfoldment and of sacred mountains. Not only does Asia contain the greatest number of sacred mountains but also a whole major range of sacred mountains; this range, the Himalayan, is fifteen hundred miles long and contains the loftiest of Earth's High Places. Asia also contains a lesser sacred range, the Tien Shan, or "Celestial Mountains," of China. Just as the Japanese Current in the north Pacific and the Gulf Stream in the north Atlantic, along with similar currents in the other Oceans, like mighty arteries, maintain the well-being of the world's waters, so the sacred mountains, in virtue of their magnetic and psychic emanations encompassing the planet, assist in maintaining the well-being of man and of every living thing embodied on Earth. The Sun of our System and each of the innumerable suns and worlds throughout the immensity of unfathomed space blends its own distinctive radiation with the radiations of the Earth and of Earth's sacred mountains; and the sage who can measure and interpret these all-enveloping radiations is the true yogin and the true astrologer.

Among these most exalted High Places, more appropriately known by its ancient Tibetan name Chomolungma, "The Goddess Mother of the World," than by its surveyor's name of Everest, the world's highest mountain (29,149 feet in altitude) is, as its rightful name implies, the supreme throne of this planet's invisible Guardians. The second highest mountain of the world and the most massive and physically impressive of Himalaya's High Places, rightly known only by its Tibetan name Kangchenjunga, "The Five Great Treasuries of the Snow," dominating Darjeeling, rises out of the semi-tropical jungles on the boundary between Sikkim and Nepal to a height of 28,295 feet, into the altitudes of eternal snow.

During my lengthy sojourn in Sikkim, Kangchenjunga was my constant inspiration. With my guru, the late Lama Kazi Dawa-Samdup, I saluted it at dawn before beginning my daily work, near Gangtok, of translating Tibetan texts which have been published as *The Tibetan Book of the Dead, Tibet's Great Yogi Milarepa,* and *Tibetan Yoga and Secret Doctrines.* The last of these three books, on pages 294–95, presents an account of the Kangchenjunga War-Dance, a Mystery-Play officially presented by the State of Sikkim in worship of Kangchenjunga. By invitation of the reigning Maharaja, I was privileged to be his guest to witness this War-Dance, celebrated in the courtyard of his palace in Gangtok during the two days of its annual celebration, the 19th and 20th of December, 1919. Popularly known as the Snowy-Range Dance, held at about the time of the winter solstice, it is performed by the Sikkimese Lamas under the personal supervision of the Maharaja for the purpose of appealing to the deities of Kangchenjunga and of the Snowy Range to expel from Sikkim all evil and to bless its people and their herds and crops during the coming year.

The Five Great Treasuries of Kangchenjunga are its five distinctive, ever snow-clad peaks, seen by its devotees as five thrones of the Shining Ones. These Five Great Treasuries, as Tanzing of Everest explains on page 96 of his *Tiger of the Snow,* have their more mundane or exoteric counterparts, symbolized by (1) salt, (2) gold and turquoise, (3) holy books and wealth, (4) weapons, and (5) crops and medicines.

Kangchenjunga's summit remains untrodden only because of the promise requested of and given by its European explorers "to leave the top and its immediate neighbourhood untouched," in order that the sanctity of the Mountain be left undesecrated, the Sikkimese regarding Kangchenjunga "as a god and protector."[17]

While immersed in the solitude of the high altitudes on the southern frontier of Tibet, during my days of exploration and research, I beheld in all its unobscured, sun-illumined majesty, Chomolhari, "The Lily-White Mother of Snow," 23,997 feet high. As its name suggests, it is one more of the many Himalayan thrones of the protecting deities; and by all its Tibetan devotees it is so visualized and venerated.

Another of the highest and most holy of the Himalayan peaks and the most inaccessible of mountains is Nanda Devi, the ever snow-white abode of the Hindu Goddess Nanda, with whom the God Shiva shares the deepest reverence of Brahmanical India. It is said that when, many thousands of years ago, the Aryan invaders of India first beheld the wondrously beautiful, ever snow-white, Nanda Devi, they intuitively recognized it as being sacred. Rising to a height of 25,645 feet, Nanda Devi dominates the Garwhal and Almora regions of the Holy Land of the Hindus; and greatly did I benefit by its uplifting influence while I dwelt in its overshadowing presence at my Himalayan Ashram on the Hill of Kasar Devi, which is itself sacred.

VIII: ARUNACHALA, THE "HILL OF LIGHT," INDIA

It was the good fortune of the writer to have been a pilgrim to Arunachala, the Holy Hill vouchsafing Divine Illumination, at Tiruvannamalai, in South India, and, in keeping with the venerable custom of its pilgrims, to have circumambulated the Holy Hill

---

[17][Ed. nt.: Cf. C. Evans, *Kangchenjunga, The Untrodden Peak* (New York, 1951), p. 13. F.W.]

barefoot. The barefootedness enables the pilgrim to absorb, uninsulated by foot-gear, the utmost benefit from the Holy Hill's magnetic and psychic emanations.

The writer was further privileged to sit in discipleship at the feet of the Sage of Arunachala, the late Sri Ramana Maharshi, regarded by many spiritually-advanced Brahmins and yogins as being the greatest of the modern Saints of India. The Maharshi, then in the full flower of saintliness, dwelt in his ashram at the base of Arunachala. For fifty-four years, from the time of his arrival at Arunachala in 1896, as a youth of seventeen, up to the moment of his relinquishment of his physical body, in 1950, the Maharshi had been unceasingly immersed in Arunachala's invisible but perceptible influences and had attained Self-Realization.

Arunachala, too, like the Himalayan abodes of the Rishis of yore, has been psychically attuned, during the course of many millenniums, by the Great Ones of the Dravidian peoples of South India, who, long before the advent of the Aryans in North India, had discovered the virtues of Arunachala and further sanctified it by their presence.[18]

The aphorisms which follow, selected from the *Skanda Purana* of the Hindu Scriptures and from the inspired verses of the Sage of Arunachala[19] suggest, as do the sayings of the Saints of all religions, that Truth, although bearing many names, is One; that the sacred High Places in every continent are alike in their elevating effects upon mankind. And mankind's responses to these effects have been in every epoch uniformly the same. This is attested by the unrecorded traditional lore, and by the recorded lore in Bibles, bequeathed by mankind in all epochs, ancient and modern, and of all races and cultural states, primitive and civilized. The Hindu Rishis, and the Sages of ancient China, Persia, Egypt, Greece, and Rome, like the Hebrew Prophets, are in at-

[18]Concerning the geology, the traditional history, and the cultural significance of Arunachala, see Paul Brunton, *A Message From Arunachala* (New York, 1936).

[19]Cf. *Five Hymns to Sri Arunachala* (Sri Romanasramam, South India, 1946) *passim,* upon which this section is chiefly based, and to which the writer gratefully acknowledges indebtedness. Some minor recension of the translated matter therein has been made, in order to make clearer to the Western World the purport of the Maharshi's message.

one-ment with the Red Men of the Americas in hymning the praise of the sacred High Places of our planet Earth.

Arunachala (*Aruna*=Light, plus *Achala*=Hill or Mountain) is symbolic of the Divine Light of Shiva, the third member of the Hindu Triad.[20] The physical mass of Arunachala is seen by its devotees as a mighty Shiva lingam, radiant with a secret transcendent radiance, and is therefore known in Sanskrit as the *Tejo-Lingam.* Its Light signifies, as does the Clear Light of the Tibetan *Bardo Thodol,* the mystical unobscured radiance of Reality, realizable only in that ecstatic state of consciousness which transcends the normal individualized mundane consciousness dependent upon bodily sensuousness.[21]

The *lingam,* the erect male generative organ, symbolizing the source of the perennial river of incarnate life on Earth, is sacred to Shiva as the Lord of Regeneration. Every spire on a Christian place of worship, every minaret of a Moslem mosque, every Zoroastrian tower of the Ever-Burning Fire, every pyramid, every menhir, and every revered High Place like Arunachala and Cuchama is a phallic symbol of that ever-becoming which sustains

---

[20]This Divine Light, or *Khvarenah,* as it is called in the *Zamyād Yasht* (see discussion under Mt. Asnavant), is in its essential characteristics synonymous with what the Iroquois know as *orenda* and the Melanesians as *mana.* Thus, among the Persians, long before our era, such an occult power was well known and applied in psychic development, as it appears to have been in ancient pre-Columbian America. According to Persia and Zoroastrian belief, *Khvarenah* can be acquired only through practising Truth and Righteousness; and the holy Mt. Ushi-darena, whereon Zarathrustra received the Law, is the chief Persian repository or center of *Khvarenah.*

The Hebrew term *Shekinah* connotes, as does *Khvarenah,* a spiritual presence that glorifies and gives superhuman power to the person upon whom it rests. Only when it rested upon the priests of Israel were they worthy of being approached for an oracle. Right living sustains and strengthens the manifestation of the *Shekinah,* while wrong living weakens and inhibits it. The *Shekinah* is the transcendent radiance of the supramundane in man; referred to as the "glory of the Lord" in *St. Luke,* 2:9. It is the innate Light, spoken of in *St. John,* 1:9, "which lighteth every man coming into the world." According to *Exodus* (24:15–18), "the glory of the Lord abode on Mt. Sinai." It "was like a devouring fire on the top of the mount," and "was in the mount forty days and forty nights." Thus was the Israelites' supreme High Place, Mt. Sinai, like that of the Iranians', Mt. Ushi-darena, a center of the *Shekinah.*

[21]See W. Y. Evans-Wentz, *The Tibetan Book of the Dead* (London, 1951), *passim.*

the never-ending pulsation of the Cosmic Heart of Brahma, the Universal One.[22]

Arunachala is also the name of the deity to whom the Temple of Tiruvannamalai is dedicated. This deity, a form of Shiva, is, like the Hill of Arunachala itself which overshadows the Temple, venerated as a symbolic manifestation of the Supreme Being.

1. The Testimony of Nandi[23] and Shiva

Nandi proclaimed:

"This is the holy place! Of all holy places Arunachala is the most holy! It is the heart of the world! Know it to be the secret and sacred heart-centre of Shiva! Therein, in the glorious Aruna Hill, He ever dwelleth!"[24]

Shiva proclaimed:

"That which requireth infinite suffering to acquire—the true import of the Vedanta—is easily acquired by all those who either behold the Hill itself or meditate upon it from afar.

"I proclaim that residence within a radius of three *yojanas*[25] of this Hill shall of itself suffice to consume, as fire consumeth, all defects [of the devotee], and effect union with the Supreme [even without formal initiation]."

[22][Ed. nt.: In her study *Spatial Archetypes,* Mimi Lobell equates the emergence of the mountain out of the sea of chaos with the rise of the ego and self-consciousness from the womb-cavern of the unconscious. There began in world history the era of mountain-worship and the erection of the pyramids in Egypt and Mesoamerica, the ziggurats of Mesopotamia, the Buddhist stupas, and the mountain-temples of Asia. The movement was reflected in the social stratification of different castes, with a divine ruler at the apex of the social pyramid. The dominant ego, according to psycho-mythologists, then often experienced spiritual enlightenment which again related it to the mother of all creation, the unconscious. Hence the religious function of the sacred mountain and the pyramid was to enable man to surmount his earthly existence at its summit and achieve transcendental unity with the universe. F.W.]

[23]Nandi is the foremost of Shiva's devotees, and herein proclaims the greatness of Arunachala.

[24]Similarly, for the initiated devotees among the Red Men, Cuchama, and other High Places which they revered, were the abodes of the Shining Beings.

[25]A distance of about thirty miles, within the radius of which Arunachala's magnetic and psychic radiations are believed to be effective.

2. The Maharshi's Testimony

"Arunachala![26] Thou dost uproot the ego of those who meditate upon Thee [enthroned] in the heart, O Arunachala!

"Arunachala! Thou dost uproot the ego of those who meditate upon their at-one-ment with Thee, O Arunachala!

"The mind by its unsteadiness preventeth my seeking Thee and finding peace; [steady the mind] and grant me, O Arunachala! the vision of Thy beauty.

"Be Thou to me as a loadstone which attracteth iron and magnetiseth and holdeth it fast, O Arunachala!

"Gem of Fire, shining in every direction, burn up my dross, O Arunachala!

"Shine Thou as my Guru, making me free from faults and worthy of Thy grace, O Arunachala!

"Glorious Mountain of Love, hymned by Gautama, govern me with Thy gracious glance, O Arunachala!

"Tear off my robes, expose me naked, then robe me with Thy love, O Arunachala!

"Vouchsafe me knowledge of Eternal Life, that I may attain the glorious Primal Wisdom, and transcend the illusoriness of the world, O Arunachala!

" 'By looking within, ever seeking the Self with the inner eye, the Self will be found': thus didst Thou teach me, beloved Arunachala!

"Let me dive into the True Self, wherein merge only the pure in mind and speech, O Arunachala!

"When, O Arunachala! shall I be as the ether and reach Thee, subtle of being, that the tempest of thoughts may cease?[27]

"My mind hath blossomed; perfume it with Thy fragrance, and perfect it, O Arunachala!

[26]Here the word *Arunachala* refers to the Supreme Consciousness of which the individual, or microcosmic consciousness, is a mode, seeking to resolve itself in its Source in the Supreme Consciousness, "so that the turbulence of the mind and senses may end, and transcendental Peace reign instead." (Cf. *Five Hymns to Sri Arunachala*, p. 10.)

[27]As suggested by the Biblical aphorism (in *Psalms* 46:10), "Be still, and know that I am God," the yogin must attain as complete control over the thought-process as a master aviator has over an airship.

"Be Thou my stay and my support lest I droop helpless like a tender creeper, O Arunachala!

"Unattached to this material body, composed of the [five] elements, let me repose blissfully in the sight of Thy splendor forever, O Arunachala!

"Protect me lest I founder storm-tossed, like a ship without a helmsman, O Arunachala!

"The moment Thou didst welcome me, didst enter into me and grant to me [participation in] Thy life divine, I lost my individuality, O Arunachala!

"As snow in water, let me melt as Love in Thee, Who art Love itself, O Arunachala!"

3. The Testimony of the "Sri Arunachala Pancharatna"

"Ocean of Nectar, full of grace and engulfing the Universe in Thy splendor! O Arunachala! The Supreme Itself! be Thou the Sun, and open the lotus of my heart in blissfulness.

"He who turneth inward, with mind unperturbed, to seek the source of ego-consciousness, realizeth the Self, and resteth in Thee, O Arunachala! as doth a river when it joineth the ocean.

"Abandoning the outer world, with mind and breath controlled, and meditating upon Thee within, the Yogi seeth Thy Light, O Arunachala! and findeth his delight in Thee."[28]

4. Arunachala Signifies Stillness Absolute

After having been immersed in Arunachala's aura unceasingly for fifty-four years, the Maharshi has bequeathed to us this remarkable testimony:

"Listen well: It [Arunachala] stands [or seems to be] an inanimate Hill; but its influence is mysterious and past human understanding. From the time of my youthfulness, I have perceived that Arunachala is something of surpassing grandeur. Yet even when I came to understand through another [devotee] that Arunachala

---

[28]This stanza has reference to the Yoga Path, as expounded by Patanjali in his *Yoga Sutras.* "The Hill, though material in outward appearance, becomes full of life, and perceptible, in the transcendental vision of the Yogi, as the Universal Glorious Light, the same as the Self." (*Five Hymns to Sri Arunachala,* p. 41.)

is synonymous with Tiruvannamalai, I failed to grasp its significance. When Arunachala drew me towards itself, stilling my mind, and I came close to it, I realized that it signifies Stillness Absolute."[29]

IX. SACRED MOUNTAINS IN ZOROASTRIANISM[30]

The Zoroastrian scriptures contain numerous references to sacred mountains, but here we shall consider only the most impor-

[29]Cf. *Five Hymns to Sri Arunachala,* p. 32.

[Ed. nt.: When in 1935 Dr. Evans-Wentz visited Sri Ramana Maharshi, he asked the sage if he had ever had a Guru, a teacher. Maharshi replied that a Guru is God or the Self, which appears to a seeker in some form, human or non-human, and that his own Guru took the form of the sacred hill of Arunachala. Dr. Evans-Wentz, commenting that there are certain psychic centers in the body and corresponding centers in the world, then asked if there were any psychic effect in visiting such sacred places like Mt. Kailas and Arunachala. Sri Maharshi affirmed this, saying what is in the world is in the body, and what is in the body is in the world also. Their complete dialogue is recorded in *Talks with Sri Ramana Maharshi.* Tiruvannamalai, S. India, 1963. F.W.]

[30]This account is based upon original source material compiled by Dastur (Dr.) Framroze A. Bode, the illustrious representative and a high preist of the Parsi Zoroastrian community of Bombay, India, and author of *Songs of Zarathustra.* He has supplied the brief note on Zoroastrianism which follows.

"Zoroastrianism is one of the world's oldest living religions. Zarathustra, whom the Greeks called Zoroaster, promulgated a monotheistic Mazdayasni faith thousands of years before the Christian era and was the earliest known World-Teacher of the Irano-Aryans. The *Gathas,* the Divine Songs of Zarathustra, and the *Avesta,* the Zoroastrian scriptures, are thus of very great antiquity, the oldest of the *Avesta* being as old as the *Vedas* and some portions even older. The Avesta and Sanskrit are sister Aryan languages. The teachings of Zarathustra have greatly influenced Judaism, Christianity, and Islam.

"The recorded sacred literature of Zoroastrianism, like that of other ancient cultures, has suffered the vicissitudes of time. When Alexander the Great, in 331 B.C., invaded Persia, known from time immemorial as Iran, he took as booty to Greece the chief manuscript records of Zoroastrianism. They were translated into Greek and afterwards burnt. Then when the Arabs conquered Persia in 651 A.D., they, too, destroyed, by burning, all the remaining Zoroastrian scriptures they could lay hands on. Such Zoroastrian scriptures as now remain are merely remnants of a great and glorious religious heritage.

"The followers of the ancient religion of Zarathustra are today represented by the Parsis of India centered in Bombay. Their ancestors came from Persia to India, to escape religious persecution, at the time of the conquest by the Arabs of their Persian homeland in the eighth century. All told, the Parsis number about one hundred and twenty thousand. Though comparatively small, this dynamic community has had a most disproportionate influence on Indian cultural developments and Indian nationhood."

tant of these mountains, our chief sources being the *Avesta,* particularly the *Zamyād* and other *Yashts,*[31] and the Pahlavi *Bundahishn.* The *Zamyād Yasht,* dedicated to Yazata Zamyād, the Genius of the Earth, describes the mountains and the Divine Glory which is invoked along with them. In Sections 1 to 8, the mountains are merely enumerated. The remaining parts of this *Yasht* are devoted to those holy personages who possessed the Khvarenah, the Divine Glory, and, in virtue of it, became illustrious. In the *Bundahishn,* which treats of the "Original Creation," and of cosmogony, mythology, and legendary history, the whole of Chapter XII of this Pahlavi text is devoted to the "Nature of Mountains." In the *Yashts,* Zarathustra and various saints, kings, and heroes are represented as making offerings and prayers on the summits of sacred mountains to the Yazatas, or Divine Powers, that thereby evil might be banished from the world. Only such prayers as were altruistically inspired were granted.

1. Mt. Ushi-darena

Mt. Ushi-darena is the most significant mountain referred to in Avestan literature. *Ushi,* derived from *ush,* means "to shine," or "to illuminate," and implies consciousness of things divine, as does the Persian term *hûsh. Darena* is derived from *dar,* "to support," or "to sustain." Accordingly, the name is translatable as "Support of Divine Consciousness," or "Sustainer of Divine Wisdom." The *Avesta* refers to two kinds of wisdom: that which is divine, or innate and intuitive, and that which is mundane, or intellectually acquired.

The *Sirōza Yasht* explains how Mt. Ushi-darena is to be invoked along with Truth and Righteousness and the Genius of the Earth. By continuous meditation on Mt. Ushi-darena, Zarathus-

---

[31] *Yasht,* derived from the root *yaz,* meaning "to worship," like *yasna* from an allied root, signifies the act of worshipping. While the *Yasna* is a book of seventy-two chapters, embracing the liturgy of the Mazdayasni religion as a whole, the *Yashts* are devoted exclusively to the worship of individual *Yazatas,* or Divine Powers. *Yasht* itself has become a technical term denoting the class of Avesta literature. These scriptures, which are of epical character, comprise very valuable records of the ancient mythology and historically-based legends of Iran.

tra was enabled to attain Illumination and to master Nature's secrets; and it was there, on the summit of this Mountain of the Holy Quest or Divine Communion, that Ahura-Mazda revealed the Law to Zarathustra. (See the *Vendidad,* xxii, 19.)

Mt. Ushi-darena appears to be situated in the Mt. Alborz Range near Ādarbaijān, Zarathustra's traditional birthplace. The *Bundahishn* places it in Seistan (or Sajêstān), east of Iran in the region referred to in the *Avesta* (*Vendidad* I, 9 to 10) as Vaēkereta, the ancient name of Kabul (or Sajêstān). The Greeks called it Dranji-ānā. In Pahlavi writings it is known as Hûshdāštār.

Another great sage mentioned in the Avestan Yasht literature as having been associated with Mt. Ushi-darena is Asmō-Khanvant, one of Zarathustra's first disciples. He dwelt on the Mountain and there attained spiritual insight.

Mt. Ushi-darena is said to be of ruby, of the substance of the sky, and placed in the midst of the widespread ocean (*Bundahishn,* xii, 6). It receives its waters through a channel of gold from the greater heights of Mt. Hukairya, so that all created things thereby derive health from Mt. Ushi-darena.

This holy High Place may be symbolic of certain mystical experiences which devotees have on various levels of consciousness, from lower levels within themselves up to the highest as represented by the Mountain's summit. Similarly, the waters referred to may esoterically imply waves of cosmic energy emanating from the Mountain.

2. Mt. Asnavant

Mt. Asnavant is the thirty-sixth of 2,244 mountains enumerated in the *Zamyād Yasht.* In the Pahlavi *Dānkart* and *Zātsparam,* Mt. Asnavant is mentioned as being one of the seven places in Ātaropātakān (or Ādarbaijān) where Zarathustra conferred with the Seven Ameshaspands, representing the seven sacred aspects of the Supreme.

It is suggestive to observe that the *Zamyād Yasht* tells of the 2,244 mountains in its first chapter and then devotes the remaining fifteen chapters to the subject of Khvarenah, translatable as "Glory," "Halo," "Illumination," or "Divine Consciousness," such as was possessed by the great sages of ancient Iran, whose names the *Yasht* records. This Gloria in Excelsis confers, upon the individual invested with it, power, virtue, genius, divine destiny, and spiritual insight. This Glory that illuminated the great and holy men of ancient Iran was thought of as having its source in the Sun. And the mountains out of which the Sun rises were thought of as being sacred because they were specially charged with the Sun's divine light and magnetic potency.

Mt. Asnavant is particularly associated with Fire (*Āthrā*), which, for Zoroastrians, is the supreme element; Fire being for them a universal etheric energy, observable in the countenances of enlightened persons. It is in the *Ātash Nyāish,* the Fire Litany, that the invocation of the Sacred Fire is associated with Mt. Asnavant, which in turn is associated with the Divine Glory.

In the *Bundahishn,* Chapter XII, on the "Nature of Mountains," it is said that the 2,244 mountains constitute a long range, connected with Mt. Albôrz; and that Mt. Asnavant is a part of this range, situated in Ādarbaijān; and, also, that Mt. Asnavant is the seat of *Ādar Gûshasp,* the Sacred Fire. The sacred lake Chaēchasta, mentioned in the *Avesta* in connection with Mt. Asnavant, is the lake now known as Urumiah. According to Rawlinson, Mt. Asnavant is the same as Mt. Ushenai in Ādarbaijān near this lake.[32]

According to legend, the Kyanian King Kai-Khosru, while endeavoring to eradicate black magical practices and idolatry in the vicinity of Mt. Asnavant, beheld a divine light appear on the mane of his horse so that darkness was dispelled and his righteous endeavour succeeded. In commemoration of this he offered up thanks to Ahura-Mazda and established the Sacred Fire in the Temple. Two passages in the *Zātsparam* (xxii, 9, 11) are of special importance, for they directly associate Zarathustra with Mt. Asnavant. They refer to it as being one of the places where he dwelt and meditated during a number of years and became inspired by the Higher Powers so that he was enabled to go forth from there among men and proclaim his pure, monotheistic, Mazdayasni teachings.

[32]Sir Henry Rawlinson, *Memoir on the Site of the Atropatenian Eobatana,* Journal of the Geographical Society of London (1841), vol. x, pp. 65–158.

3. Mt. Hara-Berezaiti

The *Zamyād Yasht* refers to Mt. Hara-Berezaiti as being the first mountain to come forth from the Earth. It is identified later on with snow-capped Mt. Albôrz, some 18,000 feet high, extending along the regions towards the sunrise which were made productive by its abundance of water. Originally the name applied to a long range of the Caucasus extending from Asia Minor on the west to the Hindukush and Himalayas on the east. In the *Bundahishn* it is said that eight hundred years were required for Ahura-Mazda to complete Mt. Hara-Berezaiti; all the other of the 2,244 mountains of Iran are believed to have grown out of Mt. Albôrz.

On the heights of Mt. Hara-Berezaiti, the Hermit Haoma, a great healer and saint, worshipped the Divine Powers and made sacrifice to Mithra (personification of the Sun, as Eternal Light, Love, and Truth) by means of the healing Haoma plant and the offering of libations to Ahura-Mazda, and to Mithra for the protection of Mankind and the triumph of righteousness.

The *Chinvato-Peretu* of the *Avesta,* mentioned several times in *Gāthās,* is described as being the Bridge of Judgment, the Bridge of Moral Discrimination, which is the pathway leading to the Otherworld. According to the *Bundahishn,* the Bridge is suspended between two mountains, Chākad-i-Daîtîk and the Arezûr ridge of Mt. Albôrz. The righteous pass over it into Paradise. The wicked fall from it into the hell-world.

On Mt. Hukairya, the highest peak of Mt. Hara-Berezaiti, in the realm of the stars, is the heavenly spring of the Celestial Waters and the Cosmic Waves. It is associated with the famed Ardvi Sura Anāhita.[33] In this spring all waters have their source and thence flow down to the Sea of Divine Magnetism known as Vouru-Kasha. This account from the *Avesta* resembles that of the origin

---

[33] Ardvi Sura Anāhita is the Iranian *yazata* presiding over the Cosmic Life-giving Waters of Regeneration and Birth and the Divine Glory which radiates from human beings who have lived righteously. In ancient times, her cult, although essentially Iranian, spread afar and became assimilated with the cult of Artemis, Aphrodite, Athene-Minerva, Magna Mater, and other goddesses. She dwells among the stars, and traverses the heavens in a chariot, the four steeds of which are the rain, the hail, the cloud, and the wind.

of the sacred Ganges in Hindu scriptures and of Lake Mānsarovar near Mt. Kailas in Tibet whence flow the sacred Sindhu and Brahmaputra.

The Zoroastrian scriptures tell of a saintly King, Yima Vivanghvant, upon whom Ahura-Mazda conferred the power of prophecy. He reigned in the Golden Age of Aryan civilization, when there was neither cold nor heat, age nor death, envy nor wickedness; and father and son walked together as though but fifteen years old. This King is depicted in the *Avesta* as making prayers and sacrifices on Mt. Hukairya so that the Kingdom of Goodness should ever flourish in the world. He had acquired the Divine Glory in virtue of his piety and noble deed, but, as the years passed, pride possessed him because of his wondrous success in establishing the Golden Age. For this pride and for speaking untruths and pretending to be a god, the Divine Glory departed from him, as the *Zamyād Yasht* declares; and he trembled and was in sorrow, and the evil mind confounded him.

4. Other Sacred High Places of Iran

Mt. Saokanta, which seems to be situated near Mt. Hukairya, is referred to in the *Avesta* (*Nyaish* I, 9) as being another of Ahura-Mazda's favored mountains. It appears to be related to Divine Wisdom, Inspiration, the Righteous Path, and the Divine Glory. It is mentioned both in Sanskrit and Buddhist literature. From its summit there is said to protrude a golden tube, extending from the depths of the Earth, whence issue waters which reach the heavens and then spread everywhere. This golden tube and the waters symbolize cosmic processes whereby certain mantric-like vibrations produce in the devotee a sort of supramundane consciousness or ecstasy.

Another of the 2,244 mountains is Mt. Taera of Hara, of the Albôrz range. (See *Yasna* XLI, 24; *Rām Yasht* 7; *Zamyād Yasht* 6.) In the *Bundahishn* (XII, 4), Mt. Taera is said to be the central peak of the range, and the celestial bodies are said to revolve around it, as they do around Mt. Meru of Hindu mythology. It thus has astronomical connotations. In the *Bundahishn* (V, 5) it is said that Mt. Taera has 180 apertures, or notches, in the east and

180 in the west, and that each day the sun rises and sets through one of them.

These, then, are the most eminent of the mountains recognized by the followers of the Great Sage Zarathustra as being sacred. The ancient Aryans of Iran, or Ariana (Avesta, *Airyana*), meaning "Land of the Aryans," obviously had religious leaders of sufficiently adept psychic insight to be able to discover, many millennia ago, the sanctity of the High Places of the Middle East. In like manner did the psychically efficient religious leaders of the Children of the Great Mystery discover the sanctity of the High Places throughout the Americas, of which Cuchama is but one of many.

X. ADAM'S PEAK, CEYLON

Adam's Peak, 7,360 feet in altitude, situated about forty-five miles east of Colombo, in Ceylon (also known since ancient times as Lanka, the Sacred Isle), has the unique distinction of being venerated by followers of the four chief faiths of mankind, Hinduism, Buddhism, Christianity, and Islam, representing almost half the world's human population. The Peak's native name is Samanala, "the abode of Samana," the diety who presides over the Mountain and sanctifies the pilgrimage.[34] The name Adam's Peak, by which this island High Place has come to be generally known, is derived from the Moslem belief that when Adam and Eve were expelled from Paradise they chose Ceylon as being the most beautiful of all the lands of Earth in which to dwell, and the Peak became their secure sanctuary.

That Adam's Peak was sacred in prehistoric times to the Veddas, the aboriginal peoples of Ceylon, is suggested by a passage in the *Mahavamsa,* the ancient chronicle of Ceylon. It tells that

[34]Mr. C. M. Austin de Silva, ethnologist, National Museum, Colombo, Ceylon, to whom I am indebted for assistance in shaping this account of Adam's Peak, informs me that butterflies are commonly called in Sinhalese *Samanalayas*, although the Sinhalese word for butterfly is *pettha*. This is because in March and April, when the prevailing winds blow in the direction of Samanala, myriads of butterflies fly thither as though on pilgrimage themselves. Similarly, Cuchama is, at certain seasons, frequented by flocks of butterflies that seem to be attracted thither by the Mountain's magnetic aura. Such butterfly migrations in the United States, like those of birds, follow a definite route year after year and this route may be magnetically defined.

Vihaya, an Aryan prince banished from India who became king
of Ceylon, invaded the island in 543 B.C., married Kuveni, a Yakka
(or Vedda) princess, and that, subsequently, Kuveni having been
murdered, Kuveni's children took refuge on the Peak and became
the progenitors of the Vedda race.[35] Such is the legend, but anthropologists are agreed that the Veddas, one of the most primitive
types of mankind, were well established in Ceylon long before the
advent of Vihaya.

On the summit platform of the Peak there is a hollow in the
rock representing a gigantic human footprint. The Hindus believe
it to be that of the god Shiva. The Buddhists believe it to be that
of the Buddha, made during his third and last legendary visit to
Ceylon. South Indian Christians, who hold that St. Thomas came
to South India and taught Christianity there, take the footprint to
be no other than that of St. Thomas himself. Moslems maintain
that the footprint was made by Adam alone, as he stood there on
the Peak on one foot, doing penance for one thousand years.

This venerable High Place, looking out like a sentinel over the
Sacred Isle, is believed to confer upon its multitudinous devotees
of the four great faiths immeasurable spiritual good. In it, as in
Cuchama, are focussed beneficent magnetic forces; and beings,
visible only to seers, sanctify it and radiate their grace-waves to
the sincere pilgrim who seeks their divine guidance. By making the
pilgrimage to the Peak's summit, the Hindu is aided in the realization of *Mukhti* (Deliverance); the Buddhist is aided in the treading
of the Noble Rightfold Path to Emancipation; and the Christian
and Moslem are strengthened in their aspiration to a Heaven of
never-ending bliss.

As there are many paths to the summit of the Mount of Immortality so there are to the summit of Adam's Peak. Some are really
dangerous, but the greater the danger faced and triumphed over
on Life's Pilgrimage, the greater the reward and encouragement
through achievement. The most perilous of these paths is up the
face of a precipice, which is ascended by placing one foot after
another in the links of an enormous iron chain, which, so tradition
asserts, was placed there by Alexander the Great—notwithstand-

[35]P. N. Crowe, *Diversions of a Diplomat in Ceylon* (Princeton and New York,
n.d.), pp. 90–91.

ing that he never came anywhere near Lanka.[36] The safest and most used path has, like incarnate existence itself, thousands of steps.

The ideal time to begin the climb is on a full-moon night. By starting around midnight, the pilgrim reaches the summit well before sunrise. There, in the dawn of a new day, which for the faithful devotee really is new spiritually, the pilgrim rings a brass bell, once for each ascent he or she has made to the symbolic goal. Then, like the youth on the vision-quest on Cuchama, the pilgrim awaits the coming forth of the Sun.

As the Sun rises, in a clear sky, the Peak frequently casts a sharply-defined shadow on the morning mists in the tropical valleys far below, with its tip touching the shore of the Indian Ocean sixty miles distant in the west. Thus does nature exhibit one of the world's marvellously impressive pageants. The most auspicious season for the pilgrimage, which the writer made in the year 1918, is March and April. But on every day of the year, even when rain and mist prevail, there are throngs of pilgrims climbing to the Peak's summit, seeking, as all men everywhere and in all ages have sought, some answer to why there is the coming into incarnation and the going out of incarnation, why there is the Dawning, the Noonday, and the Night.

XI. EXALTED HIGH PLACES IN THE AMERICAS

On the opposite side of the world, the grandest of North America's sacred High Places, 20,300 feet high, rises out of Alaska. Known to the Red Men since immemorial time as Denali, "The Great One," it has been named unwisely Mt. McKinley by the White Man. Likewise, the psychically-unawakened White Man knows Tacoma, "The Mountain That Was God," in Washington State, as Mt. Rainier (14,363 feet high, as calculated by the United States Geological Survey in 1902). To this wondrous, ever snow-white mountain, the Red Men made frequent pilgrimage. It was their Holy Land of Peace, wherein all warfare was prohibited. Upon entering into its sacred domain, the warrior laid down his

---

[36]Gordon Gaskill, "Ceylon: Isle of Delight" (*Reader's Digest,* July 1957), pp. 149–50.

arms. Like the Hebrews' Cities of Refuge and the churches of medieval Europe, it was a place to which the persecuted could flee for safety and wherein all vengeance was stayed. Tribal members found guilty of wrongdoing were commonly sent there to do penance, and profiting by the Mountain's healing influences, recovered psychic health.[37]

Not only in these two, but in many other instances, the White Man, because of his unreasoning iconoclastic zeal when confronted by a non-Christian culture, appears to have sought to obliterate the age-old sanctity of North America's sacred mountains by displacing with unfitting names of non-American origin the meaningful names given to them by the Red Men's seers who knew why the mountains were sacred. It will be for the directors of the future to restore these rightful names to their respective mountains throughout the Americas, recovering by extra-sensory means those of them now temporarily lost which are not recoverable by normal means.

Two other of the noblest of North American High Places, now, unfortunately, generally known only by inappropriate White-Man names, are Mt. Washington, 6,288 feet high, the highest of the Appalachians, in New Hampshire (which I climbed in boyhood days and on its summit received its benediction), and Mt. Hood, 11,934 feet high, the glory of Oregon.

Parallel in significance to the American Tacoma, "The Mountain That Was God," is Bogdo-ol, "God's Mountain," 11,000 feet high, which over-shadows Urga, the capital of Inner Mongolia, and extends in its stupendous massiveness along the Tola River for some twenty-five miles. Similarly, according to the Iroquois, one of the abodes of the Great Spirit (otherwise known as the Great

---

[37]J. N. Williams, *The Mountain That Was God* (New York and London, 1911), pp. 31, 89; and, for a general account of the Indian lore of the Mountain, see pp. 25–40.

[Ed. nt.: Another notable sacred mountain is Mount Shasta in California. It may be one of the oldest geological formations in the world. Five glaciers cling to its slopes, and yet from its higher crevices issue steam and molten sulphur bubbles. Neighboring Indians believed it to be the abode of the Great Spirit when on earth. Many strange tales are still told of its mysterious lights and sounds, said to come from the underground residences of the descendants of ancient Lemurians or Atlanteans. The tiny village of Mount Shasta City at its foot is reported to host more religions per capita and per square mile than any other area in the United States. F.W.]

Mystery) is Mt. Marcy, 5,344 feet high, the highest peak of the Adirondacks, in New York State.[38]

In South America, where the culture of the Red Man has not been so greatly corrupted as it has been north of the Rio Grande, the most majestic of its High Places is still known only by its ancient American name Chimborazo, derived from Chimpu-Raza, "Mountain of Snow," in the Andes of Ecuador. Chimborazo, 20,702 feet high, long thought to be the world's loftiest mountain, was aptly called by Bolivar, the great South American liberator and friend of the Red Men, "The Watchtower of the Universe."[39] Cotopaxi, 19,498 feet high, the loftiest of the world's active volcanoes, is the Ecuadorian associate of Chimborazo, for both alike, being volcanic, are sacred to the deities presiding over the element fire and its elemental beings.[40]

The third highest of North America's mountains, Orizaba, which the Aztecs called Citlaltepetl, "The Mountain of the Star," 18,200 feet high, in Mexico, is revered by all Mexicans save those of European lineage who are unattuned to the Great Mystery of the Americas. Two more of Mexico's High Places, like Orizaba, volcanic and sacred to the deities of the volcanic fires and of the Underworld, are Popocatapetl, "The Smoking Mountain," 17,887 feet high and (ten miles north of it) the sixth highest mountain of North America, 17,342 feet high, the snow-clad and volcanically-inactive Iztaccihuatl, "The Lady in White," Popocatapetl's Shakti-like companion.[41]

---

[38]F. C. Lane, *The Story of Mountains* (Garden City, N.Y., 1950), p. 26.

[39]F. C. Lane, *op. cit.,* p. 10.

[40][Ed. nt.: Mt. Misti, 19,100 feet high, is another one of some thirty Andean peaks in Peru upon which shrines have been discovered. F.W.]

[41][Ed. nt.: Popocatepetl, "Smoking Mountain," and Iztaccihuatl, "White Woman" (now popularly called "Sleeping Woman"), are covered with at least ten ancient shrines, all above 12,000 feet altitude. At one of them, Alcalican, a nocturnal ceremony is still held on May 3, attended by people from distant villages.

In ancient times an elaborate ceremony took place to honor Iztaccihuatl. Two small boys and two small girls in Tenochtitlan (now Mexico City) were richly dressed and carried in decorated litters up on the mountain, accompanied by lords and noblemen carrying gifts of precious stones, women's clothing, and food. Here the four children were sacrificed in a great cave where the image of the goddess was kept. For two days the lords remained on the heights, fasting and performing ceremonies.

1. The Holy Mountains of the Navahos[42]

It is with the much appreciated permission of Frank Waters that there is here presented this traditional and occultly significant account of the Holy Mountains of the Navahos, set forth in his *Masked Gods* (pp. 167–70).

In the Beginning the people lived in several worlds below. Successively they emerged from them to a new world above. In the middle of this new world stood a great rock. Extending through all the previous underworlds and protruding above this one, it was the core of the universe, rooted in time and space. It was oriented to the four directions, and its sides glowed with their corresponding colors—white on the east, blue on the south, yellow-red on the west, black on the north.

Emerging from the world below, the people gathered at the foot of the great rock. And when they planted seeds to make the

---

Popocatepetl was similarly revered, offerings and sacrifices being made to it throughout the year. It was particularly honored on the 29th of October during Tepeilhuitl, the "Feast of the Mountains." In homes and sanctuaries small images of amaranth seed and maize kernels were made to represent the principal mountains of the land. In the center was placed the dough image of Popocatapetl, with eyes and mouth, and dressed in native paper. Close to him was placed the image of Iztaccihuatl, who was regarded as his wife. Fine offerings were made to them, and many rites were observed. Then the little dough images were decapitated as if they were alive, and the dough eaten. Following this repast called Nicteocua, which means "I Eat God," children and slaves were sacrificed. Then the people climbed to the tops of the hills and mountains to light fires, to burn incense, and perform ceremonies.

Described by the 16th century Dominican friar Diego Durán, translated and published under the title *Book of the Gods and Rites and The Ancient Calendar* (Norman: University of Oklahoma Press, 1971). Durán comments (p. 259): "The principal aim in honoring these hills, in praying and pleading, was [not to honor] the hill itself. Nor should it be considered that [hills] were held to be gods or worshipped as such. The aim was another: to pray from that high place to the Almighty, the Lord of Created Things, the Lord by Whom They Lived. These are the three epithets used by the Indians on pleading and crying out for peace in their time. . . . " F.W.]

[42][Ed. nt.: Two spellings are widely used, the word being Anglicized by using "h" or Hispanicized by using "j," both pronunciations being the same. Their choice in the voluminous literature is dictated by the preference of writers and publishers and varies from time to time. *Navaho* is used here as it appeared in *Masked Gods: Navaho and Pueblo Ceremonialism*, first published in 1950. Since then *Navajo* has come more into vogue. The editors, therefore, have made no attempt to adhere to one spelling for the many references throughout the present text, using each according to the different sources quoted. F.W.]

Sand Painting of the Four Sacred Directional Mountains of the Navahos, made on the second day of the Shooting-Chant: Male Branch Ceremony (*Nahtohe Baka*). See also "Description of Illustrations." *Photo by Laura Gilpin. Courtesy Museum of Navajo Ceremonial Art, Santa Fe, New Mexico.*

Sand Painting of the Four Sacred Directional Mountains of the Navahos, made on the second day of the Shooting-Chant: Big House Form *(Nahtohe Kin-Be-Hatral)*. See also "Descriptions of Illustrations." *Photo by Laura Gilpin. Courtesy Museum of Navajo Ceremonial Art, Santa Fe, New Mexico.*

earth spread out, and when they called the Holy People to help them plant the Holy Mountains, it was around this great natal rock. Hence they called it simply the Mountain Around Which Moving Was Done, the Mountain Surrounded by Mountains, or the Encircled Mountain.[43]

To the east of it they planted the Holy Mountain of the East, made of sand and white shell [and sacred to the Sun]. To the south they planted the Mountain of the South, made of sand and blue-green turquoise. To the west, the Mountain of the West, of yellow-red sand and abalone. And to the north, the Mountain of the North, of black sand and jet.[44] In each they placed a Holy Person, a Talking God, to guard the mountain and to listen to the prayers and songs offered to it. Extra mountains they transplanted, and seeds of the four sacred plants.[45] They made a fire with four kinds of wood,[46] and a hogan with four logs. Everything—the stars, the winds, the seasons—they put in order and named, and they became. For "when you put a thing in order, give it a name, and you are all in accord, it becomes."

Thus the pattern of the Navaho world at the Emergence. The great central Encircled Mountain. The four directional Holy Mountains, the lesser transplanted mountains, the plants, the trees,

[43]There may be correlation between the world-wide symbolism of the lingam and yoni and the Navahos' Encircled Mountain, the great natal rock symbolizing the lingam and the circle of mountain enclosing the great natal rock, the yoni. That this symbolism was used in pre-Columbian America is attested by a Mayan figurine of a woman, probably a priestess, holding in her right hand a lingam encircled by a yoni. See S. G. Morley, *The Ancient Maya* (Stanford, California, 1956), plate 81, figure c. This Mayan Lingam-yoni symbol is quite like that sometimes held by the Babylonian Sun-god Marduk. Similar Lingam-yoni symbols are shown in Sir John Marshall's *Mohenjo-Daro and the Indus Civilization* (London, 1931), vol. III, plate CLXIV, 3: cf. plate CLIX, 9.

[44]The system of color-direction symbolism among the Diegueño, the only tribe in California as yet known to possess it, is the same here for the east and south, but for the west it is black and for the north red. Cf. A. L. Kroeber, *op. cit.,* p. 717.

[45]These are corn, beans, squash, and tobacco.

[46]The four woods most commonly used in Indian religious ceremonies are piñon, spruce, pine, and juniper, but these may vary from tribe to tribe and according to ritual usage. Such conifer-bearing trees, being perpetually verdant, symbolize for the tribes, and for the American races generally, the ever-living Great Mystery.

[Ed. nt.: The four kinds of wood vary with the rituals. For the Shooting Chant sweat-emetic, for example, aspen at the east, spruce at the south, red willow at the west, and chokecherry at the north, are used; whereas in the Night Chant the fire is made of cottonwood, piñon, juniper, and spruce. (Gladys A. Reichard, *Navaho Religion: A Study of Symbolism,* Bollingen Foundation, New York, 1950.) F. W.]

with the winds, the seasons, and the sun and moon and stars above. A world spread out like a four-petalled flower as seen from above. This today in a Navaho sand-painting is the symbol of the great axial rock, the Encircled Mountain: a four-petalled flower, like a four-leafed clover, like a lotus.

The four sacred mountains still bounding the ancient Navaho homeland are physical mountains: the Mountain of the East variously identified as Mount Blanca, in Colorado, or Wheeler Peak, above Taos in the Sangre de Cristo range, or Pelado Peak, near the pueblo of Jemez; Mount Taylor, of the San Mateo range, as the Mountain of the South; the San Francisco peaks, in Arizona, as the Mountain of the West; and a peak in the La Plata or San Juan range as the Mountain of the North.[47]

The Encircled Mountain is something else. It has been identified as Huerfano Peak, above Chaco Canyon, which bears its name. But by its very nature it cannot be so constricted. Being the core of the whole cosmos, it existed when the First People were still in the lower worlds; and spanning a time and space beyond our earth-dimensional comprehension, it is too great and too powerful to be visible. This is its metaphysical reality. El Huerfano is merely its material image, its physical counterpart.

The meaning of this is simplified by reference to the cosmography of Tibetan Buddhism, in which is found the most striking parallel to the Encircled Mountain.

The core of the cosmos is Mt. Meru. It is shaped like a truncated pyramid, three of its four sides glowing with the same directional colours of the Navaho world-axis: white on the east, blue on the south, red on the west, and yellow on the north. It is eighty thousand miles high and eighty thousand miles deep. Within it are several underworlds and several heavens. Around this mighty cosmic core are seven concentric circles of mountains separated by seven encircling oceans. Each of these fresh-water oceans and its corresponding wall of mountains is a separate universe with its own sun and moon and planets.

Outside these seven universes, and floating in the outer salt-water ocean of space, are four main continents or land masses spreading out in the four main directions. [These symbolically

[47]The Navaho names of these four High Places, made holy by the indwelling presence of the Divine Ones, are: for the High Place of the East, Sisnajinni; for that of the South, Tsodsichl; for that of the West, Doko-oslid; for that of the North, Depenitsa. The Mt. Meru-like High Place in the Center is Tsichlnaodi-chli, where were created the first Navahos. The High Place of the East, sanctified by the sunrise, was for the Navahos the chief of the sacred mountains of the four cardinal directions. The holy-song associated with it is given in part later. Cf. N. C. Burlin, *The Indians' Book* (New York and London, 1907), pp. 351, 354.

correspond to the four sacred mountains; and, like them, are directionally placed, in the four cardinal directions.][48]

Below this mighty Mt. Meru the cosmos thus spreads out like a great four-petalled flower, a lotus. Each of the world-petals is protected by a Lokapala, or World Guardian, as each of the four Holy Mountains of the Navahos is guarded by its Talking God. And just as the Navaho world and the Encircled Mountain is symbolized by a four-petalled flower, so is the Buddhistic cosmos represented as a lotus.

These are striking pictorial and mythological parallels. But their full significance would be lost without their metaphysical meaning. The whole cosmos is represented as a lotus; but this cosmos is also identical with the goddess-mother called "The Lotus"; and our earthly universe is located within her "at about the level of her waist." In its duality, then, it is both that which was created and that which created it. And each living being, himself created in the image of the Goddess Mother of creation, also duplicates within his own psyche the complete cosmos.

Only by this can we understand the cryptic opening sentence of the legend of the Navaho ceremonial *Where the Two Came to Their Father:* "When they put the extra mountains around, they took Mountain Around Which Moving Was Done out of First Woman's belt."

This too explains the Zuñi references to the Sacred Middle which their ancestors found at Zuñi after their emergence from the underworld, and the location of their corresponding Mountain of Generation as being just below the navel of the Earth Mother. Above all is their striking conception of the Earth Mother as the goddess-mother of creation, through whose successive womb-worlds they emerged to this one.[49]

The conception of this four-cornered world structure is not confined to them alone in America. In the sacred *Popol Vuh,* recording the creation myth of the Quiché Maya, the world is described as "four-pointed, four-sided, four-bordered." In the *Chilan Balam of Mani,* this cubical world-block is further alluded to as the altar of the gods. The truncated pyramid temples of the Toltecs, Zapotecs, and Aztecs themselves suggest such world axes.

Hence we understand now, at the outset, that in Pueblo and Navaho mythology we are dealing not with easily comprehended, childish legends, but with a cosmographic concept as abstract, imaginatively vast and old as that of any people on Earth. It is

[48][Ed. nt.: For Dr. Evans-Wentz's own detailed description, see *The Tibetan Book of the Dead,* pp. 62–64. F.W.]
[49]Perhaps this significance of the Zuñi Mountain of Generation may be applicable to the Mountain of Creation referred to above in relation to Cuchama.

strangely consistent that the area today still contains this mythological meaning in its name, the Four Corners. Its original prototype, its greatest physical image, may well have been, not El Huerfano, but the Colorado Pyramid, the high hinterland heart of America. Its central section, the Colorado plateau region, is still the sacred middle, their traditional homeland. The Pueblos and Navahos have always regarded life as dual: the physical and the psychical. And it is both of these realities of the Rock to which they have clung against the assault of erosion and materialism alike.

XII. DEITIES OF THE HIGH PLACES

There are, associated with all the sacred High Places of the world, not only by myth and tradition but by extra-sensory perception, races of invisible beings, apparently as multitudinous as the various species of visibly perceptible living creatures; some are inimical, some friendly and protective to man. In this connection, it is well worthwhile to take into account the remarkable testimony set forth by Bhagawan Shri Hamsa on pages 178–82 of *The Holy Mountain,* published in London in 1934, concerning his initiation on Mt. Kailas and the materialization there in palpable bodily form of his superhuman guru, who was the initiator.

William Butler Yeats, Irish poet and mystic, assured me that he had no doubt of the existence of the normally invisible beings commonly known collectively as gods and fairies. He gave unqualified support to Bhagawan Shri Hamsa's testimony by contributing to his book an introduction of thirty pages. Intimately associated with Yeats in psychic studies was the distinguished Irish poet and seer, George William Russell, whose relevant testimony, supporting that of Yeats, is to be found hereinafter.[50]

Among the Pueblo Indians, as commonly among most Indian tribes throughout the Americas, there are many sacred hills and mountains. Thus, the Lagunas formerly revered four sacred mountains: Sandia for the east, Zuñi for the west, Petaco Pinto for the south, and a mountain north of Casa Salazar for the north. In modern times, mountains nearer Laguna have been designated for these of the east and west: a sacred mountain near Suwanee for

[50][Ed. nt.: Development of the testimony of both Yeats and Russell (A.E.) is to be found in Part IV, Sections III, "Sacred Places and Their Guardians" and IV, "Otherworld Beings." C.A.]

the east and Mount Taylor for the west. In addition to four other sacred mountains for the four cardinal directions, the Keres have a sacred mountain for the zenith and another for the nadir. Each of them is under the guardianship of an invisible being, one of whose functions is weather-control. The Taos Indians revered a high peak called by them Maxwaluna, which rises immediately northeast of their pueblo. Near it is their sacred lake.[51]

[51]Cf. E. L. Hewett, B. P. Dutton, and John P. Harrington, *op. cit.*, pp. 34–38. [Ed. nt.: Taos, or Pueblo Peak, commonly known as the Sacred Mountain, rises immediately behind Taos Pueblo. Between it and Wheeler Peak—generally identified as the Navajos' Holy Mountain of the East, and the highest peak in New Mexico—lies the Pueblo's sacred Blue Lake, considered to be their place of Emergence to this world. To it, once each year, men, women, and children make annual pilgrimages to observe ceremonies never witnessed by a White Man.

Ownership of the immense mountain wilderness had been confirmed to the Indians since 1551 by Spain, Mexico, and the United States. Yet, in 1906, the federal government usurped the land for a national forest without compensation to the Pueblo. Subsequently, the Forest Service permitted desecration of the area by hunters, fishermen, and tourists, and claimed title to it. Taos Pueblo then began its long, legal fight to gain its restoration for religious purposes. The controversy reached national proportions as other Indian tribes throughout the country, church groups, civic organizations, and individuals supported the Pueblo's claim. Finally, in December 1970, the Congress passed a bill providing that the disputed 50,000 acres be kept in wilderness status under Taos Pueblo ownership. This is a unique and pleasant chapter in the history of the sacred mountains in the United States.

Other mountains immemorially sacred to the Pueblos and Navajos have been desecrated and destroyed in our materialistic march of Progress. The 3,300-square-mile Black Mesa, sacred to both tribes, is currently being strip-mined for coal, irreparably ruining the land forever. The San Francisco Peaks in Arizona, the Navajos' Holy Mountain of the West, is also sacred to the Hopis. It is the abode of those Shining Beings the Hopis call *kachinas*, "respected spirits," who come each year to bring blessings to their people. To its slopes the Hopis carry prayer-feathers and offerings, and bring back spruce for their ceremonies. Today both tribes are protesting the projected exploitation of the mountain by commercial interests for a ski resort. Sandia Mountain in New Mexico is regarded as a sacred mountain by Santa Ana Pueblo and other pueblos along the Rio Grande River. Upon it has been constructed a ski area and a tourist tramway to the summit.

Pike's Peak in Colorado, 14,110 feet high, was one of the most notable sacred mountains in the United States. The Ute Creation Myth centered upon it, and its mythical origin parallels stories of the Flood. Its spiritual forces, like a great magnet, drew people to it for centuries. It was a mecca for Utes coming down from the Rockies, and for Arapahoes, Kiowas, and Cheyennes from the Great Plains to the east, who dropped votive offerings in the medicinal spring at its foot. When the White Men came, it was a beacon peak for the "Pike's Peak or Bust" wagon caravans of the gold-seekers. Years later it still exerted its spell, drawing

It is on the sacred High Places of the Navaho and Pueblo, as on those of other nations of the Red Men, that their youth, chiefly those in training to be medicine-men, go on vision-quests. There they seek and find the Divine Ones, the Holy Persons, the Guardians, who inspire their holy-songs and in visions lay before them the lots in life. (Part III, Section II, following, deals with this aspect of the psychic training of the Red Men.)

Accordingly (and also as the outcome of my own research recorded in *The Fairy-Faith in Celtic Countries* and explained in Part IV, Section III, following), I am convinced that the world-wide folk-belief in other-world beings associated with sacred mountains ought not to be summarily dismissed, as it ordinarily is, as being purely fanciful and hallucinatory.

If there were no Otherworld, or no extra-terrestrial state of consciousness, then, indeed, there would be for man no after-death existence; and all the teachings of the Great Sages and Seers throughout the ages would be invalid. But the writer, after more than fifty years of research in the historic faiths of mankind and in matters yogic and psychic throughout both the Orient and the Occident, here places on record his own conviction that there is an Otherworld and Otherworld beings. This conviction was strengthened when the writer sat in meditation at Delphi, on the southern slopes of Mt. Parnassus, at the site of the once world-renowned national Oracle of Greece, where the Pythia, the priestess, enthroned on a golden tripod-throne placed over a fissure in the rock of her oracular cavern, inbreathed a vapor which issued

---

trainloads of visitors from all over the world. Yet neither its majestic snow-capped summit, nor the virginal beauty of its canyons, could alone account for the peace, serenity, and psychic energy it exerted as a spiritual font.

Today there is a cog-road train, and an automobile race-course highway, to its summit. The front wall of the range has been stripped bare for gravel. Cheyenne Mountain, a neighboring peak, has been hollowed out to house the operations center of the North American Air Defense Command. The Air Force Academy has appropriated the front slope to the north, while an immense Army base covers the land to the south. As a result of these military, industrial, and commercial onslaughts, Pike's Peak has withdrawn into itself its benevolent influence.

In exploiting these and many other sacred mountains throughout the country, we are, as Dr. Evans-Wentz points out, depriving ourselves of the psychic energy we could draw from them. F.W.]

from the fissure.[52] Thereby becoming entranced, the Pythia was the human medium through whom the diety of the mountain uttered his oracles, revealing the past and foreseeing the future for kings and emperors and the lowliest suppliant. Mt. Parnassus, rising 8,060 feet above the purple Aegean Sea, and sanctified by the youthful god, the Shining One, the Sun-robed Apollo, was equal, if not superior, in holiness to Mt. Olympus, 9,751 feet high, the home of Zeus, the Father of the Gods.

The secret power of these High Places of the Mediterranean world has not passed away; it only awaits the coming of a new Golden Age, as does that of the High Places of the Americas, when the Ancient Mysteries are to be restored, and man, once more, will turn to the Great Ones for guidance, re-establishing the now almost unpracticed communion with the saints and the gods.

---

[52]Although the French archaeological examination of the ruins of the oracular shrine of the Pythia, conducted from 1892 onward, failed to discover such a fissure, the unequivocal reports of its existence by Plutarch (*De Defectu Oraculorium,* c. 43) and by other well-informed classical writers cannot be ignored. More than once, in its millennia-long history, Delphi was reduced to ruin, both by invaders (e.g. the Persians in 480 B.C. and the Gauls in 279 B.C.) and by severe earthquakes (which could readily have closed such a fissure), and then rebuilt. It is obvious, therefore, that the present ruins may not be indicative of the physical state of the caverned shrine in the ancient times when the fissure was reported as existing.

The Martyrdom and Religion of the Red Men

PART III

The Worship Of The Great Mystery

The worship of the "Great Mystery" was silent, solitary, free from all Self-seeking.

Ohiyesa, in *The Soul of the Indian*

3

The Martyrdom and Religion of the Red Men

After treating of the cultural elements most intimately associated with Cuchama, in Part I, there is given here in Section I "The Martyrdom of the Red Men," as being contributory to the attaining of right anthropological perspective in this specialized study of the indigenous peoples of the Americas. In it, there is presented an epitomized historical account of the sufferings imposed upon the Red Men after the discovery of the New World, when rapacious White Men came among them and sought to destroy their culture (of which a most essential element is the cult of sacred mountains), as did Bandini and his Spanish compatriots in the territory round about Cuchama. These White Men not only seized the land and disrupted the social life of the Red Men, reducing them in many instances to starvation, but they put to death, with the utmost brutality, multitudinous thousands in order to possess their gold and silver, and overthrew their two great empires which, in some respects, were more advanced than the then contemporaneous empires of the Old World.

1. Anglo America

North of the Rio Grande, with a few outstanding exceptions (such as Pennsylvania under William Penn,[1] Manhattan Island under the Dutch, and parts of Rhode Island under Roger Williams, with all of whom, *at the outset,* the Red Men were enabled to live in brotherly peace and accord), much the greater part of the valuable agricultural, mineral, and forested lands were acquired by dishonorable means, usually by outright theft, by the White Men, who thereby amassed fabulous fortunes. Although the White Men were professedly Christian, they gave little or no heed to the Sermon on the Mount, or to the prohibitions of their Hebrew decalogue not to covet, not to steal, not to murder. Multitudes of Red Men who rose in righteous revolt were massacred.

In a letter of one of the early settlers, written in 1678, it is stated that under the wise policy adopted by William Penn, "the Indians were even rendered our benefactors and protectors. Without any carnal weapon we entered the land and inhabited therein, as safe as if there had been thousands of garrisons." Similarly, Richard Townsend, a Quaker, in about the year 1727, testified as follows: "And as our worthy proprietor, [William Penn], treated the Indians with extraordinary humanity, they became very civil and loving to us, and brought in abundance of venison. As, in other countries, the Indians were exasperated by hard treatment, which hath been the foundation of much bloodshed, so the contrary treatment here hath produced their love and affection." (Cf. The Aborigines' Committee of the Meeting for Sufferings, *Some Account of the Conduct of the Religious Society of Friends towards the Indian Tribes in the Settlement of the Colonies of East and West Jersey and Pennsylvania* (London, 1844), pp. 16, 41.)

[1] After William Penn's first purchase of land from the Indians, in 1682, "great promises passed between him and the Indians of kindness and good neighborhood, and that the Indians and English must live in love as long as the sun should give light." (Cf. George Bancroft, *History of the United States of America,* New York, 1892, I, p. 567.) This wise policy of the Quakers, of just-dealing and of total abstention from coercion and threats of violence, and with no message save peace, markedly in contrast with the opposite policy disastrously pursued in other regions of the Americas, was so successful that no blood of a Quaker was ever shed by an Indian and real fraternity prevailed in all parts of the territory as long as it remained under William Penn's truly Christian jurisdiction.

It was such savage outrages committed over and over again by White Men upon Red Men who at first had been friendly and peaceful, that transformed the Red Men into vengeance-seeking enemies, and were the direct causes of the long and bloody Indian wars both north and south of the Rio Grande. Furthermore, as the late Mr. A. Hyatt Verrill, in *The Real Americans,* page 32, states, "If we examine the matter with unbiased minds, we will find that most of the Indians' atrocities and tortures were copied from the white men." Among the atrocities and tortures so adopted were chopping off hands and feet, cutting off eyelids, tearing out tongues, burial alive in an ant-hill, after the Spanish custom in Mexico, burning at the stake, after the custom of Christians in their treatment of heretics, and the sadistic and murderous practices put into operation by Spanish Christians, ecclesiastic as well as lay, under the direction of Cortez in Mexico and of Pizarro in Peru. And as Mr. Verrill adds, on page 34, "No Indian raid in the entire history of our country could equal the unprovoked murders and massacres of peaceful friendly Indians that time and time again were perpetrated by the whites."

On a Sunday afternoon, presumably after church, New England Christians killed more than one thousand Red Men in one village of the Narragansetts. Miles Standish, quite unlike the fanciful presentation of him by the poet Longfellow, was as merciless in his treatment of the Red Men as any of his fellow Christians. On one occasion, he cut off the head of an Indian, and carried it as a trophy to Plymouth. Captain Benjamin Church, another of New England's professed Christians, had the head and hands of the body of King Philip, chief of the Naragansetts, cut off and the body quartered. The four quarters of the chief's body were hung upon as many trees. The head was publicly exposed upon a gibbet in Plymouth for twenty years. One hand was placed on exhibition in Boston. The chief's son, nine years old, was sold by the Christians into slavery overseas.[2] In New Amsterdam, the gory heads of eighty Red Men, who had been slain while sleeping by the Governor's soldiers, were placed on view on the streets, "where the governor's mother kicked them like footballs."[3]

[2] Cf. H. R. Sass, *Hear Me My Chiefs!* (New York, 1940), pp. 46, 34, 244, 41-2; C. Hamilton, *Cry of the Thunderbird* (New York, 1950), p. 132.
[3] Cf. R. M. Underhill, *Red Man's America* (Chicago, 1953), p. 73.

In 1637, while Protestant Christians set afire seventy wigwams in the Connecticut River valley wherein Pequot Red Men were sleeping unsuspectingly, many of whom perished in the flames, and shot down those that fled for safety, Captain Mason shouted, "God is over us." Dr. Cotton Mather, a clergyman, in his written account of the indefensible carnage wrote: "It was supposed that no less than six hundred Pequot souls were brought down to Hell that day."[4] Governor Bradford of the Plymouth Colony wrote of this barbarity: "It was a fearful sight to see them [the Pequots] frying in the fire and the streams of blood quenching the same, and horrible was the stink and stench thereof. But the victory seemed a sweet sacrifice, and they [the Christians] gave praise thereof to God."[5] On a seventeenth century gravestone of a Puritan there is a characteristic record that he had killed ninety-eight Indians and had hoped to make it a hundred before the year's end "when he fell asleep in the arms of Jesus."[6] After the formation of the Union of the Thirteen Colonies in 1776, the armed forces of the United States assisted the Christians in driving the Red Men from their fields and hunting-grounds and villages, and in continuing their extermination.

In 1752, the English General Jeffrey Amherst recommended that the Ottawas and Ojibways of the Great Lakes region be infected by means of sheets upon which smallpox patients had been lying, and, also, that they be hunted down with dogs. The historian of the Ottawas, Chief Andrew J. Blackbird, writing in 1887, charges the British with the deliberate use of smallpox germs in the war against the Red Men.

Sometimes, even when converted to Christianity, the Red Man was still in jeopardy. Colonel William Crawford, one of George Washington's favorite officers, by stealth and deception, placed armed troops around a church in which, on a Sunday morning, Moravian Christian Delawares were at their devotions. The troops barred all egress by door and windows, and then had the church

---

[4]Cf. John Collier, *The Indians of the Americas* (New York, 1947), p. 195.
[5]Cf. J. Underhill, *News from America* (London, 1902), p. 24; R. M. Underhill, *op. cit.*, p. 75.
[6]Cf. F. T. and J. M. Seton, *The Gospel of the Red Men* (Los Angeles, 1948), p. 60.

set afire and all within it perished. In retaliation, the Delawares burned the Colonel at the stake.[7]

In 1838, the Cherokees were forcibly removed from their ancestral homes in the Great Smokies. White Men seized their land, their cabins and their livestock; and, like ghouls, dug into the Red Men's graves to filch silver ornaments from rotting corpses. The Cherokee Removal was as wantonly wicked as it was brutal. Thirteen thousand Cherokees were forced by soldiers of the United States into exile. On the death march, some days ten to twenty men, women, and children lay down on the wayside and died. The death toll reached a total of more than four thousand.[8]

White Men in the Rocky Mountains vied with one another as to who could inflict the greatest outrages on the Red Men. On horses, "they chased them at full speed, lassoed them like cattle, and dragged them till they were dead." Of the horrible atrocities committed by soldiers of the United States during the Sand Creek Massacre of Red Men, the Indian Peace Commission of 1868 reported: "Fleeing women, holding up their hands and praying for mercy, were shot down; infants were killed and scalped in derision; men were tortured and mutilated in a manner that would put to shame the savages of interior Africa." A commission appointed in 1869 by President Grant to examine Indian affairs reported "that in our Indian wars, almost without exception, the first aggressions have been made by white men."[9]

In the United States as late as December 29, 1890, at Wounded Knee, the Federal army massacred ninety-eight disarmed warriors and two hundred women and children of the Red Men.[10] "In

---

[7]Cf. C. Hamilton, *op. cit.*, pp. 133, 145–48.

[8]Cf. H. R. Sass, *op. cit.*, pp. 233–38; T. V. Parker, *The Cherokee Indians* (New York, 1907), p. 49.

[9]Cf. H. H. Jackson, *A Century of Dishonor* (New York, 1881), pp. 339, 357–58, 381. As therein suggested, the White Men did as much scalping as the Red Men during the Indian wars. "It was from the Puritan Pilgrim Fathers that the Massachusetts Indian learned to scalp their enemies." (See E. T. Seton and J. M. Seton, *op. cit.*, p. 45.)

[10]Cf. John Collier, *op. cit.*, p. 238.

[Ed. nt.: Wounded Knee, South Dakota, is now well-known for two confrontations between the Red Men and the White.

It is now estimated that of the 350 unarmed Oglala Sioux men, women, and children, up to 300 lost their lives in the massacre in 1890. Most of them were

1917, the Assistant Indian Commissioner explained to the Indian Committee of the House that since the Indians were being liquidated, it was policy to liquidate their forests at the same time, even though these forests were the protecting cover of watersheds." The "Indian-owned timber was cut clean."[11] At the instigation of the Christian missionaries, "the Interior Department framed a criminal code forbidding Indian religious practices and established penalties. Enacted in 1884 and enriched in 1904, the code stood in force and effect until 1933."[12] Unconstitutionally, religious freedom was thus prohibited to Red Men in the United States, as it had been to the Mormons. Protestant Christianity made it a fixed policy to destroy the native American culture. Students in its mission schools were forbidden to attend Navaho religious ceremonials and even to converse in Navaho. In addition, they were subjected to uncalled-for brutality if they failed to be amenable to Christianization.[13] "The local looting of Indians became a principal business in eastern Oklahoma, continuing with

---

massacred by the Seventh U.S. Cavalry regiment using not only carbines, but Hotchkiss shrapnel guns mounted on the hillside above. An indeterminate number of the women and children died from exposure in the blizzard when they fled and hid in ravines. The soldiers lost 25 men, most of them killed by their own shrapnel fire. After the massacre, 18 cavalrymen were awarded Congressional Medals of Honor for "gallantry" and "conspicuous heroism in action." The Seventh Regiment was the regiment formerly commanded by General Custer at the time of the Custer Massacre. (*Bury My Heart at Wounded Knee,* Dee Brown, N.Y., 1970.)

The widely publicized second confrontation took place in the spring of 1973, when the little village of Wounded Knee was occupied by members of the American Indian Movement in blanket protest against the Oglala Sioux' loss of land to White ranchers, and their extreme poverty. More specifically, they were protesting the oppressive Tribal Council, supported and financed by the dictatorial Bureau of Indian Affairs; and its refusal to allow the Oglalas to hold a constitutional convention to form their own system of tribal government, and to negotiate a settlement of their grievances with the federal government. The United States' retaliation included a blockade of the community with roadblocks, Army armored vehicles and jet planes, U.S. Marshals, FBI agents, B.I.A. police, and State highway patrols, censorship of news, innumerable arrests, and months of ineffectual court trials afterward.

This second tragic affair at Wounded Knee was symptomatic of the grievous U.S.-Indian relationship that still exists today. F.W.]

[11] *Ibid.,* p. 243.

[12] *Ibid.,* p. 233.

[13] Cf. C. Kluckhohn and D. Leighton, *The Navaho* (Cambridge, 1946), pp. 82–84; E. R. Embree, *Indians of the Americas* (Boston, 1939), p. 246.

brazen openness until past 1925, and not wholly ended yet."[14] As John Collier very succinctly reports in *The Indians of the Americas,* page 214, "Between 1862 and 1867, wars with the Sioux, Cheyenne and Navaho alone, had cost the United States Government $100,000,000," all of which was expended in pursuance of that Government's avowed policy of exterminating the Red Men within its national jurisdiction. James McLoughlin, formerly United States Indian Inspector, states in *My Friend the Indian,* page 5, practically all of the regular army of the United States was in the field under General Sherman with the avowed purpose of annihilating the Red Men by "merciless and vindictive warfare." General Harney, of the United States Army, said: "I have lived on this frontier fifty years and I have never yet known an instance in which war broke out with these tribes that the tribes were not in the right."[15] And Buffalo Bill said to Ernest Thompson Seton in Washington, D. C. in 1915, "I never led an expedition against the Indians but I was ashamed of myself, ashamed of my government, and ashamed of my flag; for they were always in the right and we were in the wrong. They never broke a treaty, and we never kept one."[16]

Under the Spanish regime of Church and State in California, particularly in what is now San Diego County, where this study is centered, W. E. Smythe, in his *History of San Diego,* pages 60 and 61, reports concerning the Mission Fathers: "They did not hesitate to employ the military arm as a means of forcible conversion. There is reason to believe that whole villages were sometimes surrounded and their inhabitants driven to the Missions." The Fathers considered it better for an Indian to be converted and in

[14]Cf. John Collier, *op. cit.,* p. 217. Even now, while this book is being written, the same sort of crimes by White Men continue with equal brazen openness. In a public letter to the President of the United States, dated February 2, 1959, Herbert C. Holdridge, a retired Brigadier General of the United States Army, states: "Reports have been reaching me for many months of crimes being perpetrated against the Ute Indians of Utah violating Public Law and their sovereign rights. . . . My investigations have verified the shocking truth of these reports: confiscations of vast areas of lumber, grazing and mineral resources; misappropriation of Indian lands; impairment of hunting and fishing rights; limitation of rights of the true Utes to the advantage of the 'squatters' having no legal status as Utes."
[15]Cf. R. M. Underhill, *op. cit.,* p. 171.
[16]Cf. E. T. Seton and J. M. Seton, *op. cit.,* p. 40.

chains than to be a free heathen. Alfred Robinson, in *Life in California,* page 39, writing as an observer, reports that it was "not unusual to see numbers of them [the Indians] driven along by alcaldes, and under the whip's lash forced to the very doors of the sanctuary." And he adds: "It is not to be wondered at that many attempt to escape from the severity of the religious discipline at the Mission. They are pursued, and generally taken; then they are flogged, and an iron clog is fastened to their legs, serving as additional punishment, and a warning to others." That the Mission of San Diego, like many of the other Missions of the Californias, was frequently attacked by the outraged Indians, and finally fell into ruin when its Indian inmates could no longer be held enslaved in it to keep it in repair, was but the inevitable outcome, as it was in the Missions of Lower California. In 1775 the San Diego Mission was totally destroyed by the Indians, and then rebuilt, and then decayed.

How, even more atrociously, like the Red Men of Mexico and Peru, the Red Men of San Diego County were treated by the White Men, may be surmised from a few of the recordings by W. F. Smythe in the *History of San Diego,* page 181:

Four Indian chiefs were publicly, and illegally, executed by shooting in Old San Diego, on April 11, 1778, the charge against them being that they were preparing to attack the White Men— as they were fully justified in doing. In 1826, under the Spanish regime, Lieutenant Ybarra, in reprisal for the loss of three of his men, killed twenty-eight Indians; and, to prove his prowess, sent into the San Diego Mission twenty pairs of the slain Indians' ears. At about the same epoch, eighteen of the San Felipe Valley Indians suffered a similar fate, and their ears were cut off from their corpses. Thus it was, in San Diego County, that White Men, reared in the Christian faith, proved to be in warfare of no higher cultural level than the savage head-hunters of Borneo.

It appears that in 1637 the New England Puritans initiated scalping as a business, which soon became a widespread means of money-making among White Men, who, quite unlike the Red Men, scalped women and children without compunction, thinking only of the bounty. At first the Puritans paid bounties for whole heads of Pequots. Thirty-eight years later, bounties were paid for scalps alone. Thus, for the scalps of two braves, two women and six children, a Mrs. Hannah Dustin received fifty pounds. A Puritan clergyman preached in church on Sundays and during the week days specialized in ambushing and scalping Indian children at play as an easy way of augmenting his meagre salary. In 1671, the Governor of Canada was paying ten crowns per scalp, but, owing to an oversupply, the price was reduced to one crown. General John Burgoyne valued scalps of enemy soldiers and unfriendly Indians at twenty-eight pounds each.[17]

In 1641, New Netherlands began offering bounties for Indian scalps. In 1704, Connecticut and Massachusetts followed the precedent. Virginia and Pennsylvania did likewise. In 1764, the bounty in Pennsylvania ranged from $50 for a squaw's scalp to $150 for an Indian over ten years old captured alive. In 1814, the Territory of Indiana offered $50 each for Indian scalps. As late as 1867, a citizen of Denver, Colorado, offered to pay $10 for any Indian scalp. Residents of Central City raised $5,000 to buy scalps at $25 apiece. In 1876, the price for an Indian scalp had risen to $200, in Deadwood, Dakota Territory. At the time of the slaying of the family of the Apache warrior Geronimo, the government of Mexico was paying a bounty for Apache scalps: $100 for a warrior's, $50 for that of a squaw, and $25 for that of a child. Oregon placed a bounty on Indians and coyotes. The Indians were trailed with hounds and their springs poisoned. To save the expense of gunpowder and shot, squaws were clubbed to death and their children had their brains knocked out against trees. Not only did legislatures of the United States thus legalize these horrible atrocities, but clergy of the churches called Christian gave them public approval. The Reverend Solomon Stoddard of Northampton, Massachusetts, urged settlers to hunt Indians with dogs as they did bears; and, as the Reverend Cotton Mather had prophesied, "the woods were almost cleared of those pernicious creatures."[18]

The Spaniards, too, in their New World colonies made the hunting of the native races by bloodhounds a sport. It is said of De Soto, the explorer, that he "was much given to the sport of slaying Indians."[19] Christopher Columbus himself looked on

---

[17]Cf. T. R. Henry, *Wilderness Messiah* (New York, 1955), pp. 98–100.
[18]Cf. Frank Waters, *Masked Gods* (Swallow Press, Chicago, 1960), pp. 397–98; C. Hamilton, *Cry of the Thunderbird* (New York, 1950), p. 176.
[19]Cf. E. G. Bourne, *Narratives of the Career of Hernando de Soto* (New York, 1904), vol. II, p. 59.

while the half-starved and ferocious hounds of his Spanish com-
rades were loosed upon hundreds of defenseless Indians in Santo
Domingo, whom he had invited to come as to a feast; and he, as
well as his associates in infamy, applauded, as if witnessing a
bullfight, while the shrieking and terror-stricken men and women
were torn to pieces and the dogs glutted themselves upon their
blood-dripping flesh. It was a common practice among the Spaniards to kill an Indian to supply meat to feed their dogs. As a direct
result of the Christian conquest, not an Indian was left alive in the
Bahamas within twelve years after their discovery.[20] Of the Christians in Peru, Prescott, in his *History,* page 1120, writes: " 'Not
infrequently,' says an unsuspicious witness, 'I have seen the Spaniards, long after the conquest, amuse themselves by hunting down
the natives with bloodhounds for mere sport, or in order to train
their dogs to the game!' "

Although the Constitution of the United States proclaims that
all men are free and equal and guarantees complete freedom of
worship, the Red Men were, by fixed policy, considered to be
outside its protection. In practice, the laws of the White Men were
applicable to White Men only; and it was taken for granted by the
White Men everywhere in Roman Catholic Mexico and South
America, as well as in Puritan New England and throughout the
territory of the United States, that a White Man could rob and
murder a Red Man with impunity. Quite recently many of the
Osage tribe in the United States were murdered by White Men for
oil rights. Even the homes of the Osages were dynamited and
whole families destroyed while they slept. No one was convicted
for any of these atrocious crimes.[21] Throughout most of South
America and in Mexico the Indians fared no better than in the
United States and Canada, save where, even as yet, they have
escaped Christianization. In Guiana, under the wise administra-
tion of the British and the preceding Dutch, alone among the
nations of all the Americas, White Men and Red Men have never
been at war. There the Red Man rightly comes first. He is free to
enjoy all the natural resources of his ancestral domain, is not
required to pay any taxes, and has a right to travel on any steam-

[20]Cf. A. H. Verrill, *The American Indian* (New York, 1927), p. 59.
[21]*Ibid.,* p. 63.

boat or railway train without charge.[22] Happy, indeed, is this contrast with the awful martyrdom suffered by the Red Man in other parts of the new World.

When the White Men came to what is now the United States, there was no part not in possession of and occupied by the Red Men. One of the many dishonestly conceived laws aimed by unscrupulous White Men at the social and economic destruction of the Red Men was the infamous General Allotment Act, known also as the Dawes Act, whereby, between the years 1887 and 1933, some ninety million acres were filched from the Red Men. This represented almost two-thirds of the Red Men's land, "and in most cases the lands were covered by treaties in which the United States obligated itself to protect the tribes in their right of possession."[23] Not only were these vast areas of land thus unjustifiably taken away from the Red Men, but the very *use* of most of the allotted land left in their possession and occupancy was lost to them.[24] The lands taken away were transferred to White Man ownership without cost to the federal government, the tribes so despoiled being made to pay the costs of the surveying and allotting.[25] In arguing for the enactment of the Dawes Act, Senator Pendleton of Ohio, declared "that these Indians must either change their modes of life or they will be exterminated." As late as 1911, about 3,500,000 acres were wrested from the Navahos, placed in the public domain, and then, by prearrangement, opened exclusively to non-Indian stockmen, despite the fact that every acre was fully occupied and stocked to maximum capacity by the Navahos' own herds.[26]

2. Spanish America

In the Peruvian empire of the Incas, agriculture was more highly developed than in any part of Europe. There was "maximum human use of the land and water, with total conservation,"

---

[22] *Ibid.*, pp. 69–72.
[23] Cf. D. McNickle, *Indian and European: Indian-White Relations from Discovery to 1887,* in *The Annals of the American Academy of Political and Social Science* (Philadelphia, 1957), vol. 311, pp. 10–11.
[24] Cf. John Collier, *op. cit.,* p. 227.
[25] Cf. D. McNickle, *op. cit., Ibid.*
[26] Cf. C. Kluckhohn and D. Leighton, *op. cit.,* p. 11.

and yet a population possibly denser than that of the same area now. "None were in want, where today millions are in chronic want." Under the Incas, "from generation to generation the soil and water resources became more, not less. Today, as ever since the European conquest, the Andean area marches with most of the rest of the world on its way to the destruction of these resources." Apart from maize, "the most remarkable achievement in agricultural history," and the potato, the Red Men enriched mankind with the tomato, the sweet potato or yam, manioc, whence tapioca is derived, the pineapple, avocado, artichoke, peanuts, buckwheat, the cultivated strawberry, lima, frijole, kidney, and tonka beans, the squash and pumpkin, chocolate, vanilla, aloes, rubber, quinine, cocaine, and tobacco. Forty lesser crops were first developed and cultivated by the Red Men; "for example, maté, maple sugar, pecans, brazil nuts, butternuts, and sarsaparilla. From Virginia to California they processed acorns into important food." They were also the first to domesticate the turkey, the guinea pig, the llama, and vicuña. In Mexico and Yucatan, astronomical calculations had resulted in a calendar more accurate than ours today. The Mayas developed the concept of zero, or nought, used in their vigesimal numbering system, long before it was known in Europe. Inca mummies show that in the knowledge of surgery, anatomy, dentistry, trepanning, and amputating, the surgeons of the Incas surpassed those of Europe, at the time of the conquest. Teeth were filled, crowned, and bridged by the Inca dentists centuries ago.[27]

Yet, the Holy See took upon itself the right to give away the land of the Red Men to any temporal potentate who would champion Roman Christianity and assume the burden of conquering and dispossessing the Red Men.[28] Very rightly did the Inca Emperor Atahuallpa, when about to be put to death by the avaricious and inhumane Pizarro, exclaim, "As for the Pope of whom you speak, he must be crazy to talk of giving away countries which do

[27]Cf. John Collier, *The Indians of the Americas* (New York, 1947), pp. 33, 72; A. H. Verrill, *Our Indians* (New York, 1935), p. 3; A. H. Verrill and R. Verrill, *America's Ancient Civilizations* (New York, 1953), pp. 153–54; C. Wissler, *The American Indian* (New York, 1938), pp. 15 ff; and especially, A. H. Verrill, *Foods America Gave the World* (Boston, 1937). See, also, Mary Austin, *The Indian's Contribution to Culture in the United States,* in *The Genius of Mexico* (New York, 1931), pp. 71–76, edited by H. C. Herring and K. Terrill.
[28]Cf. W. H. Prescott, *op. cit.,* p. 275.

not belong to him."[29] Indeed, the Spanish Crown and the Papal Church held "the property of the infidel, in common with that of pirates, as fair spoil for the true believer."[30] "The lands, the persons, of the conquered races were parcelled out and appropriated by the victors as the legitimate spoils of victory; and outrages were perpetrated [by the Spanish Christians] every day, at the contemplation of which humanity shudders."[31]

In the West Indies there were similar atrocities, so horrible that the native population was almost annihilated within the space of a few years. Of this, John Collier, in *The Indians of the Americas,* pages 98–99, writes: "In the West Indies it was not decimation that befell the Indians—the people whom Columbus had found to be gentle, merry, and walking in beauty—it was annihilation. Since the supply was supposed to be unlimited in the beginning, these chattel slaves were worked to death. So terrible was their life that they were driven to mass suicide, to mass infanticide, to mass abstinence from sexual life in order that children should not be born into horror. Lethal epidemics followed upon the will to die. The murders and desolations exceeded those of the most pitiless tyrants of earlier history; nor have they been surpassed since." The natives of the Bahamas were sold into slavery for four pesos apiece. In various other islands of the West Indies, the Red Men who resisted being enslaved were destroyed by hanging and by fire; those who escaped were hunted down by man-killing dogs.

In Peru, "The people became the serfs of the Conquerors. Their dwellings in the capital—at least after the arrival of Alvarado's officers—were seized and appropriated. The temples were turned into stables; the royal residences into barracks for the troops. The sanctity of the religious houses was violated. Thousands of matrons and maidens, who, however erroneous their faith, lived in chaste seclusion in the conventual establishments, were now turned abroad, and became the prey of a licentious soldiery. A favorite wife of the young Inca was debauched by the Castillian officers."[32]

[29] *Ibid.,* p. 940.
[30] *Ibid.,* p. 275, n. 8.
[31] *Ibid.,* p. 1120.
[32] *Ibid.,* pp. 1015–16.

Too few of the Roman priests pleaded for genuine Christian treatment of the Red Men. One of the most outstanding of them who did was Bartolome de Las Casas (1474–1566), who argued that the Red Men were by the law of nature free, that as vassals of the Spanish Crown they were entitled to protection, and that the Spaniard had no right over the land or person of the Red Men, since "God does not allow evil that good may come of it." The powerful pleadings of the humanitarian Las Casas happily resulted in a code of ordinances intended to ameliorate the sad condition of the Red Men. But unfortunately, the Spanish colonists, who were in possession of the land and of the Red Men's gold and silver mines, and had enslaved the Red Men, refused to obey the ordinances. When Blasco Nuñez, the first Spanish Viceroy of Peru, attempted to enforce the ordinances, the colonists revolted against him. A black slave of one of the colonists beheaded him, two years after he had arrived in Peru from Spain.[33]

Gasca, chosen in 1545 to go to Peru to bring order out of this disorder, proved to be a wise administrator. Although he failed to attain the ideals hoped for by Las Casas, much was accomplished by him to improve the lot of the Red Man. After Gasca had returned to Spain, Peru's racial troubles were renewed; and even today, like those of Mexico, are far from being resolved.[34]

"Everywhere Pizarro made proclamation that he came in the name of the Holy Vicar of God and of the Sovereign of Spain,"[35] demanding of the Red Men submission to both the Church and the State, as Cortez did in Mexico. The Church deemed it better to save the souls than to save the bodies of the Red Men. Cortez told his troops, "We are fighting battles of the Faith, fighting for our honor, for riches, for revenge."[36] A truer statement could hardly have been made; the riches, as we shall see presently, were more important than the Faith.

Prescott writes: "Mass was performed with great solemnity by the ecclesiastics who attended the expedition; the God of battles was invoked to spread his shield over the soldiers who were fighting to extend the empire of the Cross, and all joined with

[33] *Ibid.*, pp. 1123–24; 1153.
[34] *Ibid.*, pp. 1166 ff., 1232.
[35] *Ibid.*, p. 910.
[36] *Ibid.*, p. 551.

enthusiasm in the chant 'Exsurge, Domin,' 'Rise, O Lord! and judge thine own cause.' One might have supposed them a company of martyrs, about to lay down their lives in defense of their faith, instead of a licentious band of adventurers, meditating one of the most atrocious acts of perfidy on the record of history!"[37]

In Mexico, in like sacrilegious manner, the priests of the Christians daily performed Mass and invoked the blessings of the Christian Godhead upon the treacherous and murderous enterprises of the destroyer Cortez.[38] "Too often the ecclesiastic became infected by the general spirit of licentiousness; and the religious fraternities, who led a life of easy indulgence on the lands cultivated by their Indian slaves, were apt to think less of the salvation of their souls than of profiting by the labour of their bodies."[39]

The paramount passion of the Spaniard was not Christianity, though he professed it and proclaimed himself a faithful son of the Church of Rome, but the lust for gold. "For this he shrank from no toil himself, and was merciless in his exactions of labor from his Indian slaves."[40]

It was the militant Dominican friar Valverde, Pizarro's chaplain, who commanded Pizarro to begin the awful massacre of multitudes of unarmed and peaceful Red Men massed in the plaza of the Peruvian city of Caxamalca: "Set on, at once; I absolve you." There are varying accounts of the number of the massacred. Pizarro's secretary makes it 2,000. A descendant of the Incas—a safer authority than the secretary—makes it 10,000. An old Inca said that the blood ran like water. Of this massacre of Red Men, Prescott says that it was "as wanton as it was wicked."[41]

Similarly in Mexico, Alvarado, one of the Spanish destroyers under Cortez, fell upon the Aztec nobles while they were performing a sacred dance in a temple enclosure and massacred them, so that the pavement "ran with streams of blood, like water in a heavy shower." This atrocious deed, according to some contemporaries, was born of pure avarice on the part of the Christians, who,

[37] *Ibid.,* pp. 935–36.
[38] *Ibid.,* p. 343.
[39] *Ibid.,* pp. 1121–22.
[40] *Ibid.,* p. 1121.
[41] *Ibid.,* pp. 940, 943, 978.

while the Aztec nobles lay dying, proceeded to strip their bodies of their ceremonial gold ornaments and jewels.[42]

It required many Indian goldsmiths a full month, working night and day, to melt down the gold and silver paid in ransom by Atahuallpa, the last of the Inca Emperors. The value of the gold alone is estimated by Prescott at about $15,500,000. Although presumably so ransomed, Atahuallpa remained a prisoner of the Christians, who put him to torture in continuous efforts to procure further treasure, and finally put him to death. Of this ill-gotten treasure, the Church of San Francisco, the first Roman church erected in Peru, was allotted an endowment of 2,220 gold pesos.[43]

Of the unjustifiable torture and execution of Atahuallpa, Prescott has well said, "The blood-stained annals of the Conquest afford no such example of the cold-hearted and systematic persecution, not of an enemy, but of one whose whole deportment had been that of a friend and benefactor."[44]

Guatemotzin, or Guatemoc ("Swooping Eagle"), the last of the Aztec emperors, who, like the Inca Emperor Atahuallpa, had been plundered of the national treasures, been subjected to torture, and then treacherously put to death, said, as he was about to die, addressing the inhumane Cortez, his murderer, "Why do you slay me so unjustly? God will demand it of you!"[45]

Upon entering Cuzco, the beautiful and spacious capital of the Inca Empire, estimated to have had then a population, including the suburbs, of approximately 400,000, the Christians "lost no time in plundering the palaces of their contents, as well as in despoiling the religious edifices. The interior decorations supplied them with considerable booty. They stripped off the jewels and rich ornaments that garnished the royal mummies in the temple of Caricancha. In some instances, indignant at the concealment of their treasures, they put the inhabitants to the torture and endeavoured to extort from them a confession of their hiding-places. They invaded the repose of the sepulchres, in which the Peruvians

---

[42] *Ibid.*, pp. 404–6. Accounts vary as to the number of the nobles. The smallest computation is six hundred. "Some writers carry the number as high as eight hundred or even one thousand." Las Casas swells it to two thousand. *Ibid.*, p. 404, n. 15.

[43] *Ibid.*, pp. 965–66, 968.

[44] *Ibid.*, p. 978.

[45] *Ibid.*, pp. 647–48.

often deposited their valuable effects, and compelled the grave to give up its dead. No place was left unexplored by the rapacious Conquerors."[46]

Such wholesale looting and desecration of temples and tombs of the dead is probably unparalleled in the annals of Christendom. The amount of the booty is variously estimated by those who shared it. According to some, it greatly exceeded in value the ransom of Atahuallpa. Sancho, the secretary of Pizarro, estimated it at 580,200 gold pesos and 215,000 marks in silver, or several million of present-day United States dollars. The total value of the gold and silver wrested from the Incas and the Aztecs, and of that later produced from the mines stolen from them between the years 1493 and 1803, has been estimated at about ten billion United States dollars, truly a fabulous sum. Of this the Spanish received one-fifth, and the Church was allotted rich endowments.[47]

Pizarro died as he had lived, in the midst of human brutishness and human gore; he reaped as he had sown. To him, unlike his colleague in iniquity, Cortez, the even-handed justice ever meted out by the higher than human law came swiftly. He received a wound in the throat at the hand of one of the warring Spanish conspirators who but a short time before had been his companion in arms. Reeling, he sank to the floor, while the swords of several of the conspirators were plunged into his body. "Jesu!" exclaimed the dying Pizarro; and "tracing a cross with his finger on the bloody floor, he bent down his head to kiss it, when a stroke more friendly than the rest, put an end to his existence." Prescott adds the annotation: "Pizarro y Orellana seems to have no doubt that his slaughtered kinsman died in the odor of sanctity."[48]

Cortez, who, in the eyes of his fellow countrymen, died a good Christian, is held in such detestation both by the native-born Mexicans and many of the descendants of the conquerors throughout Mexico that, in 1823, the patriotic mob of Mexico City, celebrating the era of independence from Spain, were preparing to break open his tomb there and scatter the ashes to the winds. Only because the ashes had been secretly removed from the

---

[46] *Ibid.*, pp. 992–94.
[47] Cf. John Collier, *op. cit.,* p. 135.
[48] Cf. W. H. Prescott, *op. cit.,* pp. 1088–89.

tomb by kinsmen of Cortez, who had been apprised of the plan, did the plan fail of accomplishment. As Humboldt observes, there is nowhere in Spanish America a national monument which public gratitude has raised to Hernando Cortez.[49] But Cortez, like Pizarro, is, according to the Christian historian Diaz, presumably to be thought of as being so good a Christian as to be worthy of emulation; for, in the words of Diaz, Cortez "was a good cavalier, most true in his devotion to the Virgin, to the Apostle St. Peter, and to all the other Saints."[50]

Although in itself little more than a convenient camouflage for the exercise of human brutishness, sadistic orgies, and pillage, the excuse advanced by the Christians for their savage massacres of the Aztecs was that among the Aztecs human sacrifice was a national institution which required, as did the massacres by the Christians, hecatombs of victims. In Peru, where human sacrifice was not in vogue and seldom practiced at the time of the Conquest, no excuse was advanced other than the invalid one that the Peruvians were idolatrous heathens. Had the Christians been anthropologists they would have realized that many, if not all, peoples at the semi-barbaric stage of culture of the Aztecs have practised human sacrifice of like sacramental character and that the sacrifice of the Mass is a sublimated heritage from that stage of culture.[51]

[49] *Ibid.*, p. 680.
[50] *Ibid.*, p. 187: Diaz, *Hist. de la Conquista* cap. 203.
[51] Although of uncertain origin, but cited in the year 788 by Aetherius, Bishop of Osma in Spain (cf. E. R. DuMont, *Voltaire's Philosophical Dictionary,* vii, 231), the following citation is of unusual interest anthropologically as being suggestive of the transition from pre-Christian human sacrifice in actuality (with its usual accompanying ritualistic cannibalism), through substituted animal sacrifice, which is much akin to that of Lamaism:

"I offer up every day, on the altar of the only true God, not the flesh of bulls, nor the blood of goats, but the unspotted lamb, which still remains living and entire after it is sacrificed, and all the faithful eat the flesh."

In the pre-Christian eucharistic ceremonies, human or animal blood, or else red wine or a fluid colored red by ochre to simulate blood, symbolized life. According to ancient Egyptian belief, the blood of the sacrificed one conferred life itself, even upon the dead, and restored youth to aging kings. Since remotely distant times, all such rites, involving the eating of the flesh of the god and the drinking of his blood, are indicative of mankind's persistent quest throughout the ages to prolong and protect the active life of the living, to restore youthfulness, and especially, as in the Christian rite, to confer immortality. Cf. G. F. Smith, *The Evolution of the Dragon* (Manchester University Press, 1919), pp. 114, 118, 145, 194.

That the Aztecs were at the beginning of that evolutionary transition, such as the Tibetans completed, from sacrifice in actuality to human sacrifice in effigy and symbol, is attested by their own eucharistic ceremony, of which Prescott writes: "An image of the tutelary deity of the Aztecs was made of the flour of maize, mixed with blood, and after consecration by the priests, was distributed among the people, who, as they ate it, 'showed signs of humiliation and sorrow, declaring it was the flesh of the deity.' "[52]

So universal was the awful martyrdom designedly imposed upon the Red Men by the Christians, Roman Catholic and Protestant alike, that to treat it in any degree exhaustively would require a library of volumes.

This account of the martyrdom of the Red Men may very fittingly be concluded in the wise words of John Collier, formerly Commissioner of Indian Affairs of the United States, in his humanitarianly-inspired book, *Indians of the Americas,* pages 27–28:

The Indian knew the meaning of society as creator of personality and as organizer of man with universe, through many aeons before ever the White Man came. He kept alive, and was made alive by, a multiplicity of contrasting societies. The white conqueror, for reasons military, economic and religious, pronounced sentence of death on the Indian societies. Through century-long years of slavery, expropriation, physical decimation, and propaganda directed towards the Indian against the Indian Spirit, the conqueror worked hard to carry out the Indian's death sentence. . . . When so very, very late, and perhaps for only a brief term of years (none can be sure as yet), some of the white man's societies lifted their sentences of death from these all but invisible Indian societies, the response was a rush of human energy, a creativity, industrial, civic, esthetic. How swiftly, with flashing brilliance, with what terrible joy, these long-immured, suddenly reprieved little societies demonstrated the truth which our age has lost: that societies are living things, sources of the power and values of their members; that to be and to function in a consciously living, aspiring, striving society is to be a personality fulfilled, is to be an energy delivered into the communal joy, a partner once more in the cosmic life.

[52]Cf. W. H. Prescott, *op. cit.,* p. 969. For a fuller discussion of the anthropological significance of human sacrifice, the student is referred to *Tibetan Yoga and Secret Doctrines,* by the writer, pages 295–99.

II. THE RELIGION

Apart from the vision-quests, to which special consideration has been given, little is known of the religion of the Red Men who inhabited the territory round about Cuchama prior to the coming of the White Man, except indirectly by reference to the religion of the Yuma nation to which they were ethnologically related.

Comparative study reveals that all pre-Columbian religions of the Americas have much in common, independently of their diversities of nomenclature and ritual, whether studied in simpler form north of the Rio Grande or in more sophisticated form in Mexico, Yucatan, and Peru. Hence it may be inferentially assumed that the Red Men tributary to Cuchama also shared in this commonness of belief. Their vision-quests, being not only like those of the Yumas, but, generally, like those of the Red Men as a whole, especially in North America, give support to the view that they were partakers in the cultural elements common to all the American religions. Accordingly, this suggestive rather than exhaustive account of the religion of the Red Men may assist in better understanding of what the essential religious characteristics are assumed to have been of the Red Men of the Cuchama area.

1. Health as Harmony

Among Hindus and Buddhists, religion is expressed chiefly through yogic meditation; among Moslems, through prayer performed in the direction of Mecca; among Roman Catholics, through the ritual of the Mass; among Protestants, through sermons and prayers; and among the Red Men, through holy-songs and ceremonial dances.

Among the Navahos, the religion of the Red Man is practically viewed as a psychological technique for maintaining or restoring harmony, or at-one-ment, between man and the cosmos. In other words, the Red Man's realizable, naturalistic religion is basically dependent upon knowing how to maintain or restore right relationship between all things, animate and inanimate.

For this reason, unlike the White Man, the Red Man recognizes health, or harmony of the physical body, as inseparable from religion; and many of his ceremonial practices are directed to restoring harmoniousness to the physical organism as well as to the mental and psychic man. The Navahos sing a holy-song over an ill person, declaring all things to be perfect as when first created. Thereby the sufferer is mentally placed in a state of perfection and so regains his or her original wholeness or harmony.[53]

In psychosomatic therapy and in the therapy associated with psychoanalysis, the White Man is beginning to follow in the footsteps of his more psychically alert brother practitioner, the medicine-man of the Americas. In many of the religious societies of Christendom, similar methods of healing, including the laying on of hands and prayer, are, rather belatedly, making great advances.

In their ceremonials, as Frank Waters discovered, the Red Man experiences "that simple and sublime feeling that comes to a people who submerge for a moment their individualities in the collective unconscious, which is not only tribal, but universal; the simple sacred ecstasy of spiritual communion whose obverse or perverted duality is the hysteria of mob violence."[54] Similarly, when on pilgrimage to some long-revered shrine, river, or holy mountain, the multitudes of pious Hindus or Buddhists become, at times, merged in the collective unconscious and thereby enjoy ecstatic uplift; just as the Mexicans do when on pilgrimage to the shrine of the pre-Christian mother-goddess Tonantzin. This ecstatic condition, too, is dependent upon the attainment of that harmoniousness which results in psychic health and wholeness.

2. Man's True Being and At-one-ment

A Cheyenne Indian of Oklahoma, known by the English name of Alfred Wilson, who was the head of the Native American Church, taught that the earth-part of man is merely that which gives to him visibility: man's true being is invisible; it is the breath, or energy, of the Great Spirit. Because man participates in the universal spiritual essence, his mind, or consciousness, is not limited to mundane consciousness. This supraconsciousness of man's mind dominates the conscious mind. The Indians know nothing

[53]Cf. N. C. Burlin, *The Indians' Book* (New York and London, 1907), p. 371; C. K. Kluckhohn and D. Leighton, *The Navaho,* p. 165.
[54]Cf. Frank Waters, *op. cit.,* p. 335.

of a beginning nor of an ending of the cosmos. They cannot conceive of the Christian Hell. They say that mankind must follow the path of right living, and live in accordance with the moral laws of nature. If man fails to do so, he alone is the sufferer and the cause of his sufferings. There is no other punishment.[55]

The chief rules of the Shawnees governing human conduct were not to kill or injure one's neighbor, because it is not he that is injured but oneself; and not to wrong or hate one's neighbor, because it is not he that is wronged but oneself. The Great Spirit loves one's neighbor as he loves oneself.[56]

Generally, the Red Man is taught to recognize his kinship with all living things. He must not destroy any living thing without good reason; and then, when he does so, he must ask its consent. Of the deer or any animal he is planning to kill, he must first ceremonially ask such permission.[57] Likewise in Tibet, if a villager kills even a venomous snake, he prays that it may attain at its next birth a higher form. The writer had working on his ranch in San Diego County, a Red Man of the Yuma Tribe who would not kill a rattlesnake because of an ancient tribal totemistic taboo, nor cut down any useful or beautiful tree or bush growing amidst the brush being cleared.

Very much as the Hindus view the world, the Red Men as a whole, and the Navahos in particular, see it as an at-one-ment, undivided, as is the White Man's world, into secular and religious compartments. They conceive spiritual forces as being everywhere present, although invisible to all save seers. To the Navahos, who call themselves the Earth Surface People, no doubt exists as to an Otherworld (inhabited by various orders of beings inclusive of the dead) being an integral part of this world. To them, as to all religiously uncorrupted Red Men, the dead and the living are an indivisible social unit. Although many Navahos profess Christianity nominally, most of them, like most Red Men, wisely remain faithful to their own more satisfying and realizable American religion.[58] As Edwin R. Embree in his *Indians of the Americas,* page 6, has observed, "to the Indians it was as shameful

[55]Cf. John Collier, *op. cit.,* pp. 240–41.
[56]*Ibid.,* p. 181.
[57]Cf. Frank Waters, *op. cit.,* p. 180.
[58]Cf. C. Kluckhohn and D. Leighton, *op. cit.,* pp. 81, 122.

to lose their faith and independence as it was to give up their land."

3. Dance Ceremonials

Since Indian dances are not dances as the White Man understands dances, but ceremonials, symbolic representations, and prayers, they constitute an integral and important part of the religion of the Red Men. Most Indian dances and ceremonials are concerned with food-crops, agriculture in general, rain-making, and thanksgivings to the beneficent cosmic forces, especially to Father Sun and Mother Earth. Likewise, many European peasant ceremonials and dances are equally agricultural and astronomical. Among these are the May Day dances, those observances associated with the Celtic November Day, with the great festival of the Sun at the winter solstice on the 25th of December, and with the joyous spring-tide festival of resurrection and rebirth, sacred to the Germanic goddess Eostre (or Ostara), whence is derived the name Easter. Some of the Red Men's dances and ceremonials celebrate successful vision-quests of their initiated youths. Thanksgiving Day is a direct adaptation by the Pilgrim Fathers of the Algonquins' autumnal dance ceremonial of thanksgiving to the beneficent spiritual forces associated with the Great Spirit and to the Earth Mother, who gives sustenance to man.

Among the Ojibways it was customary for the members of a tribe to assemble on a bright midsummer day at a place whence a view of the surrounding country could be had and with joyous singing and dancing give thanks to the Earth Mother. The medicine-man sang first:

> Behold! Our Mother Earth is lying here;
> Behold! She giveth of her fruitfulness.
> Truly, her power she giveth unto us;
> Give thanks to Mother Earth who lieth here!

Then all the tribe sang in chorus:

> We think of Mother Earth who lieth here;
> We know she giveth of her fruitfulness.
> Truly, her power she giveth unto us;
> Our thanks to Mother Earth who lieth here!

The entire holy-song, which is thus antiphonal, consists of eight stanzas, the phraseology of one stanza varying but little from that of another, four being sung by the medicine-man and four by the assembly. Nowhere among the races of mankind, primitive or civilized, is there a more beautiful and fitting service of thanksgiving, and there is none more inspiring among man's various faiths.[59]

The dance called by the White Man the Sun Dance is known to the Arapahoes as the "Offering" and to the Cheyennes as the "New Life Lodge"; it implies new life, rebirth, and life itself. The dance recreates, reforms, and reanimates the Earth and all life thereon, vegetable and animal.[60]

Some dances, found in all parts of the Americas, are exorcising ceremonials, very much like the Devil Dances of Tibet. In both there are masked figures representing gods of war. Knives and bows and arrows are brandished to scare the evil away from the man whose illness is taken to be due to demon possession. The masked dancers move around him, chanting and dancing.

As a whole, the Red Man's dances are representative of a universally human urge to attain rhythmic attunement with the vibratory law at the base of all objective things, animate and inanimate, ranging from the dancing particles forming the atom to the rhythm of the vast forests, the mighty oceans, and the planets in their dance around the Sun. The Hindus personify this Universe-embracing rhythm as Shiva dancing the Dance of Life.

John Collier, who was privileged to witness one of the Pueblo Indians' little known ceremonial dances on the Sacred Mountain at Taos, New Mexico, testified to the Indian Committees of the House and Senate in support of a bill, which is now law, to protect the Pueblo Indians in their age-long exclusive use of their sanctified area in the National Forest as follows:

"On this night, at this place, the spirit of Pueblo religion could have been mistaken by none. Forces or beings normally invisible, only half-personal yet connecting with the hidden central springs of the empirical life, are a dominating fact in the Pueblo (in the

[59]Cf. J. M. Buttree, *The Rhythm of the Redman* (New York, 1930), p. 171; A. C. Fletcher, 22nd Ann. Rep. Bur. Eth., p. 335.
[60]Cf. J. M. Buttree, *op. cit.,* p. 145.

tribal Indian) mind. The Indian's relationship to these forces or beings is not chiefly one of petition or adoration or dread, but of a seeking and sharing in joy. It is a partnership in an eternal effort whereby, from some remote place of finding and communion, the human and the mechanical universes alike are sustained."[61]

4. Ohiyesa's Testimony

Perhaps the most outstanding recorded account of the religion of the Red Men is by Ohiyesa (who later took the name of Charles Alexander Eastman), a Santee Sioux of the Dakota nation. Very fittingly, the Indian name, Ohiyesa, which he inherited, means "Winner" or "Successful One." Although most of his testimony, set forth in *The Soul of the Indian,* relates to the Red Men of the Great American Plains, it has, as will be seen, much in common with the religion of the Red Men of the Southwestern United States, as our own research has confirmed.

Jim Chaleco of the Yumas and his son Arsenius, a tribal poet, previously referred to as two of our chief sources on Cuchama, were in agreement with what Ohiyesa has written concerning the Great Mystery:

> The original attitude of the American Indian toward the External, the "Great Mystery" that surrounds and embraces us, was as simple as it was exalted. To him it was the supreme conception, bringing with it the fullest measure of joy and satisfaction possible in this life.

[61]Cf. John Collier, *op. cit.,* p. 188.

[Ed. nt.: As mentioned in the Editor's footnote on page 81, no White Man ever has been permitted to witness the secret ceremonies performed at Blue Lake. The occasion described so beautifully by John Collier took place, as he states, at the overnight campground on the annual pilgrimage. Here, next morning, he was turned back and not allowed to continue. Nevertheless, the ceremonial gathering undoubtedly reflects the spirit of the events at Blue Lake—the joyful exchange and merging of psychic energy with universal forces, the sublimation of the individual self in the collective unconscious. It is the same feeling experienced by the Yaquis on their annual pilgrimage to Magdalena, Sonora, on October 4, and by Mexicans on their national pilgrimage to the hill of Tepeyac on December 12. It must be the same feeling called *darshan* by the Hindus on their pilgrimages to the Ganges, and sacred shrines.

The Congressional bill referred to in John Collier's quoted account simply gave Taos Pueblo restricted use of the Blue Lake area for religious purposes. Since then, Congress, in 1970, awarded the Pueblo clear title to the area. F.W.]

The worship of the "Great Mystery" was silent, solitary, free from all self-seeking. It was silent, because all speech is of necessity feeble and imperfect; therefore the souls of my ancestors ascended to God in wordless adoration. It was solitary, because they believed that He is nearer to us in solitude, and there were no priests authorized to come between a man and his Maker. None might exhort or confess or in any way meddle with the religious experience of another. Among us, all men were created sons of God and stood erect, as conscious of their divinity. Our faith might not be formulated in creeds, nor forced upon any who were unwilling to receive it; hence there was no preaching, proselytising, nor persecution, neither were there any scoffers or atheists. There were no temples or shrines among us save those of nature. Being a natural man, the Indian was intensely poetical. He would deem it sacrilege to build a house for Him who may be met face to face in the mysterious, shadowy aisles of the primeval forest, or on the sunlit bosom of virgin prairies, upon dizzy spires and pinnacles of naked rock, and yonder in the jeweled vault of the night sky. He who enrobes Himself in filmy veils of cloud, there on the rim of the visible world where our Great-Grandfather Sun kindles his evening camp-fire, He who rides upon the rigorous wind of the north, or breathes forth His spirit upon aromatic southern airs, whose war-canoe is launched upon majestic rivers and inland seas, needs no lesser cathedral.[62]

Of the White Man's misunderstanding of the Red Man, Ohiyesa very rightly states:

The native American has been generally despised by his white conquerors for his poverty and simplicity. They forget, perhaps, that his religion forbade the accumulation of wealth and the enjoyment of luxury.[63] To him . . . the love of possessions has appeared a snare, and the burdens of a complex society a source of needless peril and temptation. Furthermore, it was the rule of his life to share the fruits of his skill and success with his less fortunate brothers. Thus he kept his spirit free from the clog of pride, cupidity, or envy, and carried out, as he believed, the divine decree—a matter profoundly important to him.

[62]C. A. Eastman, *The Soul of the Indian* (Boston and New York, 1911), pp. 4–6.
[63]In this respect, the Kwakiutls, of northwest Canada, are exceptional among Red Men because of their accumulating of and fondness for private possessions, or, as Paul Radin expresses it, because of their being capitalists. Cf. Paul Radin, *The Story of the American Indian* (New York, 1927), p. 323.

It was not, then, wholly from ignorance or improvidence that he failed to establish permanent towns and to develop a material civilization. To the untutored sage, the concentration of population was the prolific mother of all evils, moral no less than physical. He argued that food is good, while surfeit kills; that love is good, but lust destroys; and not less dreaded than the pestilence following upon crowded and unsanitary dwellings was the loss of spiritual power inseparable from too close contact with one's fellow-men. All who have lived much out of doors know that there is a magnetic and psychic force that accumulates in solitude and that is quickly dissipated by life in a crowd; and even his enemies have recognized the fact that for a certain innate power and self-poise, wholly independent of circumstances, the American Indian is unsurpassed among men.[64]

The Red Man's psychological understanding of mind, and of his religious rites, was profound and rational.

[He] divided mind into two parts—the spiritual mind [of the psyche] and the physical mind [of the ego]. The first is pure spirit, concerned only with the essence of things: and it was this he sought to strengthen by spiritual prayer, during which the body is subdued by fasting and hardship. In this type of prayer there was no beseeching of favor or help. All matters of personal or selfish concern, [such] as success in hunting or warfare, relief from sickness, or the sparing of a beloved life, were definitely relegated to the plane of the lower or material mind, and all ceremonies, charms, or incantations designed to secure a benefit or to avert a danger, were recognized as emanating from the physical [or egoistical] self.

The rites of this physical worship, again, were wholly symbolic, and the Indian no more worshiped the Sun than the Christian does the Cross. The Sun and the Earth, by an obvious parable, holding scarcely more of poetic metaphor than of scientific truth, were in his view the parents of all organic life. From the Sun, as the Universal Father, proceeds the quickening principle in nature, and in the patient and fruitful womb of our Mother, the Earth, are hidden embryos of plants and men. Therefore our reverence and love for them was really an imaginative extension of our love for our immediate parents; and with this sentiment of filial piety was joined a willingness to appeal to them, as to a father, for such good gifts as we may desire. This is the material or physical prayer.[65]

[64]C. A. Eastman, *op. cit.,* pp. 9–12.
[65]*Ibid.,* pp. 12–14.

Of the Red Men's view of nature as being the embodiment of an all-pervading impersonal cosmic spirit, Ohiyesa writes: "The elements and majestic forces in nature, Lightning, Wind, Water, Fire, and Frost, were regarded with awe as spiritual powers, but always secondary and intermediate in character. We believed that the spirit pervades all creation and that every creature possesses a soul [or partakes of an all-pervading spirit] in some degree, though not necessarily a soul conscious of itself. The tree, the waterfall, the grizzly bear, each is an embodied Force and, as such, an object of reverence."

The Red Man rose superior to the external life of the White Man: "It is simple truth that the Indian did not, so long as his native philosophy held sway over his mind, either envy or desire to imitate the splendid achievements of the White Man. In his own thought he rose superior to them. He scorned them, even as a lofty spirit absorbed in its stern task rejects the soft beds, the luxurious food, the pleasure-worshipping dalliance of a rich neighbor. It was clear to him that virtue and happiness are independent of these things, if not incompatible with them."[66]

5. Prayer

The Red Man's daily devotions, especially his daily salutation to the Sun at dawn, are remarkably parallel to those of the Hindu. "In the life of the Indian there was only one inevitable duty—the duty of prayer—the daily recognition of the Unseen and Eternal. His daily devotions were more necessary to him than daily food. He wakes at daybreak, puts on his moccasins and steps down to the water's edge. Here he throws handfuls of clear, cold water into his face, or plunges in bodily. After the bath, he stands erect before the advancing dawn, facing the Sun as it dances upon the horizon, and offers his unspoken orison. His mate may precede or follow him in his devotions, but never accompanies him. Each soul must meet the morning Sun, the new, sweet Earth, and the Great Silence alone."[67]

The Red Man offers prayer in many ways: by the ceremonial smoking of tobacco, symbolizing the breath of life; by scattering

[66] *Ibid.*, pp. 14–15, 18–19.
[67] *Ibid.*, pp. 45–46.

holy corn-pollen, symbolizing fruitfulness and productiveness; by planting plumed prayer-sticks, upon the feathers of which he breathes the prayer to be carried to the Great Spirit on the wind. These prayer-sticks thus serve the same purpose as do the prayer-flags of the Tibetans. The Red Man also prays by means of his symbolical designs in woven fabrics, in bead-work, on pottery, by decorations of numerous sorts, and by means of sacred dances, rituals, and songs.[68]

Sun worship was universal throughout the Americas, as attested by the religion of the Incas, Mayas, Toltecs, Aztecs, and the Indian nations north of the Rio Grande. An interesting illustration of sun-worship is found here in San Diego County. The Indians of the village of Helshow Nawa, at the foot of the Cuyamaca Peak, annually went on pilgrimage to the summit of Viejas Mountain, just on the other side of their village, to watch Inya, the Sun, come out of the East, and to glorify him with joyous song and dance. On account of this celebration they called the mountain Kwut-ah Lu-e-ah, meaning "Song-Dance." The youth of the tribe, during the many months of training for a foot-race to the mountain's summit which initiated the great festival, ate no flesh-food, nuts or oily substance, and daily bathed and rubbed their bodies with an alumlike crystalline material called *cha-hoor,* meaning "clear-rock," which gave to them lightfootedness and the swiftness of deer. The sun-dance itself was performed in a circular space on the summit in the increasing light of the dawn. There, awaiting the coming forth of Father Sun, "The people chanted songs of praise in honor of his wonderful light, and made obeisance in the dance in homage of his great power over all things."[69]

To the summit of Grossmont in La Mesa, near San Diego, not many miles westward from Viejas Mountain, as to many other high places throughout California and the United States, the White Man likewise now makes pilgrimage annually, during the dawn of Easter Sunday, to greet with song and prayer the Sun as it rises. Although the White Man is apt to be, hereditarily, like most of human kind, psychically responsive to an innate urge to do homage to the Sun, in these instances of neo-American sun-worship he seems to have been unconsciously influenced by the

[68]Cf. N. C. Burlin, *op. cit.,* pp. xxiii–xxiv.
[69]Cf. Mary E. Johnson, *Indian Legends of the Cuyamaca Mountains* (San Diego, 1914), pp. 24–25.

Red Man's psychic shaping of the American environment. And so it is that the Red Man's appropriate way of revering the Sun is today also the White Man's.

6. Initiations

The initiatory practices of the youth of the Red Men on the Sacred Mountain of Cuchama were much the same as similar practices of the youth of the Aztecs. The Aztec youth "learned the chants which contained the esoteric lore, and the organization of the great dramatic pageants. He joined the ceremonial fasts, lit the incense at midnight, and journeyed at night alone and nude to a neighboring mountain, carrying incense, a torch, a conch-shell trumpet, and a bunch of the aloe spines used in ritual self-torture."[70] Among the Incas of South America, as among the Red Men north of the Rio Grande, the Sun was the symbol of the Supreme; and the initiation of the youth was nationally directed as it was in ancient Greece. Among the Red Men of the Southwestern United States, boys at puberty were immured for as much as two years, in order to instruct them in the secret lore of the tribe. They had no practical need of the White Man's culturally-corrupting education, which the United States Government, with the connivance of the Christian missionaries, forced upon them.[71]

Efforts have been made to show that the various secret societies of the Red Men are akin to those of the Masonic Order. They probably are, just as are similar secret societies among all primitive races.[72] It has been said often that no race of men, even the least in culture, has been found without some sort of religion.

---

[70]Cf. John Collier, *op. cit.,* p. 80. See, in this connection, Section IV, "Vision Quests."

[71]In the true meaning of education, as a drawing out of innate knowledge, the Red Man is better educated than most White Men whose education has been, on the contrary, a process of filling the mind from without. The nearest to the Red Man's educational discipline is that of our boy scouts and forest rangers in so far as it consists of disciplining the faculties and parts of the physical body as a whole. In addition, the Red Man's education, especially during his initiation, is quite unlike the White Man's, for it is directed to the awakening of the psyche, to the end that the highest life, the mystic spiritual life. of which man is capable may be attained.

[72]Cf. R. C. Wright, *Indian Masonry* (Ann Arbor, Mich., 1907).

The Medicine-Man Guru and the Suppliant Disciple on a Sacred High Place of Initiation. Reproduction of Charles M. Russell's painting, "The Medicine Man."

Universally, too, among all peoples there have flourished, as they flourish now, Mysteries, which orthodox Western scientists may discount, but of which only initiates have knowledge.

Black Elk, a holy-man of the Oglala Sioux, famous for his success as a healer, recalled in his old age his own initiatory experiences: "There," he said, pointing to the sacred Harney Peak, "when I was young, the spirits took me in my vision to the center of the Earth and showed me all the good things in the sacred hoop of the world." Then, standing reverently on Harney Peak, and holding the symbolic sacred pipe before him in his right hand, Black Elk made appeal to the Great Spirit: "I am sending a voice, Great Spirit, my Grandfather, forgetting nothing you have made, the stars of the Universe and the grasses of the Earth. You have said to me, when I was still young and could hope, that in difficulty I should send a voice four times, for each quarter of the Earth, and you would hear me. Today I send a voice for a people in despair."[73]

Black Elk was one of the most remarkable of psychically-developed Red Men of whom there is trustworthy record. The psychic phenomenon of going out of the physical body he frequently experienced at will, rather than during a ceremony of initiation, when it is usually experienced. On one occasion, when in Paris, France, where he had employment in a Buffalo Bill show, he was out of the body for three days, breathing only at intervals and sometimes with no perceptible heart-beat. While thus disembodied, Black Elk was quite conscious of journeying westward, on what seemed to him to be a cloud, until he was hovering over the place where his parents were encamped in the United States. His mother was aware of his invisible presence there. As if from an airplane, he looked down and recognized the parts of the Earth, the cities and fields and the Great Waters of the Atlantic, over which he traveled, both on his journey to America and on his return to Paris. He testifies to having experienced a number of other consciousness-projections.[74]

According to Crashing Thunder, a Winnebago Indian, reincarnation, which was a widespread belief among his people, is a privilege reserved to those who have been initiated into the sacred

[73]Cf. J. C. Neihardt, *Black Elk Speaks: Being the Life Story of A Holy Man of the Oglala Sioux* (New York, 1932), pp. 277–79.
[74]*Ibid.,* pp. 230–33, 245–47, 248–51, 22ff.

Medicine Dance. He tells of such initiates who recalled past incarnations. Medicine Dance initiates are credited with ability to kill a fellow member and then restore him to life, which appears to be an esoteric way of saying that in virtue of the initiation one becomes master of death and life and of the power to reincarnate consciously.[75]

Of Tirawa, the Father Above, the Pawnees said, "We know only that He made all things, that He is everywhere and in everything, and that He is almighty." Among the Dakotas, the Supreme Being was called Wakan-Tanda, usually translated "The Great Spirit," although "The Great Holy-Mystery" is a more correct rendering.[76] To other tribes and nations, this fundamental, impersonal, transcendent force, underlying all phenomena affecting man's destiny, and permeating all nature, was known by other names. It was called *manitu* by the Algonquins, *pokut* by the Shoshonis and *orenda* by the Iroquois.[77] Viracocha, the Uncreated Creator, the pre-Inca Sun-god whom the Incas recognized, personified this supreme power, as did Pachacamac, another Sun-god of the pre-Inca peoples of Peru.[78]

The Mescal, or Peyote, Cult, which flourished in Mexico and the Southwest United States, taught that each man acquires truth for himself, through dreams induced by the sacramental eating of the mescal button.[79] The spiritual pathway is revealed to each devotee of the Mescal Cult as being within his own heart.

---

[75]Cf. P. Radin, *Crashing Thunder: The Autobiography of an American Indian* (New York and London, 1926), pp. 5–7, 110.
[76]Cf. N. C. Burlin, *op. cit.,* pp. 94, 32.
[77]Cf. National Geographic Society, *Indians of the Americas* (Washington, D.C., 1955), p. 41.
[Ed. nt.: *Orenda* is further discussed in Part III, Section II, 9, "Yogic Powers"; Part III, Section II, 12, "Psychic Influences on Modern American Cults"; and is described in detail in Part IV, Section II, "Occult Forces." C.A.]
[78]Cf. P. Radin, *The Story of the American Indian,* pp. 123–24.
[79]The mescal button, otherwise known as the pellote, or peyote, grows on the top of a cactus which flourishes in Mexico, where the cult probably originated in pre-Columbian times, and in the Southwestern borderland of the United States. Each of the mescal devotees usually eats four of the mescal buttons, four being the Red Man's sacred number. The mescal button is, in the Mescal Cult, a symbol of the Sun, which in shape it resembles, with a circle in the center surrounded by white spots resembling the Sun's rays. The student is directed to *Doors of Perception,* a remarkable record of Aldous Huxley's own personal experiences while for twelve hours he was experimentally under the influence of mescaline, an alkaloid extracted from peyote.

The Mescal Cult displaced among many modernized young Indians the more psychically-efficient vision-quest of those who went into solitude to fast and pray. Old conservative Indians fear that mescal-produced visions, unlike those produced naturally in the vision-quests, can bring to their people little or no good.

Peyote addiction is said to be responsible for insanity and shortening of the life-span among the devotees of the Mescal Cult, by G. E. E. Linquist in *The Red Man in the United States,* pages 69 to 76. On the other hand, John Rave, a Winnebago, who lived in Oklahoma during 1893–94 with peyote eaters, of whom he was one, reports that whosoever will eat peyote will be cured of all evil propensities. He cites curing of a consumptive and of his own Walking-Priest's illness by peyote eating.[80]

As stated in *The Real Americans* by A. Hyatt Verrill, page 58, "Whatever else we may think of this strange (peyote) cult, it has one feature that is most laudable and is lacking in the majority of religions. Only strict teetotalers can become members of the sect, and any member caught using alcoholic liquor is blackballed for life." Big Elk, a hereditary chieftain of the Oglala Sioux, said that the use of peyote has been of inestimable value in decreasing alcoholism among his people. He himself, once a heavy drinker, took the peyote initiation, and nothing, thereafter, could induce him to take an alcoholic drink.[81]

Akin to the Mescal Cult was the Toluache Cult, in which the sacramental drinking of a decoction made of the root of the jimson-weed was an initiation practice, found chiefly in what is now southern California. Of like nature is the very holy rite of the

[80]C. Hamilton, *Cry of the Thunderbird,* p. 94.
[81][Ed. nt.: Much has been written about peyote during recent years. It is a small hallucinogenic cactus (Lophophora williamsii) found growing close to the ground in the deserts of northern Mexico. Blue-gray in color, the tiny buttons, when eaten, produce dreams and visions. It has been determined that peyote is a non-addictive drug, and hence is not a narcotic.

Peyote has been used in Mexico since pre-Columbian times. The Huichol Indians still make a ritual five-day journey on foot from their mountain villages down into the desert in the state of San Luis Potosi to gather the peyote buttons. The ritual use of peyote spread northward to the Great Plains tribes in the United States, and thence to Taos Pueblo, New Mexico, where it flourished and then virtually died out. It has since spread among the Navahos in Arizona. Some thirty years ago, peyote ritualism was incorporated as the Native American Church, embracing both Indian and Christian beliefs. F.W.]

eating of sacred mushrooms, quite recently reported as being practiced in rural parts of Mexico.[82] All three of these cults are peculiarly American. They recall the practice of the priestess of the Oracle of Apollo at Delphi in ancient Greece, who, to attain clairvoyance and foretell the future, inhaled an intoxicating vapour.

At least once during his lifetime the Red Man sought a guardian spirit or power. The medicine-man, or shaman, who was appealed to for guidance in all such psychic quests, usually gave aid to the devotee to shape his own personal secret rite. Similarly in India or Tibet a guru gives to a disciple a mantra, or word of power, to be held in inviolable secrecy. Precisely as it was in Oriental countries, this personal relationship of the individual Red Man to his spiritual director, guru, or medicine-man, is fundamental to his religion and ritualistic procedure.

Many rituals of the Red Men are symbolic mystery-plays to demonstrate the psychic enlightenment of a specially successful devotee, either of ancestral antiquity or of modern times. Underlying the rituals is the concept of the devotee's spirit-guardian that usually appears in the symbolic form of a totem animal of the devotee's tribe. It is by virtue of special proficiency in gaining psychic powers by means of a vision-quest that a medicine-man is recognized, and then becomes a healer both of body and of mind, and a tribal prophet and seer. Very similar is the training of the medicine-men among the Red Men of Central and South America.[83]

7. Death and Rebirth

Throughout the Americas, the Red Men are convinced that the dead are still alive and can, under right conditions, communicate with their kinsfolk still incarnate. Thus, for the Red Men, the world of the living and the world of the dead are one. It is generally true that the Red Men, especially if they have had successful vision-quests, unlike the psychically undeveloped White Man, exhibit no fear of quitting the earth-plane body in the process called death.[84] However, rather exceptionally, there is among the Nava-

---

[82]Cf. A. Puharich, *The Sacred Mushroom* (New York, 1959), pp. 67–70.
[83]Cf. C. Wissler, *op. cit.,* pp. 206–7.
[84]Cf. A. H. Verrill, *The American Indian,* p. 81; J. M. Buttree, *op. cit.,* pp. 201–3.

hos who have failed to attain psychic self-sufficiency since the coming of the White Man's religion, a fear of death where primitively it did not exist.

In former days, before being corrupted by White Men, every Indian brave committed to memory a Death Song, often of his own composing, for use when he knew that the inevitable end had come. He sang the Death Song, as did the famous Apache Medicine-Man and War Chief Geronimo (circa 1834–1909), and died, not with fear and trembling, as many White Men do, but heroically, "like a hero going home."[85] From youth he was trained to be prepared to meet death, as the Oriental yogin is, with the assurance of having made the best use of the opportunities afforded by human birth.

Both the Luiseños and Diegueños made images to represent deceased members of their tribes and used them in a commemorative ceremony for the dead.[86] Quite like Tibetan effigies of the dead, described in *The Tibetan Book of the Dead* on pages 20–24, these images were dressed in the clothes of the deceased and, after the completion of the ceremonial dancing and singing, were cremated, just as the bodies of the dead had been.

In complement to what has been set forth above in Part I, the following account of more than ordinary anthropological significance is presented here, from Father Boscana's *Historical Account of the San Juan Capistrano Indians of Southern California,* as translated from the original Spanish by John P. Harrington:

"They also had the custom at the time of the new moon, the first day that the new moon appeared, [that] some old man began to shout, saying, 'Boys, start your moon-running!' And immediately the youths began to run like crazy men, without order or arrangement, and the old men to dance [and sing] as a sign of joy, saying in their song that even as the moon died and lived again, even so, though they were also to die, they were to live again." That this implied a return to life here in the human world and not in an after-death world is suggested by Father Boscana's comment

[85]Cf. E. T. Seton and J. M. Seton, *The Gospel of the Red Man* (Los Angeles, 1948), pp. 11, 24.
[86]Cf. C. G. Dubois, *The Religion of the Luiseño Indians of California* (Berkeley, 1908), University of California Publication in American Archaeology and Ethnology, vol. 8, no. 3, pp. 100–1.

thereon: "This very clearly manifests the resurrection of the flesh, but how they understood it I have not been able to determine."[87] Had Father Boscana been more an occultist than a believer in the orthodox Christian resurrection (itself a corruption of the doctrine of rebirth or reincarnation), he would have understood the Indians' belief better.

8. Sages and Culture Heroes

In various contexts throughout this treatise, attention has been directed to seers, prophets, and culture heroes among the Red Men. The great culture hero of ancient Mexico and Central America known to the Mayas as Kukulcan appears to have been adopted and renamed Quetzalcoatl by the Aztec conquerors. The name Quetzalcoatl, meaning "Feathered Serpent," refers esoterically, as does the traditional association of any other heroic teacher with serpent-worship, to a Sage possessed of supramundane wisdom. The first Quetzalcoatl (or his prototype Kukulcan) is believed to have come to the New World from the region of the sunrise. Although at first apparently the name of an historical culture-hero, Quetzalcoatl seems to have come to be applied, as a title, to the high priest of the cult of Quetzalcoatl (or Kukulcan).[88]

In South America, the chief culture hero was Manco Capac, the founder of the Inca dynasty of the divine Children of the Sun. North America, too, north of the Rio Grande, in ancient as well as in modern times, has had its own prophets and inspired teachers, commonly of lesser and sometimes of only tribal-wide influence. Two outstanding representatives of these are Chinigchinix, whom the San Juan Capistrano Indians of Southern California

---

[87]Cf. John P. Harrington, *op. cit.,* p. 48.

[88][Ed. nt.: The concept of the mythical god and culture-hero Quetzalcoatl (from *quetzal,* the brilliantly colored bird of the Mexican tropics, and *coatl,* snake), literally, the "Plumed Serpent," seems to have first appeared at Teotihuacan among the Toltecs, who preceded the Aztecs, about the beginning of the Christian era. The religion of Quetzalcoatl, based on the union of the primal opposites of earth and sky, as the name suggests, spread throughout the great Toltec empire from northern Mexico to Central America. A new version was introduced to the Mayas in Yucatan a thousand years later, where Quetzalcoatl was known as Kukulcan. F.W.]

revered as a prophet while he lived and deified after his departure from this world, and Degandawide.

Chinigchinix is very humanly represented as having been at first an ordinary man, a non-initiate known as Saor, then an initiate known as Tobet, and finally an incarnate teacher known as Quoar. "The prophet was born at the *ranchería* of Pubu in Los Angeles County, California, only a couple of miles inland from Alamitos Bay, there accomplished his principal teaching, and, when he died, was from there merely translated to the heaven of the stars, leaving no earthly bodily remains."[89] In like manner was the Hebrew Prophet Elijah translated, triumphing over death. Chinigchinix is thus an outstanding instance of a truly Great Guru among the Red Men comparable to the Great Gurus of Tibet and India.

Degandawida, "He the Thinker," the Iroquois Redeemer, traditionally said to have been born of a virgin, like other Great Teachers, together with his chief disciple, Hiawatha, founded the Iroquois Confederacy of the Five Nations (the Mohawks, Oneidas, Onondagas, Cayugas, and Senecas).[90] These two sages of the Red Men visualized the human race as One Family. "All the peoples of mankind," in the words of Degandawida, are destined to dwell redeemed from war, "in peace and tranquillity," under the Great Tree of Peace, with all weapons of war buried in the depths of the earth forever.

Another Iroquois prophet was Ganiodaya, or "Handsome Lake," who preached what was fundamentally the ancient Iroquois faith as it had been modified by Degandawida and Hiawatha and into which were absorbed the elements of Christianity.[91]

9. Yogic Powers

Demonstrations of yogic powers have been observed among Red Men. The harmless handling of fire and plunging of the hand into boiling water, feats comparable to the fire-walking ceremony

---

[89] *Ibid.,* p. 2.

[90] [Ed. nt.: This is not the Hiawatha celebrated by Longfellow, but a wizard, a shaman, who was associated with Degandawida. F.W.]

[91] Cf. T. R. Henry, *op. cit.,* pp. 32–44ff, 145–147; a book of paramount importance, to which the writer gratefully pays tribute.

of South Sea Islanders and of Oriental yogins, were demonstrated by the Sioux tribes of the Great Plains. A yogic plant-growing technique was found among the Pawnee and Navahos quite like that practiced in India.[92]

A Luiseño medicine-man cut off his tongue and the blood covered his breast. He held out the cut-off tongue for everyone to see. Then "he put it back and it grew together again." On another occasion, a medicine-man was shot with bow and arrow. The arrow penetrated so deeply into his breast that he vomited blood and fell down as if dead. A second medicine-man, apparently exercising supernormal power such as that with which an adept in yoga is credited, pulled out the arrow, "doctored him and blew upon him and he got perfectly well and went on dancing." A Luiseño named Turiyo threw his feather headdress up on a briskly burning fire. All who were present saw and smelt the feathers burning. Then he walked and looked about and there lay the same feather headdress on the ground undamaged.

Upon the completion of a *toluache* initiation ceremony, sacred to the culture-hero and prophet Chungichnish (whom the San Juan Capistrano Indians knew as Chinigchinix), several of the old Luiseño men would jump into the very midst of a big fire lit for the ceremony, in order to extinguish it magically, and then stand there for several minutes. One could smell the feathers of the regalia burning, but the old men would jump out of the fire unburnt. Flaming logs would be pulled out and the fire extinguished by stamping upon it. The chief prohibited all use of water to put out the fire. The fire was to be put out by that magical power which the Iroquois derive from the employment of *orenda,* or, as the Melanesians call it, *mana.* With these magical practices associated with fire-extinguishing, all initiated members of the tribe were familiar. After having fasted from salt and flesh-food for two or three weeks, neophytes, usually boys at the age of puberty, were initiated and then taught how to perform these practices. A medicine-man of the Diegueños of Mesa Grande would hold a red-hot stone in his hands, lick it with his tongue, and suffer no ill effect.[93]

[92]Cf. C. Wissler, *op. cit.,* p. 203; N. C. Burlin, *op. cit.,* pp. 39–40; Erna Fergusson, *op. cit.,* pp. 227–28; and especially G. B. Grinnell, *Pawnee Hero Stories and Folk-Tales* (New York, 1889), pp. 379–81, 383, 388.

[93]Cf. C. G. Dubois, *op. cit.,* pp. 81–82, n. 19.

Major Frank North, who was in command of the Pawnee Scouts, testified to having seen the Pawnee medicine-men make maize kernels grow. In the middle of the medicine-lodge, a medicine-man dug up a bit of the hard-trodden floor "about as large as a dinner plate, and broke up between his fingers the hard pieces of soil, until the dirt was soft and friable. The ground having thus been prepared, and having been moistened with water, a few kernels of corn [or maize] were buried in the loose earth. Then the doctor [or medicine-man] retired a little from the spot and sang, and as the place where the corn was buried was watched, the soil was seen to move, and a tiny green blade came slowly into view. This continued to increase in height and size, until, in the course of twenty minutes or half an hour from the time of planting, the stalk of corn was a foot or fifteen inches in height." The stalks continued to grow until they were of full height and then tasseled out and put forth one or more ears of corn, which grew to full size. Then the medicine-man approached the plant, plucked an ear, and passed it to the spectators.[94]

A similar feat was performed with a cedar berry. The berry was passed around among the spectators for examination, as the maize kernels had been, and then planted. After a short time there was seen to have grown from the berry a cedar twig nine or ten inches high, whence side branches were beginning to appear. A cedar

---

[94]It is highly significant to note here that a magical plant-growing technique of very arcane character, but akin to that of the medicine-man of the Red Men, appears to have been practiced by the Hierophants of the famed Mysteries of Eleusis of ancient Greece:

"The ear of wheat growing and maturing with a supernatural suddenness is just as much a part of the mysteries of Demeter as the vine growing in a few hours is part of the revels of Dionysius. And the veneration of the Mysteries by such men as Sophocles and Euripides is hardly compatible with the easy notion of a fraud practised by the priests. We find the very same plant miracles in the nature festivals of primitive peoples. The ear of wheat, suddenly grown, silently harvested, and displayed to the mystes, is then really a revelation and pledge of the goddess, who first gave this fruit to mankind through the Eleusinians. More than that: it is an epiphany of Persephone herself, her mythical *first* recurrence in the shape of the grain, after her descent to the realm of the dead. We need not ask what thoughts and hopes the mystes associated with an epiphany of this sort. It transported him into the realm of miracles, into the presence of the great goddesses themselves in the moment when they bestowed the ear of grain upon men." Cf. Walter F. Otto, *The Meaning of the Eleusinian Mysteries,* Bollingen Series XXX.2, *The Mysteries* (New York, 1955), pp. 25–26.

branch, sharpened and stuck in the ground, became so deeply rooted within the space of a few minutes that the strongest man of the tribe could not pull it up. Then a blind man, apparently endowed with *orenda,* succeeded in pulling it up. Its roots were six feet long, and fresh and growing. A Pawnee girl could make plums and other fruit grow on trees devoid of fruit, as Hindu and other yogis can.[95]

Pawnee medicine-men are also credited by Grinnell with exercising other remarkable yogic powers. One of them handed to a group of spectators, for their examination, his bundle of arrows. The arrows upon being examined were found to be of the usual sort with sharp sheet-iron points. Then he shot them with the full force of the bow and struck a number of tribal initiates in the sides or on the legs as they danced the sacred elk-dance. "The arrows, instead of penetrating the flesh, bounded back, some of them flying fifteen or twenty feet in the air." When picked up and examined by the onlookers, "the sheet-iron points were found to be doubled back as if they had been shot against a plate of iron, and the shafts of some of them were split." The dancers suffered no injury whatsoever.

Another Pawnee medicine-man, by means of a tomahawk, ceremonially inflicted on one of the tribesmen a scalp wound so deep that the spectators saw the gray brain-matter oozing out and streams of blood running down the injured man's face and dripping from his hair behind. A boy's belly was cut open by such a medicine-man so that the liver was exposed and a bit of it cut off. An Indian representing a bear was shot at by Indians who were not medicine-men and "an arrow pierced him through the bowels, and the wound was plainly seen on each side." All three of these wounded ones were restored to bodily wholeness and health

[95]Cf. G. B. Grinnell, *op. cit.,* pp. 379–81, 383, 388. Louis Jacolliot, who resided in India for many years, where he was Chief Justice of the former French possession of Chandenagore, near Calcutta, has placed on record, in *Occult Science in India* (New York, 1884), pp. 38–39, 259–64, trustworthy accounts of his own personal experiences in India in relation to these plant-growing phenomena. There appear to be two methods in vogue: (1) the production of spontaneous vegetation, apparently in actuality, and (2) the employment of what in psychic research are called "apports" (material objects which have transported after having been atomically disintegrated and thereafter reconstituted) to simulate the first method.

within a few days. Similarly, a second Indian also disguised as a bear was slashed across the abdomen so that his bowels protruded. "The bear was carried off, and in a short time was healed, and went about as usual."

During a sacred dance, a medicine-man shot ten Indians, one after another, who represented deer. "They fell down wounded, and then got up and limped off half dying. He drove them around the dance ring so that the people might see their wounds. After they had looked at them, he went up to the first and slapped him on the back, and the ball dropped out of him on to the ground, and the man straightened up, healed. So he did to all, up to the tenth man, and they were all healed. This was wonderful." A brave in a medicine-man's dance had four youths disguise themselves as horses. He loaded and cocked a gun, to which a scalp was tied, and laid the gun on the ground pointing towards the four horses, and walked some steps away. "Then he motioned to the scalp and the gun went off, and one of the horses went down wounded. It seems that the ghost of the scalp obeyed his motion, and shot off the gun. . . . This was repeated until all the horses were down. The people examined them and saw that they were really wounded in the breast. The man went up to them and they seemed to be dying and vomited blood, and the young man slapped them, and the balls came out of their mouths, and as soon as the balls came away from them they were healed."[96]

These remarkable feats were witnessed and vouched for by Major Frank North, and by his brother Capt. L. H. North, who was for many years associated with Major North in command of the Pawnee Scouts. Both these United States Army officers, like George B. Grinnell, were, unlike most White Men, genuine friends of the Red Men, and for this reason were enabled to attain right understanding of some of the deeper aspects of the Pawnees' life. It was to his friend Major Frank North that George B. Grinnell dedicated the book. Grinnell testifies concerning the feats as follows: "It is further to be noted that clear-headed, intelligent white men, whose powers of observation have been highly trained, have confessed themselves wholly unable to explain these startling

[96]Cf. G. B. Grinnell, *op. cit.,* pp. 377–79, 384–87.

performances, or to hazard a guess as to the means by which they were accomplished. That these things happened as detailed is well authenticated by the testimony of many perfectly credible witnesses."[97]

A remarkable account of how the present Hopi Sun-Chief of Oraibi, Don Talayesva, experienced consciousness (or "astral")-projection, when a boy, is given by Frank Waters in *Masked Gods,* pages 115–16. "Don felt himself lifted like a feather and swept over the mountains by a gust of wind; 'like flying,' he said it was." While thus out of the fleshly body, the boy walked into his own home. "They didn't see him . . . Don walked out—into what? The Department of Sociology of Yale University, the Institute of Human Relations do not know. It was beyond sociology, beyond rationalization, beyond the limit of human relationship. It was a realm of myth and legend, a time-space dimension in which everything that had existed and was to exist had being in a perpetual, unified, living now." Geronimo, the famous Apache warrior, tells of a similar experience of his own of consciousness-projection. Thunder-cloud, a Winnebago medicine-man, told of how he consciously entered the womb and was reborn with no break in the continuity of his consciousness, after the manner of a great yogi.[98]

As among practitioners of Mantra Yoga, which is dependent for its efficacy upon the correct application of mantric, or magical, sound, so among the Navahos, sacred chants "*must* be sung exactly as directed by tradition, since any error or inefficiency might be fatal." The omission, or wrong intonation, or misplacement of a single syllable or word would neutralize the spiritual benefit which otherwise would accrue to the hundreds of participants in a ceremonial. Similarly, seeing that thought itself also sets into motion far-reaching vibratory waves, it should be used only rightly, as the Navaho medicine-men wisely teach; for an evil thought can be powerful enough to inflict death upon the person against whom it is directed, and a good thought can produce harmoniousness and health.[99]

[97] *Ibid.,* p. 375.
[98] Cf. P. Radin, *American Indian Life* (New York, 1922), p. 77.
[99] Cf. S. H. Babington, *Navahos, Gods, and Tom-toms* (New York, 1950), pp. 187, 202.

10. Extrasensory Perception

Among Red Men, the foreseeing of future events and telepathy appear to have been, as they still are, rather widely practiced, especially by their medicine-men. Concerning such prophetic powers among his fellow Red Men of North America, Ohiyesa has placed on record, in *The Soul of the Indian,* pages 157–58, the following testimony:

"A Sioux prophet predicted the coming of the white man fully fifty years before the event, and even described accurately his garments and weapons. Before the steamboat was invented, another prophet of our race described the 'Fire Boat' that would swim upon their mighty river, the Mississippi, and the date of this prophecy is attested by the term used, which is long since obsolete."

As to similar foreseeing among Red Men in South America and their ability to describe telepathically happenings taking place at a distance, the late A. Hyatt Verrill, in *The Real Americans,* pages 56–57, states that he has incontrovertible evidence, some of which he sets forth, of such extrasensory powers being exercised by Indians in British Guiana and in Peru. He reports two such evidential experiences of his own, as follows:

"In Peru, some of the Andean Indians have an amazing ability to report events transpiring many miles distant. I have known them to state that soldiers were arriving at a distant village and they even told how many were mounted, how many afoot, and described their equipment. When, later on, we reached the village we found matters exactly as had been stated."

On another occasion, a medicine-man in British Guiana declared that Verrill and his party of Indians would be killed or injured by a falling tree if they made camp where they had planned. "There were," Verrill states, "no dead trees near and no sign of a tree having reason to fall. Personally, I would have paid no heed to the fellow's warning, but my Indians insisted upon camping at another spot. During the night there was a violent thunderstorm and in the morning we found that the upper portion of a huge tree, thickly overgrown with air plants and other parasitic growths and weighing many tons, had been splintered by lightning and had fallen on the precise spot we originally had selected for our camp."

11. Images and the Virgin of Guadalupe

Like mankind of other faiths, the Red Men made images of their gods and goddesses, often in miniature, like the Kachinas of the Pueblo Indians. In Roman Catholic churches of Mexico, Central and South America, similar small images of such American deities have been found secreted under altars and elsewhere. In parts of Bolivia, the Red Men openly carry into the churches such miniature images on their person.[100]

The Virgin of Guadalupe, officially endorsed by the Vatican and proclaimed the patroness and protectress of New Spain, is, as Father Sahagún perceived, no other than the goddess Tonantzin (meaning "Our Mother") whom, it appears, the Aztecs adopted from the pre-Aztec races and made the mother of all their gods. Even her ancient feast-day, the twelfth of December, continues to be observed. Tonantzin's new Spanish name of Guadalupe did not deceive the Red Men. As Frank Waters adds, "It only lent official and ecclesiastical sanctity to their forbidden pagan worship." Thus, just as Roman Christianity took over without the least acknowledgment the pre-Christian cult of the mother-goddess Isis and her divine child Horus in Italy, as well as elsewhere in Europe, and renamed them the Virgin Mary and the child Jesus, so it took over that of Tonantzin. And "today, clad in her sky-blue mantle 'dotted with stars like toasted maize grains' and under her new name of the Virgin of Guadalupe," the dark-visaged ancient Earth-Mother is still the celestial guardian of all Indian America.[101] Her present Christian shrine graces the High Place, the Hill of Tepeyac, which has been sacred to her for unknown centuries, perhaps for unknown millenniums, before the coming of the Spaniards. Sharing in this guardianship is another dark-visaged pre-Columbian American goddess, the Virgin of Zapopan.

[100]Cf. Frank Waters, *op. cit.,* p. 49; A. H. Verrill, *op. cit.,* p. 91.
[101]Cf. Frank Waters, *op. cit.,* pp. 51–52, 197–98.

12. Psychic Influences on Modern American Cults

Attention will now be directed to the remarkable similarities between the religious practices of the Red Men and those new cults which arose among White Men immersed in the American environment psychically conditioned by the Red Men. As Frank Waters clearly discerns, the earliest White trappers, whether Spanish, French, or English, became wholly Indian in spirit and feeling. They "had confronted here that great psychic entity which was the spirit-of-place, the heart of a new continent. The impact was tremendous. It shattered them completely. But each succumbed in a different way,"[102] according to his own social psychology. The outcome of our examination, however, should be taken as being little more than suggestive.

Thus, in 1820, near Manchester, New York, Joseph Smith, then in his fifteenth year, knelt down in a solitary place in a wood, and began to pray for spiritual guidance, quite as the youths of the Red Men under yogic instruction of medicine-men had in the same or contiguous environment during the course of uncounted centuries. Of the vision vouchsafed to him then, he said, "I saw a pillar of light exactly over my head, above the brightness of the sun, which descended gradually until it fell upon me. . . . When the light rested upon me, I saw two personages, whose brightness and glory defy all description, standing above me in the air. One of them spake unto me."[103]

A second vision came to him three years later, when, it is asserted, Moroni, a heavenly messenger, appeared and revealed to him the secret hiding place of the gold tablets, engraved with the texts, said to have been in reformed Egyptian, which when translated under inspiration by Joseph Smith became *The Book of Mormon.* Joseph Smith experienced seven such visions extending over a period of seven years.

Having been mentally conditioned by Christian teachings, Joseph Smith saw the two personages of the first vision as God the Father and Jesus Christ the Son, and the personages of the other

[102] *Ibid.,* pp. 59–60.
[103] Cf. *Writings of Joseph Smith,* 2.16–17, in *The Pearl of Great Price.* See also A. E.'s description of the Shining Beings, in Part IV, Section IV, "Otherworld Beings."

visions as angelic or heavenly. Had these personages been seen on Cuchama by a youth of the Red Men on a vision-quest, they would have been recognized as of the order of Shining Beings, known to Hindus and Buddhists as Devas.

Inasmuch as *The Book of Mormon* is believed to have been so hidden and safeguarded for the good of succeeding generations, Joseph Smith in discovering and giving it to the world performed a mission precisely like that of a Tibetan *terton,* or "taker-out," of secreted scriptures.[104]

The Book of Mormon purports to record the "Sacred History of Ancient America," along with lost teachings of Jesus Christ addressed to the peoples of America. It asserts that the American Indians are remnants of a tribe of Israelites who settled in America about 600 B.C. Joseph Smith reports that he dug out of an Indian mound a "peek-stone," as he called it, which aided him in translating the script on the golden tablets. This peek-stone, "which became the later Urim and Thummin" (or talisman used in making the translation), itself suggests the marked influence of the Red Men in the life of the founder of the Church of Jesus Christ of Latter Day Saints.[105]

Joseph Smith's peculiar method of revealing what the heavenly visitants taught to him would be quite understandable to the youth of the Red Men whose vision-quests had been successful. He was accustomed to hide behind a blanket, and, inducing in himself a state of reverie or ecstasy by fixing his gaze upon his talisman, "he dictated to his scribes communications of supposedly supernormal origin."[106]

Internal evidence suggests that *The Book of Mormon,* whatever may have been its original source, is, in at least some degree, indigenously American. As is suggested, this is probably because of its having taken shape in an environment which long before had been psychically conditioned and Americanized by the Red Men. The youthful Joseph Smith dictated *The Book of Mormon;* to assume that he, the unlettered son of an unlettered father, wholly untutored in history and anthropology, could have done so in his

[104]See *The Tibetan Book of the Dead,* by the writer, pp. 75–77.
[105]Cf. I. Woodbridge Riley, *Latter-Day Saints, Encyclopaedia of Religion and Ethics* (New York, 1921), edited by James Hastings, pp. xi, 85.
[106]*Ibid.*

normal mental state appears to be quite untenable. Even as he gave to the Christian world a new Bible in *The Book of Mormon,* so Mohammed, similarly unlettered, gave to the Moslem world its Bible, the *Koran.* [107]

In this connection, it is important to take into account the fact that the Fox sisters started American Spiritualism only ten miles from the place where Joseph Smith lived, and were his contemporaries. Unconsciously to him, they were his psychic associates; partakers, as he was, of the same Indian-conditioned psychic environment.

The Book of Mormon, no less than American Spiritualism, thus took shape under the direct influence of an American environment which had, long before, been conditioned psychically by the preceding Red Men. The youth Joseph Smith, by his recourse to meditation and prayer in the solitude of that American environment, precisely like a youth of the Red Men on a vision-quest, invoked, and was granted, visions of guidance.

Mary Baker Eddy, too, was immersed in the Red-Men-shaped aura of the new world, and, being psychically gifted herself, could no more escape its influences than Joseph Smith or the Fox sisters. Frank Waters points out the striking parallelisms between the Navaho and Christian Scientist teachings concerning the true Eternal Mind and the illusory mortal mind.[108] The Christian Scientist, like the Indian medicine-man, seeks to cure illnesses by restoring harmony to the patient. The medicine-man sings a holy-song over the patient; the Christian Scientist practitioner prays over the patient. Both seek to direct aright the thought of the patient, to the end that the all-potent power of Eternal Mind may prevail and health be restored. Equally to the medicine-man and the Christian Scientist practitioner, health, or harmoniousness, and religion are rightly one. It is, as Frank Waters observes, "strange, indeed, that between the oldest and newest religious

[107]Another American spiritistically-inspired Bible is *Oahspe,* wherein are contained numerous references to the racial origins and remote antiquity of the Red Men. Its scribe, John Ballou Newbrough, was a Spiritualist, who, about 1881, declared that he had received revelations inspired by shining beings, whom he called angels.
[108]Cf. Frank Waters, *op. cit.,* pp. 388–89.

systems truly indigenous to America there is so close a resemblance."[109]

In this relation, very remarkable are some of the songs of the Red Men practitioners which are sung to restore the patient's health, the Singer requesting of the Holy Beings that the feet, the mind, and the voice of the patient be restored. There is repeatedly proclaimed that all is well, that the patient's feet and head are better, and that the patient is better in every way. "Finally, it is said over and over again that all is being made beautiful and harmonious." Once complete harmony has been restored, the illness of the patient has vanished, and there is health.[110]

Phineas P. Quimby, an American-born mesmeric healer (with whom Mrs. Eddy, when known as Mrs. Patterson, was closely associated, at first as a patient of his and then as his disciple), acquired from his favorite subject, a youth named Lucius Burkman, a method of healing based upon the application of a force which was the same as the *orenda* of the Iroquois and the *mana* of the Melanesians. Quimby called this occult force "the Wisdom," which he invoked by silent prayer just as an Iroquoian medicine-man would by chanting. In its manifested aspect he called it "the Power." As he proceeded in his new-found method of healing, he arrived at the conviction that disease is due to a departure from, or loss of, man's natural, or primordial, harmoniousness, or state of bodily, mental, and spiritual wholeness. This was the same conviction which the medicine-men long before him in the same psychically-shaped environment had held. Therefore, man's disorders are the creation of his own undisciplined and misdirected mind and thus unnatural and unreal. He urged his patients to refuse to give to their ills any reality.[111] Here was the American foundation upon which Mrs. Eddy, after the death of Quimby in 1865, built her admirable system known as Christian Science.

That the Founder of Christian Science understood rightly and appreciatively the psychic import of the naturalistic religion and

[109] *Ibid.,* p. 388–89.
[110] Cf. A. H. Leighton, D. C. Leighton, *The Navaho Door* (Harvard University Press, Cambridge, Mass., 1945), pp. 34, 55.
[111] Cf. Max Freedom Long, *op. cit.,* pp. 316–22.

the correlative poetic insight of the Red Men is obvious from the following significant reference contained in *Science and Health:* "The Indians caught some glimpse of the underlying reality, when they called a certain beautiful lake 'the smile of the Great Spirit.' " Being part of a recapitulation of the first edition of her classbook, copyrighted in 1870 and produced "after much labor and increased spiritual understanding," this passage referring to the Red Men is of special value psychologically. As the passage's context adds, "absolute Christian Science pervades its statements."[112]

Although mental therapy is for the medicine-man the ideal or divine therapy, as it is for Christian Science, he is always prepared, unlike the Christian Scientist, to resort to the lower or mundane therapy of medication when the patient is incapable of applying or profiting by mental therapy. Or the medicine-man may make use of the middle-path method of homeopathy, with his own equivalent of the harmless "sugar-pill" to serve as the catalytic agent for inspiring the patient's faith in the method's efficacy. All three therapies are, of course, wholly dependent upon the omnipotence of mind to restore that harmoniousness or wholeness which is health.

The teachings of Christian Science are so largely in agreement with the Red Man's teachings, not alone with respect to the omnipotence of mind and the theory of disease and methods of healing but also in relation to *orenda,* that the Red Man may, indeed, rightly be credited with being their psychic progenitor. As Frank Waters very aptly expresses it in *Masked Gods,* page 17, "If there exists such a thing as a spirit-of-place, imbuing each of the continental masses of the world with its own unique and ineradicable sense of rhythm, mood, and character, and if there exists an indigenous form of faith deriving from it, then it is to the Indian we must look for that expression of life's meaning which alone differentiates America from Europe, Africa, and Asia."

The German Baron de Palm, who arrived in the United States in 1862, spent much time among the Red Men of the far West, and was so deeply impressed by their spiritistic practices that he often

---

[112]Cf. Mary Baker Eddy, *Science and Health with Key to the Scriptures* (Boston, 1934), chapter xiv, Recapitulation, pp. 465, 477.

spoke of his sojourn among them as having been the most spiritually profitable period of his life.[113] This experience of the Baron is of historic importance and anthropological significance. Later on he was automatically attracted by the new spiritism of the White Man, then taking shape around him as an outcome of the psychic phenomena associated with the Eddy brothers in Vermont and with various mediums in New York State. He felt it to be quite in harmony with the indigenous spiritism of the Red Men, with which he had been so intimately acquainted.[114] Thus viewed, the new spiritism of the White Man appears to have been a spontaneous outgrowth of its American environment, whence it was carried to all parts of the world, and became, in large measure, one of America's modern contributions to mankind's cultural achievements.

The Baron was one of the early and most active members of the reformed spiritism of the Theosophical Society, founded in New York City in 1875, by Madame H. P. Blavatsky, a Russian-born woman, and Colonel H. S. Olcott, a veteran of the United States Civil War. Both Madame Blavatsky and Colonel Olcott were then ardent investigators of the Fox sisters and of American Spiritualism in general; and, like the Baron, had been, sometimes consciously, immersed in the aura of the spiritism of the Red Men.[115]

The writer, when a small boy in Trenton, New Jersey, the place of his birth, a region inhabited by many Red Men before the coming of the White Man, had a German-born nurse who was a medium. He often saw her go into trance and describe what to her

[113]Cf. E. H. Britten, *Nineteenth Century Miracles* (New York, 1884), p. 442.

[114]As stated in *Tomorrow* (New York, Spring 1956), in the article "Influence of Spiritualism," p. 128, "The first Spiritualists [in the United States] were the Shaker communities who believed that they received visitations from the neighboring dead Indians collectively, as a tribe." The Shakers passed on the technique to professional spirit mediums in the United States. And the tent of the Indian sorcerer has given place "to the 'cabinet' or darkened seance room of thousands of modern mediums who have taken over the secrets of the humble medicine-man."

[115]Colonel Olcott, in close friendship and psychic understanding with the Baron, although severely critical of him in *Old Diary Leaves* (I, 159–65), acted as chief officiant and orator at the Baron's public funeral, held in New York City in 1878, and attended by a vast concourse. The cremation of the Baron's corpse, which followed, was the first scientific cremation in the New World. Cf. E. H. Britten, *op. cit.,* pp. 440–43.

were the disembodied spirits of Red Men who, when incarnate, had formerly dwelt there. Her chief spirit-control was Black Hawk, a deceased chief of the Red Men.[116] Such spirit-control by deceased Red Men was at that epoch, and still is, common throughout the United States. An anthropologist might ask, Does the medium really see spirits of deceased Red Men, as the spiritualists believe? Or, as the Theosophists believe, does the medium merely "read" psychic records of Red Men of the past?

The German-born medium was entranced in the environment which the Red Men undoubtedly had conditioned psychically; and, as a result, saw what she described as spirits of Red Men. Had she been entranced in her native Germany, it is not likely that she would have seen American spirits or have had an American spirit-control.

Apparently, there is some as yet undetermined psychic relationship, more or less direct, between the Red Man's spiritistic practices and the White Man's American-born Spiritualism, and, in turn, with the higher Spiritualism of the American-founded Theosophical Society.

It is for whatever they may prove to be worth that these observations are made a part of this examination of the Red Man's heretofore much misunderstood psychically-based life and self-realizable religion.

13. The Secret Greatness of the Red Man's Religion

As Edwin R. Embree has fittingly written, "The Indian's close acquaintance with nature, his reverence and deep feeling for the mysterious, begin to look like pleasant oases in a world made desert by pavements, clattering machines, and fixed rules and schedules. . . . No longer satisfied with a standard of living based solely on the number of things a man possesses, we view with more appreciation the Indian's ability to build a colorful and satisfying

---

[116]Black Hawk, a chief and distinguished warrior of the Sauk and Fox tribes of the Algonquin Nation, was born in the Sauk Village at the mouth of the Rock River, Illinois, in 1767. In the Black Hawk War of 1832, he won great renown as the leader of his people. He died near Iowaville on the Des Moines River in 1838. Cf. J. W. Moyer, *Famous Indian Chiefs* (Chicago and New York, 1957), pp. 17–22.

life without the constant aid of gadgets. We are beginning to look longingly at his ancient zest for life, boiling over in drama and dance and thrilling at the presence of danger, at the artistry of his social organization and the grateful courtesy of his personal relationships."[117]

In the words of John Collier, the Red Men "had what the world has lost. They have it now. What the world has lost, the world must have again, lest it die. Not many years are left to have or have not, to recapture the lost ingredient."[118]

III. HOLY-SONGS AND HIGH PLACES

Throughout the Americas there are many High Places which, like Cuchama, were revered by the Red Man for untold millenniums before the coming of the White Man. In Mexico and Yucatan truncated pyramids were reared in honor of the Sun and Moon; and on them, after the Aztec conquest, human sacrifice was made to the deities of the Aztecs.

To a High Place, the Dakota initiate went alone, as did the Coochimí initiate to Cuchama, and, likewise, the Aztec initiate, to acquire divine insight. Without food and drink, he remained there fasting, usually from one to four days and nights, and prayed for power to be vouchsafed to him, whether from animate or inanimate nature, "from bear or snake or rock."[119] Having received the divine inspiration, he returned to teach men what the Great Mystery had commanded him to teach them. Among the Pawnee, when the youth desired to learn how rightly to live, he went into solitude, often on a mountain, and cried aloud until some animal, inspired by the Great Mystery, appeared to him in a vision and enlightened him.[120]

The Winnebagos tell of a youth who went into the hills in solitude and fasted twelve days, when a spirit came to him in a dream and "gave him knowledge and taught him wonderful words

[117]Cf. E. R. Embree, *op. cit.,* p. 244.
[118]Cf. John Collier, *op. cit.,* p. 15.
[119]An Indian society "may bear the name of some animal whose virtue or psychic power it incorporates." The animal is often purely emblematic of the spirit animal. See N. C. Burlin, *The Indians' Book,* pp. 31, 61.
[120]*Ibid.,* pp. 39, 61, 96.

[of mantric-like power] that brought health, welfare, and long life." When he returned to his people he taught them the wisdom transmitted by the spirit. This is the holy-song he sang:

> (Saith the Spirit,
> "Dream, oh, dream again,
> And tell of me;
> Dream thou!")
> Into solitude went I

> And wisdom was revealed to me.
> (Saith the Spirit,
> "Dream, oh, dream again,
> And tell of me;
> Dream thou!")
> Let the whole world hear me,

> From the beginning
> Know I all; hear me!
> All was revealed to me!
> (Now saith the Spirit,
> "Tell of me;
> Dream thou!")[121]

Great is the song's power, the secret significance of which is understood only by the medicine-men. During the medicine, or religious, ceremony of the Winnebagos, which lasts four days and nights, the people are taught the paths of goodness. That the people may not grow tired or drowsy, the ceremony is enlivened by dancing. "So the slow part of the holy-song is followed by a quick part which is the music of the dance." Such a sacred dance-song follows:

> I have won the world,
> The world is won,
> I have won the world
> The world is won;
> I am come,
> I am come here now!
> I have won the village,

> Yea 'tis won,
> I have won the village,

---

[121] *Ibid.,* pp. 254–55.

> Yea 'tis won,
> I am come,
> I am come here now!

"The [Winnebago] medicine ceremony used to be very solemn and sacred in the olden times, and its mysteries were known only to the initiated."[122]

In similar manner, the medicine-man who sings holy-songs receives intimation in youth that he will attain holiness. "The Great Mystery makes him to know this. Sometimes it is the Spirits who tell him. The Spirits come not in sleep always, but also when man is awake. When a Spirit comes, it would seem as though a man stood there, but when this man has spoken and goes forth again, none may see whither he goes. . . . With the Spirits the Holy-Man may commune always, and they teach him holy things."[123] During a famine, the Kiowas obtained an abundance of food by virtue of the miraculous wisdom that a boy had been taught in a dream and practically applied by singing.[124]

Geronimo, one of the most famous of Apache warriors, told of an initiatory song taught to him when he was a little lad: "This is a holy-song [medicine-song], and great is its power. The song tells how, as I sing, I go through the air to a holy-place where Yusun [the Supreme Being] will give me power to do wonderful things. I am surrounded by little clouds, and as I go through the air I change, becoming spirit only."[125]

This is the holy-song sung by Geronimo:

> O, ha le!
> O, ha le!
> Through the air
> I fly upon a cloud
> Towards the sky, far, far, far.
> O, ha le!
> O, ha le!

[122] *Ibid.*, pp. 255–56.
[123] *Ibid.*, p. 39.
[124] *Ibid.*, pp. 226–28.
[125] *Ibid.*, p. 324. Comparison can profitably be made here with the doctrine of consciousness-transference, or projection of the "astral," or subtle, body, as practiced in Tibet and known there as *phowa*. See *Tibetan Yoga and Secret Doctrines*, by the writer, pp. 253–76.

There to find the holy place.
Ah, now the change comes over me!
O, ha le!
O, ha le!

In illustration of the song, Geronimo made a drawing of himself passing through the air to the holy-place. He represented himself by a circle surrounded by an aura, and the holy-place by a sun ornamented by a horned head-dress symbolical of divine power. "Such head-dress is the insignia of the Holy Man."[126]

The Dakotas recognized two kinds of songs: songs made by man and songs inspired by the Great Power that is beyond man's understanding. The Bear Society, or Religious Fraternity, of the Pawnee, made salutation to the rising Sun, as the Hindus do, and sang:

Now the rising Sun hath sent his rays to Earth,
A many coming
Yonder coming,
Yonder coming;
Lo, the many yonder, he—
Yo!
Sunbeams o'er the ground are speeding!

Lo, the many yonder, he—
Yo![127]

Esoterically the song, which is a very ancient sunrise song, represents the Bear Warriors of the Bear Society as being the victors in virtue of the great Spirit-Bear who receives his power of victory from Father Sun. The victors are returning from war just as the Sun is rising, and the women of the village go forth to greet them. "The hidden meaning of the song is the victorious power of the Sun." The following stanzas of a similar sunrise song of the Bear Society illustrate this:

They are coming,
They are coming.
Lo, the victor hosts, ya he—
Yo!

[126]Cf. N. C. Burlin, *The Indians' Book,* p. 324.
[127]*Ibid.,* p. 105.

Forth to meet them go the women
With the rising Sun, ya he—
Yo!
Now the Sun

Hath sent to Earth his hosts of sunbeams
Swiftly speeding
Who are coming,
Who are coming
With the rising Sun, ya he—
Yo!
Radiant now the warriors' triumph

In the rising Sun, ya he—
Yo![128]

Among the followers of the Mescal Cult, all holy-songs are esoteric, and are sung as invocations to the Great Mystery to vouchsafe divine understanding. The songs contain no words. Their secret import is known only to initiates, or, sometimes, only to the singers or to the makers of the songs, which are inspired by spiritual experiences of the devotees.[129]

The Navaho sings to his chief of all mountains, Sisnajinni, as to a divine being, "for the mountain is pure and holy; there is freedom above it, freedom below it, freedom all around it. Happiness and peace are given by the mountain, and the mountain blesses man when in the song it calls him 'son' ":

Thither go I!
Chief of all mountains,
Thither go I,
Living forever,
Thither go I,
Blessings bestowing,
Thither go I,
Calling me "Son, my son."
Thither go I!

In explaining a mountain-song of the Navahos, the aged Singer said, "The song that I will sing is a holy-song. In olden times it was the first song that a boy learned. It was taught to him by his

128 *Ibid.*, pp. 104–6.
129 *Ibid.*, p. 164.

father, for every boy should know this song before starting into life." Of the Sacred Mountain of the East, Sisnajinni, named in the song, he in part and other Navahos in part said, "To the East they [the gods] placed the Sacred Mountain Sisnajinni. They adorned it with white shell, and fastened it to the Earth with a bolt of lightning. They covered it with a sheet of daylight, and put the Dawn Youth and the Dawn Maiden to dwell in it."[130]

The holy-mountain songs are often sung over a sick man, to heal him, by their mantric-like sound-waves. The songs tell of a journey in the subtle body (as in Tibetan consciousness-transference or "astral-body" projection, referred to above) to a holy place of everlasting life and blessedness beyond the sacred mountains. "The Divine Ones who live in and beyond the mountains made the songs, and so they tell of the journey as of a home-coming." The spirit of the ill man makes the journey described in the song sung over him. Upon the rainbow he goes, from mountain to mountain, as the Divine Ones do. Sometimes these songs are sung in order to bless runners prior to a great race and so confer upon them the speed with which the end of a rainbow moves.[131]

As a god does, a sacred mountain shields and protects its devotee. When the devotee sings with initiatory and mantric correctness of the sacred mountain, he quits his earth-body, and as swiftly as lightning, goes to the holy place beyond the mountain. There, like the mountain itself, he becomes pure and . . . holy; when the mountain calls him "son," he is blessed thereby, and filled with blissfulness and life unending.[132]

From *The Indians' Book,* pages 354–55, the first two stanzas of the Navaho mountain-songs are quoted, in their English rendering, as follows:

[130]As set forth on pages 74–78, the Navahos have three other sacred mountains, appertaining to the four cardinal directions, dedicated to the South, West, and North. White, as here, is associated with the East, blue with the South, yellow with the West, and black with the North. Sisnajinni is presumably Pelado Peak in Bernalillo County, New Mexico, and its meaning is probably "Dark Horizontal Belt," according to N. C. Burlin, *The Indians' Book,* pp. 350–1, 552.
[131]Cf. N. C. Burlin, *The Indians' Book,* pp. 352–53.
[132]*Ibid.,* pp. 352–53.

-1-
Swift and far I journey,
Swift upon the rainbow.
Swift and far I journey.
Lo, yonder, the Holy Place!
  Yea, swift and far I journey,
To Sisnajinni, and beyond it.
  Yea, swift and far I journey,
To the Chief of Mountains, and beyond it.
  Yea, swift and far I journey,
To Life Unending, and beyond it.
  Yea, swift and far I journey,
To Joy Unchanging, and beyond it.
  Yea, swift and far I journey.

-2-
Homeward now shall I journey,
Homeward upon the rainbow.
Homeward now shall I journey.
Lo, yonder the Holy Place!
  Yea, homeward now shall I journey,
To Sisnajinni, and beyond it.
  Yea, homeward now shall I journey,
To the Chief of Mountains, and beyond it.
  Yea, homeward now shall I journey,
To Life Unending, and beyond it.
  Yea, homeward now shall I journey,
To Joy Unchanging, and beyond it.
  Yea, homeward now shall I journey.

IV: VISION-QUESTS

As has been suggested above, it was the cultural practice among the Red Men of the Western Plains, as it was among the Yumas of the Southwest, for the youth to prepare for a life-directing vision-quest. Although such vision-quests appear to have been generally universal among the many nations of Red Men, especially north of the Rio Grande, there were minor differences in the yogic procedure between one nation and another.

Unlike the Plains Indians, for whom it was normal for every youth to go on a vision-quest, among the Navahos such vision-quests were usually limited to Singers or medicine-men and initiates in training. As Frank Waters has informed me, "From birth to death, through all illnesses of body and mind, even in the puberty rituals, the Navahos are dependent upon the Singer, who conducts the great nine-day sings. It is he, or one who is learning to be a Singer, who goes on vision-quests and obtains holy-songs, not the ordinary Navaho." The Singer supervises the dances, prayers, and sand-paintings associated with the sings.

In his *Indians of the Americas,* Edwin R. Embree records a very illuminative account of these vision-quests among the Sioux,[133] which is presented here for comparative study with the vision-quest of the Yuma youth on Cuchama, The Exalted High Place. In this instance, the vision-quest was undertaken by one of the two sons of Standing Buffalo, a famous chief of the Red Cloud Bank of the Oglala division of the Teton-Dakota tribe.

He was old enough now to commune with the great spirits above and seek from them guidance for his future life. The Wakan Tanka (the Sacred Spirit) would send him a vision of the guardian spirit who would teach him to protect himself from his enemies and perhaps help him to become a leader of the tribe. Lest he make some slight mistake and thus antagonize the Wakan Tanka, he scrupulously performed each task prescribed in the seeking of a vision.

He brought the horse his father had given to him to Fast Whirlwind, a medicine-man, offered him a pipe, and asked his guidance, [quite as a Hindu or Tibetan youth would of a famous guru].[134] For almost a moon, Fast Whirlwind taught the youth what he must know and do in order to seek a vision. The boy purified himself by prayer. He went to the sweat-lodge, where he crouched, sprinkling water on the heated stones pushed through the opening [by the medicine-man], until the little house was filled with steam; and then, naked, the sweat pouring from his body, he ran to a nearby stream to plunge into the cold water. At last, purified in mind and body, he was ready for his ordeal. When the setting sun was but

[133]Cf. E. R. Embree, *Indians of the Americas,* pp. 140–42.
[134]Throughout the Orient it is, and has been for unknown millenniums, customary for a youth when requesting guidance of a guru, or spiritual director, to present to him, in token of respect, some gift, great or small, according to the disciple's circumstances. The son of Standing Buffalo presumably offered to his guru, the medicine-man, the horse, the youth's most prized possession, along with the symbolic tobacco-filled pipe; and, the medicine-man, precisely as a guru in India or Tibet would do, accepts the youth as a disciple, and becomes his guide in psychic development and self-realization.

a hand's breadth above the edge of the world, accompanied by the medicine-man, the youth set out for a distant hill. There the old man left him alone to fast and pray, promising to return each morning and evening.

For two days and nights the youth remained there, praying incessantly that the Sacred Spirit would vouchsafe to him the life-directing vision. And his prayer was:

> Wakan Tanka, *Onshimayala* (Great Mysterious One, have pity upon me). I reverence the Sun and the Moon, and the Stars, and the Blue Sky, and the Thunder Trails, and the Mountains, and my Grandfather the Rocks and the Waters which give life, and everything that standeth upright. Thanks I give unto thee for all these, and for the Earth-Mother with all her creatures that crawl upon the face of the Earth. Great Mysterious One, have pity upon me.

When the third day had come, the youth returned, as did the youth of the Yumas from the summit of Cuchama, to his people. He was "lean and haggard. His arms were covered with gashes from flesh-offerings to the Sun, but he was singing a song of victory."

The youth, in his vision, having seen and talked with a black-tailed deer, went at once to a medicine-man of the black-tailed deer cult to ascertain the import of this, as Milarepa did to his guru Marpa to ascertain the import of his own similarly symbolic dream.[135] The medicine-man "explained that now, like the deer, the youth would be able to scent any danger, that he must publicly perform a dance dressed as the deer, and that ever afterward he must carry sage, the deer's food, as a protection from harm. The medicine-man prepared a medicine-bundle [or religious talisman] for him, which the boy must never let out of his keeping."

The youth felt that he had been favored by the Great Mysterious One, "for though all men tried, at some time in their lives, many did not succeed in their vision-quests. Now that he had power, he could either become a mighty warrior or even a *shaman,* or medicine-man, himself, and be, in his own turn, a

[135]Cf. W. Y. Evans-Wentz, *Tibet's Great Yogi Milarepa* (Oxford University Press, 1951), pp. 149–54.

teacher of the tribal mysteries to the youth of coming generations."[136]

In like manner, War Chief Joseph of the Nez Percé Indians dreamed his own big medicine-dream when as a youth he was on a vision-quest, fasting and alone, on a High Place. A personage in a yellow blanket, who personified the occult significance of thunder, appeared in the vision and blessed him with a name meaning "Thunder-rolling-in-the-mountains." This name indicated that the boy Joseph was divinely appointed to become, as he did, a great leader of his people, and that, accordingly, he was under the protection and guidance of the divine forces. There was also bestowed upon the youth whatever the dream-personage may have been carrying, symbolically indicative of the bestowal of *orenda,* or psychic power. In the dream, Joseph was taught a holy-song which once he sang upon the very solemn occasion of a tribal dance in honor of the tribe's Guardian Spirit; but the content of his dream as a whole he never revealed, apparently because of its profound esoteric character.[137] Such reticence is quite in keeping with the practice common among all the American races, as in the Orient, of maintaining silence with respect to personal psychic experiences much too sacred to be made public.

Ohiyesa's account of the *hambeday,* or religious retreat among the Dakotas, which presents another aspect of the vision-quests, confirms what our own informants, Jim Chaleco and his son Arsenius and Feliciano Manteca, reported concerning the similar institution among the Yuma tribes, religiously associated with Cuchama:

[136]Among the Orāon tribesmen of the Bihar Province, India, there are vision-quests essentially the same as those among the Red Men. Under the urge of religious fervor, directed by his guru, an Orāon "repairs to some solitary place, and, after an absence of days, returns home with new-found occult powers." Jatra, an Orāon youth of the Ranchi District, in April, 1914, in a dream was vouchsafed inner illumination. He became a religious teacher and gathered together more than a thousand disciples. Like a medicine-man of the Red Men, he taught them holy-songs and words of divine power, which came to him through inspiration. An Orāon woman, too, was similarly inspired and became a prophetess, and her teachings were substantially the same as the teachings by the youth Jatra. Cf. Rai Bahadur S. C. Roy, *Orāon Religion and Customs* (Ranchi, 1928), pp. 304, 341–43.

[137]Cf. H. A. Howard, *War Chief Joseph* (Caldwell, Idaho, 1941), pp. 38–41; Spinden, *The Nez Percé Indians,* memoirs of the American Anthropological Society, vol. II.

That solitary communion with the Unseen, which was the highest expression of our religious life, is partly described in the word *hambeday,* literally, "mysterious feeling," which has been variously translated "fasting" and "dreaming." It may better be interpreted as "consciousness of the divine."

The first *hambeday,* or religious retreat, marked an epoch in the life of the youth, which may be compared to that of confirmation or conversion in Christian experience. Having first prepared himself by means of the purifying vapor-bath, and cast off as far as possible all human or fleshly influences, the young man sought out the noblest height, the most commanding summit in all the surrounding region. Knowing the God [or the Great Mystery] sets no value upon material things, he took with him no offerings or sacrifices other than symbolic objects, such as paints and tobacco. Wishing to appear before Him in all humility, he wore no clothing save his moccasins and breech-clout. At the solemn hour of sunrise or sunset he took up his position, overlooking the glories of Earth and facing the "Great Mystery," and there he remained, naked, erect, silent and motionless, exposed to the elements and forces of His arming, for a night and day to two days and nights, but rarely longer. Sometimes he would chant a hymn without words, or offer the ceremonial "filled pipe." In this holy trance or ecstasy the Indian mystic found his highest happiness and the motive power of his existence.

When he returned to the camp, he must remain at a distance until he had again entered the vapor-bath and prepared himself for intercourse with his fellows. Of the vision or sign vouchsafed to him he did not speak, unless it had included some commission which must be publicly fulfilled. Sometimes an old man, standing upon the brink of eternity, might reveal to a chosen few the oracle of his long-past youth.[138]

Of the vision-quest of the Comanches and Apaches, Edwin Eastman, who lived among them in captivity for a number of years, makes record on page 80 of his autobiography entitled *Seven and Nine Years Among the Camanches* [sic] *and Apaches,* published in 1873, as follows:

When a youth has arrived at the age of sixteen it becomes necessary for him to "make his medicine";[139] to this end he leaves his father's lodge, and absents himself for one or two days and nights; entering the woods, where he may be secure from interrup-

---

[138]Cf. C. A. Eastman, *op. cit.,* pp. 6–9.
[139]In other words, the youth must awaken into activity the psychic powers innate within him by his own efforts, a practice akin to that of the neophyte in Zen Buddhism.

tion, he seeks some quiet nook, and stretching his length upon the ground, remains in that position until he dreams of his medicine. During this time he abstains from food and water. Then, in his dreams, the bird, reptile, or animal, that is to act as his guardian angel through life appears to him.

Of like character was the vision-questing among the Lenni Lenape, a branch of the great Algonquin Nation, who occupied what is now eastern Pennsylvania, New Jersey, and part of Delaware. Each of the youths was taught that a guardian spirit, usually a totem animal, watched over him and would in due course reveal itself in a dream. Having prepared himself to meet his guardian spirit, the youth "sought out the noblest height in the region and for days and nights, without food, silent, motionless, alone, awaited the revelation. From the terrors of this mysterious vigil he returned a man, ready to assume grave responsibilities with the help of his spiritual protector."[140]

The Indian youth of the flat prairie regions, not having been favored like the Indian youth of mountainous regions with easy access to sacred High Places, found his solitude in woods or isolated places. In the vision-quest of the youth of the Yuma tribes, the Shining Beings rather than symbolic totem animals appeared and advised him concerning the responsibilities of the mature life upon which he was about to enter.

A very remarkable vision was vouchsafed to Plenty-Coups, chief of the Crows (Asarokees), when he was but nine years old. After having fasted and purified his body, he went to a sacred mountain. From there, on the fourth night of his vision-quest, he was taken to an assembly of the Little-People, as Irish seers who have similar psychic experiences also call them, and their chief taught him that greatness comes from exercising one's innate powers, that by dependence upon himself alone, which would lead him to success, he would become, as he eventually did, the chief of his tribe. Plenty-Coups testified that during the seventy and more years of his life he was conscious of the aid of the Little-People, and he begged their pardon if in telling of them he erred.

Having told of this strange experience, Plenty-Coups said in conclusion, "I *know* myself now." How many White Men, proud

---

[140]Cf. E. E. Gray and L. R. Gray, *op. cit.,* p. 10.

of their book learning and literacy and academic degrees, are as truly educated as was Plenty-Coups?

In another vision, when he was not yet ten, on the same mountain, where four real eagles stood round about him fearlessly as though guarding him, he was shown a vision of himself as an old man and how the black buffalo would go forever and be replaced by the spotted buffalo of the White Man who would possess the land, and that although he would be childless, which proved to be true, he would, indeed, become the chief man of his people. In this vision, he was admonished that it is not strength of body but the mind that leads a man to power.

Plenty-Coups told of tribal seers who long before his time had dreamt of the coming of railroads and iron horses and flying wagons and many-storied buildings. Traditions tell of pre-Columbian Red Men who foresaw the advent of the White Man and described the sort of clothing he would wear and the weapons he would have. The art of planting tobacco-seed is said to have been revealed in a Red Man's dream. Plenty-Coups reported how even a White Man, living as a member of the Crow tribe, had a true vision, such as a Red Man immersed in the same psychically-charged environment might have.[141]

To Linderman's book, *American,* which makes possible this authentic insight into the psychic life of a great Red Man, Plenty-Coups, the writer here expresses his indebtedness. He heartily recommends *American* to all students who believe, as he does, that the Red Man can be understood aright only by understanding him psychically, quite apart from his physical and mundane propensities. Accordingly, the most culturally valuable approach to the right knowing of the Red Man is through psychic research. To this end, ethnology and archaeology are merely subsidiary and not, as anthropologists are apt to assume, all-important.

[141]Cf. F. B. Linderman, *American, The Life Story of a Great Indian* (New York, 1930), pp. 34–47, 60–75, 97, 124–25, 240–41.

Reflections

PART IV

The Magic of the Red Deer Dance
and the Taos Sacred Mountain

The Red Deer Dance began, and the Sacred Mountain which haunts the sky northwestward from Taos shuddered and poured out a cold, flaming cloud to the sun and all the stars. It seemed that way. And veritably, within its own affirmation, through a multitudinous, stern, impassioned collective outgiving, the tribe's soul appeared to wing into the mountain, even to the Source of Things.

John Collier, in *The Indians of the Americas.*

4

Reflections

The fundamental doctrines of the naturalistic religion of the Red Men seem to have arisen as a direct outcome of self-realization, in the Hindu meaning of self-realization, born of yogic practices peculiarly American but akin, in some instances, to those of the Hindu and Tibetans. In other words, the non-Christianized Red Men believe only that which they realize through their own psychic experiences, mainly in dreams and in the disembodied state of "astral-body" projection. They cannot comprehend any religion divorced from such psychic experiences and based upon mere belief.

It may be assumed that the Red Man is not aware of the psychological import of his naturalistic religion. Probably, he does not know that his psychic practices, conducted in the solitudes of the wilderness or on sacred High Places, which induce his dreams and visions and inspire his holy-songs and give to him his assurance of repeated births and deaths, are an efficient means of entering into and exploring the arcane realm of the Unconscious, wherein lies the storehouse of memory, not of this life-time alone but of myriads of life-times in innumerable states of existence. As

Plato would add, the Unconscious is also the reservoir of all archetypal ideas, or, as modern Jungian psychology teaches, the source of that universal symbolism underlying all mythologies and transcendent cultural manifestations.

Quite unlike the devotees of almost all other religions, the non-Christian Red Man holds no essential belief based wholly upon Bibles, traditions, or dogmatic theology. To him, Bibles, traditions, and dogmatics are not essential to the Inner Wisdom. In this way, the uncorrupted Red Man is in accord with the Buddha when He advised His disciples not to believe anything merely because it is recorded in scriptures, handed down by tradition, or taught by gurus, but to hold fast only to that which by their own spiritual realization they knew to be true.

II. OCCULT FORCES

Apparently their High Places, as well as lesser places, became sacred to the Red Men not by haphazard choice but because their actual magnetic and psychic forces were perceptible by psychically-awakened medicine-men. As noted, the essentiality of these forces was called *orenda* by the Iroquois, literally meaning "[holy] chant" or "[holy] song," implying a mysterious, indefinable power invocable by means of magical or mantric sound. The Sioux word *wakan,* implying "power which makes or brings things to pass," and the Algonquin word *manitu,* translatable as "mystery," convey substantially the same meaning. In other cultures, geographically far apart, there are terms with similar meaning, such as *baraka* in Morocco, referring to the sanctity associated with holy persons, sacred places and objects; and *mangyur,* used among the Kabi tribe of Queensland, Australia, to express the "vitality" with which a medicine-man is charged and effects his miracles.[1] The Sanskrit term *prāna* likewise refers to an impalpable but psychically perceptible principle or essence which, as in yoga, may be derived by man from the air, water, and earth; and it is in virtue of *prāna* that the yogin or saint attains supernormal powers.[2] That

[1] Cf. R. R. Marett, *Mana, Encyclopedia of Religion and Ethics* (New York, 1916), viii, pp. 375–80.
[2] According to Patanjali (*Yoga Sutras* III, 41), it is by controlling the force which governs the prana that a yogin acquires the power to surround his body with a blaze of light.

which is known as *mana* by the Melanesian and other Pacific races also appears to be practically synonymous with what the Red Men know as *orenda, wakan, manitu,* or by other means.

The late J. N. B. Hewitt of the Smithsonian Institution's Bureau of American Ethnology, himself a Tuscarora Indian of the Iroquois family, defined *orenda* as an immaterial, impersonal force, principle, or magic power "assumed to be inherent in every body or being of nature." It is a dynamic energy associated with all natural phenomena affecting mankind's welfare, although limited in its function and efficacy, local rather than omnipresent, and objectively embodied. Its possession is a distinctive characteristic of all deities.[3]

A medicine-man may attract, accumulate, localize, and transfer *orenda.* As a magnet magnetizes iron, or radium or atomic energy makes a locality radioactive, so *orenda,* either spontaneously or through magnetic and psychic radiations from human and non-human beings, makes a locality magnetically and psychically effective for all living things that come within the radius of its influence. Every animate thing coming into birth adds its own *orenda* to the collective total of the Earth's *orenda.*

Similarly, following R. H. Codrington in *The Melanesians, mana* has been described by the late Dr. R. R. Marett, Reader in Social Anthropology in the University of Oxford and the writer's Oxford tutor, as a power or excellence which is supernatural in so far as it is "what works to effect everything which is beyond the ordinary power of men, outside the common processes of nature." It is an impersonal force resembling electricity in that a material object may be its vehicle. Essentially, this power belongs to personal beings [incarnate and discarnate] to originate or manifest, but it is not fixed in anything; it is indiscriminately at the service of religion for social good or of the black art for social ill. Although not personal, *mana* adheres to personal beings. In some aspects it amounts to intelligence and will-power. It is present in greater or lesser degree in all beings of the invisible realms as in all beings of this world, in mankind and in animals; and in plants, stones, meteors, clouds, storms, and processes of nature. Acquir-

[3]Cf. T. R. Henry, *op. cit.,* pp. 11, 62–63; J. N. B. Hewitt, *Handbook of North American Indians,* Bureau of American Ethnology, Smithsonian Institute (Washington, D.C., 1907).

ing *mana* or its benefits for oneself, or for the family or tribal unit, is the aim of all Melanesian prayers, sacrifices and religious observances generally, as it is among the Red Men to acquire *orenda* or its equivalent. *Mana* is the most appropriate term "to express magico-religious value as realized in and through ritual." *Mana* and *tabu* always denote each other. The civilized man's notion of luck is a genuine, although degraded, member of the *mana* group conception.[4]

Perhaps we may regard *mana* or *orenda* as an unseen influence behind all cosmic operations and thus the life-directing principle in man and in gods, and in all inanimate things. One possessing it in superabundance and knowing how to use it wisely, as does a medicine-man, a master yogin, or a Tibetan oracle-priest, may heal, interpret dreams and omens, read the mind, foretell the future, and perform miracles, including the restoring of life to an organic form assumed to be dead.

It is this occult power, principle, or quintessence that gives sacredness to sages, totem animals, trees, plants, gems, material substances, inanimate objects, springs, bodies of water, places, and mountains wherein it is superabundantly present or finds focus and whence issue its emanations. It also has astrological correlations, in such manner that certain days, seasons, and epochs are holy solely in virtue of its then greater outpouring upon, or throughout, the Earth and its consequent increased influence in human affairs. Hence, among the pre-Columbian Red Men as among other psychically-awakened races in all known ages, there were celebrated at such sacred times the most solemn esoteric rites and the greater initiations. By partaking of the flesh and blood of an incarnate divinity, or symbolically of a discarnate one, as in world-wide eucharistical ceremonies, ancient and modern, the devotee shares in the divinity's *orenda*. By means of *orenda*, heavenly beings may bestow divine grace and protective guidance upon men.

Even today, despite the cultural chaos imposed upon them by their Christian despoilers, the surviving Red Men throughout the Americas intuitively recognize the esoteric import of their profound doctrine of *orenda*. Anciently, the European races were in

[4] Cf. R. R. Marett, *op. cit.*

psychic at-one-ment with the Red Men in this recognition. Then, when the Mystery Schools were closed in Europe, and Christendom, in the ensuing Darkness, exulted in its self-imposed ignorance and anathematized the Children of the Light in the Old World, the ancient at-one-ment was disrupted.

Had the European peoples fostered that True Light which lights every man who comes into incarnation, Columbus and all who came after him to the New World would have come as Children of the Light to the Children of the Light, reverencing every one of human kind of every race and faith. But now, alas, it will require immeasurable time, perhaps many centuries, to restore the ancient at-one-ment, and overcome the racial arrogance and religious intolerance to which its disruption gave rise, because of Christendom's wrong understanding and tragic errors.

In accord with our own interpretation, Max Freedom Long, in *The Secret Science Behind Miracles,* sets forth the teachings of the Hawaiian priests called *kahunas* concerning *huna* (meaning "secret"), synonymous with *mana* or *orenda*. He, too, recognizes it as a universal secret power. He states, as the outcome of his careful research, that it works independently of men's religious beliefs and is the motivating force of magical and psychical practices, inclusive of fire-walking, neutralization of gravity so that physical objects can be moved regardless of their size and weight (as appears to have been done by the builders of cyclopean structures throughout the world), and also of materialization, clairvoyance, telepathy, thought-reading, crystal-gazing, mental-healing, and weather-control, including rain-making.

By means of mind-directed *mana, prāna, huna,* or *orenda,* the human body can be levitated and transported through the air, as in the instance of Milarepa. Material things can be disintegrated and then transported and then reintegrated. By the transfer of this electric-vital force from medicine-man to patient, through the laying on of hands, magical intonations, and mental concentration, disease is neutralized and the body's natural harmony restored. If the disease be due to a loss of this force, the loss can be compensatorily repaid by the practitioner. It can be beneficially transmitted from the living to the dead and vice versa, as implied by *The Tibetan Book of the Dead.* It may be stored for a time in living tissue, in material objects, and in water. By its stimulating and inspiring presence, one becomes, within karmic limits, a magnetic personality capable of great deeds, or a world-moving genius. The degree of *mana* or *huna* present in any living creature, or in any object or place, may be determined by its respective aura. Spiritual non-human beings of numerous species may influence mankind for good or ill by employing this force. Many peoples, including the cultured Greeks and Romans, maintained that from whatever is offered in sacrifice, be it a human being, an animal, or food, the invoked deities and lesser spirits absorb, by a process of psychic osmosis, these subtle vital essences.

III. SACRED PLACES AND THEIR GUARDIANS

To the problem of the existence of orders of normally invisible beings, such as the Red Men call Shining Beings and the Hindus Devas, and believed by them to inhabit sacred places, the author devoted his first book, *The Fairy-Faith in Celtic Countries*. As a result of nearly four years of psychic research among the Celtic peoples of Ireland, Isle of Man, Scotland, Wales, Cornwall, and Brittany who believe in various species of fairies inhabiting an invisible Otherworld, he concluded that there is trustworthy evidence for the existence of such beings.

These Shining Beings, or Devas, are perceived by the medicine-man to be the guardians of the sacred places. A European student of the occult sciences reports that great devas "magnetize the Earth and guard certain sacred spots on the Earth's surface, holding them in trust for a future of wonders. . . . One such spot is in County Wicklow, Ireland, another is the heart of covenanting Scotland; close to Amiens, in France, is a third, and still another is in the Campagna, near Rome. The vast steppes of Russia have a sacred spot, and in India there are several. America hides three, of which one is located in California in a spot not yet disclosed, but the healing effect of the entire south (of California) is due to its presence."[5] Canada has two, Australia one, and New Zealand one. Apart from these, which are the most important, there are a few others of major importance. Many of more or less minor

[5]Cf. "The Involutionary World Process," by the Old Professor, in *The Beacon* (Tunbridge Wells, England, Nov. 1955), p. 185.

importance exist throughout all the continents. Cuchama seems to be, to whatever degree, another such magnetized spot.

The late George William Russell (1867–1935), the well-known Irish poet-seer, often referred to as A. E., described to the author the resplendent appearances of great devas which he had seen in the mountains and elsewhere in Ireland, the Sacred Isle, and of which he painted likenesses. He also reported his awareness of sacred spots in Ireland, some of them High Places, guarded by such devas.

The late William Butler Yeats (1865–1939) told the author of having seen fairy beings in Ireland and of his conviction of the existence of magnetized and psychically-charged places there inhabited by fairies. In County Sligo, he took the author to such fairy haunts. The testimony of both these modern seers is recorded in *The Fairy-Faith in Celtic Countries.* A. E.'s is given under "An Irish Mystic's Testimony," on pages 59 to 65, and that of Yeats on page 66.

IV. OTHERWORLD BEINGS

A. E. and Yeats, as well as other seers among the Celtic and the Oriental peoples, are in agreement with the Red Men, that in the Otherworld—unlike in the human world where man is the only species of visible beings possessed of superior intelligence—there are many species of intelligent beings, some of which appear to be endowed with intelligence greater than that of man.

Anthropologically it is important to note that not only was A. E. a cultured seer, but also a man conspicuously successful in practical affairs in Dublin, where for many years he edited *The Irish Homestead,* which sponsored and brought into being co-operative associations throughout rural Ireland. Sometimes A. E. induced in himself the state of clairvoyance and at other times the visions arose spontaneously. He reported that it was usually after being away from cities and towns long enough to throw off their auric influences and to become attuned to the rhythm of the Irish countryside that he saw Otherworld beings. Similarly, by attaining psychic equilibrium, far from the haunts of men, the youth of the Red Men, too, were vouchsafed their visions of guidance. "The whole west coast of Ireland," A. E. explained, "from Donegal to Kerry seems charged with a magical power, and I find it easiest to see while I am there. I have always found it comparatively easy to see visions while at ancient monuments like New Grange and Dowth, because I think such places are naturally charged with psychical forces, and were for that reason made use of long ago as sacred places." A. E. also reported visions in which he and other persons collectively participated. Having known these percipients intimately, I am able to state that as percipients they fulfilled all essential pathological conditions required by psychologists in order to make their evidence acceptable.

A. E. distinguished between what he called Shining Beings and Opalescent Beings: "The beings whom I call the Sidhe [the ancient Irish name of these Otherworld beings], I divide, as I have seen them, into two great classes: those which are shining, and those which are opalescent and seem lit up by a light within themselves. The Shining Beings appear to be lower in the hierarchies; the Opalescent Beings are more rarely seen, and appear to hold the positions of great chiefs or princes."

In answer to my question, "Can you describe the Shining Beings?" A. E. said:

> It is very difficult to give any intelligible description of them. The first time I saw them with great vividness I was lying on a hillside alone in the west of Ireland, in County Sligo: I had been listening to [fairy-like] music in the air, and what seemed to be the sounds of bells, and was trying to understand these aerial clashings in which wind seemed to break upon wind in an ever-changing musical silvery sound. Then the space before me grew luminous, and I began to see one beautiful being after another.

Concerning the Opalescent Beings, which A. E. believed correspond in a general way to what the pre-Christian Irish called gods, and which, in the writer's view, are akin to the gods of the High Places and other sacred localities of the Red Men, A. E. contributed the following remarkable testimony:

> The first of these I saw I remember very clearly, and the manner of its appearance: there was at first a dazzle of light, and then I saw that this came from the heart of a tall figure with a body apparently shaped out of half-transparent or opalescent air, and throughout the body ran a radiant electrical fire, to which the heart seemed the

center. Around the head of this being and through its waving luminous hair, which was blown all about the body like living strands of gold, there appeared flaming wing-like auras. From the being itself light seemed to stream outward in every direction; and the effect left on me after the vision was one of extraordinary lightness, joyousness, or ecstasy.

V. SELF-REALIZATION

To the impartial anthropologist, it is quite understandable why the Red Men were looked upon by their arrogant and ruthless White conquerors and despoilers, who professed to be Christian, as being illiterate and uncouth savages. Literacy, conventional bodily attire, and "civilized" ways of living are not, as has been shown in *The Tibetan Book of the Great Liberation,* prerequisites for the attaining of spiritual insight. Although all those who profess and call themselves Christians ought to know this, they almost invariably have refused to acknowledge it in practice when in contact with natural, or primitive, peoples.

Although illiterate and unsophisticated (as were many of the Great Sages of India and Tibet), save for a small minority of nobles and priests chiefly in Mexico, Central America, and Peru, and unattached to the accumulation of private property, the Red Men possessed the invaluable technique for attaining self-realization. The singer of one of their holy-songs sang of how, by going into solitude, wisdom was revealed to him. Such wisdom must be differentiated from knowledge, or intellectual understanding.[6] It is the natural product of that self-knowing which is born of Right Meditation and not of the pursuit of that knowledge, which, being of the mundane, the transitory and the perishable, is often an impediment in the pursuit of the Truth.

Thus did the pre-Columbian races of the Americas practice a yoga as efficient, in some respects, as that of the Orient; and, like the present-day peoples of India and Tibet, were more spiritually evolved than the peoples of Europe who plundered them and

[6]This is made clear in *The Tibetan Book of the Great Liberation* on pages 15–24.

cold-bloodedly sought their total destruction. The White Man, rather than the Red Man, is rightfully to be regarded as the savage, despite his literacy and what he considers to be civilization.

Like the Oriental yogin, the Red Man knows that emphasis upon the world of appearances, wherein the consciousness of the White Man is centered, is not essential to the enjoyment of the good life. The Red Man has, as John Collier points out, that which the White Men have lost because of their attachment to intellectualisms rather than to wisdom: Namely, the psychic means to enter at will into the Otherworld, as the also psychically-endowed Celtic peoples call it, where time and space and consciousness are not of this world of incarnate humanity.

Unlike the White Man, the races of the pre-Columbian Americas commonly had no fear of death, because, having a religion based upon realization rather than upon faith, they knew that death in this world is birth into another world, and that birth into this world is death in the Otherworld. Like the Druids of Gaul, Britain, and Erin, the Red Men perceived, as the Buddha did, that man is involved in the Circle of Necessity, is bound to the Wheel of Life, and that, therefore, the living do come from the dead and the dead from the living unceasingly.

In another respect like the Druids, most of the Red Men north of the Rio Grande reared no shrines or temples. Their temples were the solemn music-filled forests, the vast sun-enhaloed prairies, and the sacred High Places. No need had these Red Men, the psychically self-educated and intuitive Children of Nature, of written books. Very rightly would they be in attunement with Milarepa, the great yogin and saint of Tibet, when he sang:

> I am Milarepa, great in fame,
> The direct offspring of Memory and Wisdom.
>
> * * * * * *
>
> From my lips springeth forth a little song,
> For all Nature, at which I look,
> Serveth me for a book.[7]

[7]Cf. W. Y. Evans-Wentz, *Tibet's Great Yogi Milarepa* (Oxford University Press, 1951), p. xviii.

The singers of the holy-songs of the Red Men might sing, as did Milarepa, of the non-necessity of books and intellectual acquirements in the seeking of wisdom:

> Accustomed long to meditating on the Whispered Chosen
>   Science,
> Knowledge of erring Ignorance I've lost.
> * * * * * *
> Accustomed, as I've been, to meditation on this life and the
>   future life as one,
> I have forgotten the dread of birth and death.
> * * * * * *
> Accustomed long to application of each new experience to mine
>   own growth spiritual,
> I have forgot all creeds and dogmas.[8]

Like the youths of the Red Men, Milarepa, as a young man, went into solitude to acquire Right Understanding, as he did most successfully, and in fullness, in caves of the high Himalayan ranges of Tibet. He also sought out there the sacred High Places of pilgrimage. Of this he sings, just as the Red Men would:

> Accustomed long to studying, all by myself, mine own
>   experiences,
> I have forgot the need of seeking the opinions of friends
>   and brethren.
> * * * * * *
> Accustomed long to keep my mind in the Uncreated State
>   of Freedom,
> I have forgot conventional and artificial usages.[9]

The Great Sage, the Buddha, likewise discarded books, and even gurus, and, in solitude, beneath a bo-tree in the jungles of India, attained the Nirvanic State of One Fully Awakened.

When Milarepa made the Great Renunciation, in emulation of the Buddha, he sang a holy-song of his determination to go into solitude amidst the eternal snows of the Himalayas. He vowed to remain there until either death or the Awakening should come to him. In similar manner, the youth of the Red Men feared neither dangers nor hardships nor death itself, in the supreme endeavour to know the Great Mystery.

[8] *Ibid.*, p. 246.
[9] *Ibid.*, p. 246.

VI. THE WHITE MAN'S SPIRITUAL INFERIORITY

The religion of the European White Man is, for him culturally, a foreign importation, alien to his Aryan racial heredity. It represents, in large measure, the outcome of a struggle for social adjustment and cultural integration, through half-hearted acceptance and practice of a super-imposed theology based upon scriptures and tradition, rather than upon a science of self-realization.

Apart from the Mysteries and the philosophically-shaped religions of Greece, all of which were, in essentials, direct outgrowths of Orientalism, and apart also from the religion of the half-Aryan Celtic peoples, which, like that of the Red Men, is psychically based and psychically efficient, the European White Man, quite unlike the Red Man, has not as yet evolved a satisfying, self-realizable religion of his own. In this respect, he is, in relation to religion as a scientific method of right-living, parasitical, while the Red Man is constructive. This religious parasitism of the White Man has resulted in his present-day spiritual impotence, the inevitable outcome of his failure to exercise his psychic faculties.[10] In terms of applied spirituality, psychic efficiency, and social psychology rather than of applied science and technology the White Man is, therefore, inferior to the Red Man.

[10]After this conclusion had been set forth here, I found confirmatory support for it in the following account by Mary Austin, a psychic, in *Experiences Facing Death* (Indianapolis, 1931), page 100: "I have tried out in my own practice every psychic device discovered among American Indians, and find them superior in most cases to what was known by the general public twenty-five years ago. . . . and the Amerind use of rhythm for healing and for raising the plane of group activity is far in advance of anything of ours."

And, correlatively, of the superiority of the Red Man as a social being, the late A. Hyatt Verrill, in *The Real Americans,* page 52, after having had vast and intimate acquaintance with the Red Men in most parts of the Americas, testifies as follows: "I have never yet met a primitive Indian, or one who had not been ruined by civilization, who knowingly lied, who intentionally broke his word or a promise, or who was dishonest."

Not only have the Red Men generally, when living in their natural ancestral environment, been found to surpass the White Men in psychic ability and morality, but intelligence tests conducted jointly by the Indian Bureau and the University of Chicago between Indian children and white children of a rural area of the Middle West of the United States showed the Indian children to be equal and in most instances superior to the white children. In one test, every Indian group had a higher average than the white children. Cf. H. E. Fay and D. McNickle, *Indians And Other Americans* (New York, 1959), pp. 117–18.

In India, the Aryans, unlike those of Europe, have never suffered a break of cultural continuity. Their culture has been unitary and integrated from the prehistoric time of the evolution of the naturalistic religion of the *Vedas,* which is very much like the naturalistic religion of the Red Men, to that of the unsurpassed yogically-based religion of the *Upanishads* and of Buddha. This state of India's cultural wholeness still prevails. But in Europe the Aryan cultural continuity was shattered irreparably by the impact of the same Semitically-shaped faith which sought and still seeks to destroy the cultural heritage of the Aryans of India and of the Red Men of the Americas.

It is because of this deplorable shattering of their ancestral culture that the Aryan peoples of Europe became religiously and psychically confused and so failed to make, save fragmentarily, their rightful Aryan contribution to mankind's spiritual growth. Whereas, in contrast, the Red Man made a very remarkable contribution.

VII. THE RED MAN'S CULTURAL TRIUMPH

Christianity, after its triumph in Europe, incorporated in its own synthetic system (shaped, as St. Augustine perceived, of many heterogeneous elements originally pagan) outstanding fragments of Europe's shattered Aryan culture. Notable among these are the primeval Celtic November Day, in honor of the dead and of beings of the Otherworld, which became two separate days, All Souls Day and All Saints Day; the Day of the rebirth of the Sun, at the winter solstice, which became Christmas; and the joyous festival of the resurrection of life in the springtime, in honor of the Germanic goddess of rebirth, Eostre, which became Easter. Similarly, by its spoliation of the American religions, the Church of Rome enriched itself more exoterically and materially than esoterically and spiritually; thus, in Mexico and Peru, with no true understanding or gratitude, it built its churches on the Red Man's holy-sites and sacred High Places. But, compensatorily, throughout the Americas, the Red Men, in religious self-defense, only nominally adopted the Christianity of their despoilers. They frequently did so that the new religion might serve more as a protective, camouflaging veneer for their own psychically satisfying and realizable religions than as a substitute for them. In other parts of the world it was this same sort of militant Christianity which absorbed or compromised with the non-Christian cults of the aboriginal races. In the Americas, it is the non-orthodox cults which have compromised with, and to some undeterminate degree absorbed, exoteric Christianity.[11]

Roman Christianity, however grave its errors in Mexico and South America in supporting Cortez and Pizarro, was far wiser and more worthy of respect in allowing compromise (as is well illustrated by the still flourishing pre-Columbian cults of the Virgin of Tonantzin and the Virgin of Zapopan directly under the auspices of the Church of Rome) than was Protestantism north of the Rio Grande in its uncompromising and irrational iconoclastic zeal for destroying outright the Red Man's religious and cultural heritage; and, in too many instances, by allying itself with governmental policies directed to the extermination of the native American races.

What need has the psychically developed Red Man of unrealizable creeds and mere belief when he can investigate and know the Otherworld itself at first-hand?[12] Like the Celtic peasant seers, he has no need of mere belief or argument as to whether or not there exists an after-death state, for he can realize it.

[11]As shown by the distinguished ethnologist, Pablo Gonzales Casanova, this process of compromise and absorption is particularly marked in Mexico. See *The Indian Heritage* in *The Genius of Mexico,* edited by B. C. Herring and K. Terrill (New York, 1931), pp. 47–57.

[12]A Navaho headman, furious at the aggressive methods of Christian missionaries to destroy American culture, expressed himself in the following forcible words: "Why don't these missionaries go home? Why do they come here? Why do they bother us? We have a good religion. It is a religion of good. It teaches good. It tells us not to bother anyone. It is the same religion for all the People. Now come these missionaries with seven religions. They all talk different. They divide our people. They make trouble among us. Why don't these missionaries go home?" Cf. Erna Fergusson, *op. cit.,* p. 198.

Well aware of this very justifiable anti-Christian attitude of many of the Indians, the late Father Carey Ellis, a much-beloved Catholic missionary in British Guiana, frankly and succinctly told the late A. Hyatt Verrill, "You cannot Christianize an Indian without civilizing him and you cannot civilize him without ruining him." Correlatively, the Hopi Indian Thomas Banyacya testifies: "Our young people are educated. They then come home and look down on our religious teachings." Cf. *Indian Views,* League of North American Indians, no. 4, p. 15.

In league with the same Christian forces of cultural disruption and destruction which overwhelmed the Aryan culture of Europe, the government of the United States, despite its Constitution's guarantee of freedom of religious worship, employed its armed forces to massacre the non-conforming Red Men, in compliance with an established policy about which John Collier has given testimony. In the end, however, this inhumane policy failed; the Red Men and their religion could not be annihilated, as have been almost all the aboriginal races and religions of Australia and Tasmania by Christians.

Today, on most of the reservations within the United States, and generally in the villages throughout Mexico and South America, the Red Men are increasing in number. Perhaps nowhere else in the world at any time has an imposed religion of a conquering race been so half-heartedly accepted as Roman Catholicism south of the Rio Grande and Protestantism north of the Rio Grande by the Red Men.

Although throughout the Americas all too many of the advocates of Christianity fanatically sought either the conversion or else the destruction of the Red Men, as they generally have that of all non-Christians throughout the world, they failed to uproot completely the native American religions. Now, happily, the Red Men, no longer under the Christians' sentence of death, can dance their holy-dance in honor of Father Sun, their Spirit Dance in invocation of the beings of the Otherworld, and their Snake Dance to call upon the cosmic forces to vouchsafe rain and fruitage of Mother Earth. Freed from the massacre-threatening proscriptions with which the White Man unjustly and illegally fettered them, the children of the Great Mystery can now sing with a joyful voice the holy-songs and the mountain-songs. They can sing in praise of the beneficent and protective powers sanctifying the solitudes and sacred High Places.

VIII. THE SPIRIT OF AMERICA

Although well over four centuries have passed since Spain, supported by the Holy See, brought pillage, desecration, and death among the Red Men south of the Rio Grande, the survivors have not forgotten the awful martyrdom. Perhaps no one of them in our generation has given better expression to their resentment than Señor Abraham Arias-Larreta. He summarized their pressing social needs for liberty of conscience and emancipation from the oppressive fetters fastened upon them by such professional Christians as the Dominican Valverde (who absolved Pizarro and his soldiers from the massacre of approximately ten thousand innocent and unarmed Red Men massed in the plaza of the Peruvian city of Caxamalca) and the Jesuit Arriaga (who, exulting in the destruction of the culture and religion of the Incas by his fellow Christians, wrote the fanatically-inspired work entitled, *Estirpacion de la Idolatria de los Indios del Peru*). As its title suggests, this work of Arriagas is one more recorded account bearing witness to that martyrdom. It is in the following words that Señor Arias-Larreta thus speaks, mainly on behalf of the Red Men of today south of the Rio Grande:

> [The Statue of] Pizarro, set up in the portico of the Cathedral, is the symbol of the races who [have continued to] subjugate the Republic ever since [the time of] the colony. . . . And while confronting the problem of the Indian, let us not forget that economic and cultural advantage will mean nothing without restitution of his liberty of conscience. . . . Bread and learning are not enough for us Indians. His [the Indian's] sense of justice must be freed from the oppressive fetters that the Valverdes and the Arriagas, of the time of the Conquest, fastened upon it. The same must be done with the half-breed, who inherited the fetters. . . . What we need is to redeem our conscience and its free will, effacing secular enslavement from memory. Then the spirit of America will speak.[13]

IX. WORLD FEDERATION: AN AMERICAN IDEAL

The great religious ideal of universal brotherhood by means of political union was indigenously American, as shown by the Iroquois Confederacy brought into being by Degandawida and Hiawatha.[14] The English colonists were directly inspired by it, as suggested by Benjamin Franklin's reference to the Iroquois scheme of union as being applicable to the Thirteen Colonies; and the Thirteen Colonies became the nucleus of the United States of

[13]Cf. Abraham Arias-Larreta, *Literaturas Aborigines, Azteca, Incaica, Maya-Quiche, Coleccion Sayari* (Los Angeles, 1951), pp. 11–12.
[14]Cf. Luis Quintanilla, *A Latin American Speaks* (New York, 1943), pp. 243–46.

America. Simón Bolivar, the South American Liberator, was also inspired by it and, along with Degandawida and Hiawatha, is counted among the pioneer seed-sowers of Pan-Americanism and of the League of Nations, which has been reborn as the United Nations.

When the twenty-one republics of the Americas and Canada are federated, as they are destined to be, in fulfillment of Degandawida's great vision, then may come the federation of Europe, of Asia, and of Africa, and, at last, the Federation of the World. And of this glorious realization of mankind's age-old dream of social at-one-ment, the Red Men, especially Degandawida and Hiawatha, will have been in no small measure among the prime inspirers.

Among the Oklahoma Shawnees there is still current the prophecy that Tecumseh (1768–1813), their great hero and dreamer of an all-Indian confederacy, will be reborn and achieve this ideal, for which he gave his life in battle against the White Men at the age of forty-five.[15]

X. THE WISDOM PATH OF SELF-CONQUEST

The secret virtues of the Red Man's religion and the mysteries of his sacred High Places will yet be universally acknowledged, and mankind will go to the sacred High Places among all nations and throughout all the continents for the healing of the earth-body, the restoration of the long-lost tranquillity of mind, and the attaining of that joyous Freedom which the Enlightened Ones proclaim. Then will the peoples of the world come to recognize in the naturalistic religion of the Red Men, whose Bible is Nature and whose method of attaining salvation is wholly dependent upon self-realization, a way of living here on Earth far more satisfying and scientific than that circumscribed by sophistical creeds and dogmatic theologies.

Thus, in addition to the many and invaluable contributions of the Red Man to the world's food resources, its art, architecture, and philosophy, he is also to be credited with having evolved a

[15]Cf. J. M. Oskison, *Tecumseh and His Times* (New York, 1938), p. 236. It is strangely interesting to observe that *Tecumseh,* the name of this noble and clear-seeing Red Man, means "Falling Star," or "Meteor," which in fact Tecumseh was in his swift and light-giving flight across the world from birth to death.

religion more psychically efficient and realizable than that of the White Man. And as has been suggested, this religion appears to have been fundamentally influential in the shaping of various cults more or less indigenously American which arose in the United States during the nineteenth century.

Because of centuries of conditioning by intellectually-shaped modern Christianity, the average White Man is now incapable of entering into the arcana of the Red Man's realizable religion. Lacking in psychic development, he cannot fathom the esoteric significance of Father Sun and Mother Earth. His city environment has separated him from their manifold beneficences. The world of the Red Man is a world apart. Though the White Man may try to enter it, he cannot, for the gods guard the entrance; and he does not possess the secret password. Nor will he ever possess it until he becomes, as ancestrally he was ages ago, a Child of Nature. His machines and his gadgets have become his fetters; and his cities will become, as they have in the past, the graveyards of his civilization. When the White Man's cities are but ruins, buried under the accumulated dust of the centuries for future archaeologists to explore, the life of the Red Men, so their seers prophesy, will still be flourishing. The youth of the Red Men will continue to seek the Vision of Guidance. He will continue to hear the Shining Beings call him "son." He will continue to attain Right Education and Right Guidance without books and without a written language. He will continue to attune himself to the voice of the silence of High Places; and there, he will be empowered to enter upon the Wisdom Path of Self-Conquest.

There is always a gate to any history. The Indians entered a certain gate, one which Columbus opened when he presented to Castille and to Leon a New World. On this imagined gate there was to be carved the verse from Dante: "Through me thou enterest into endless sorrow."

For those among the great Red Indian civilizations who entered the gate, the verse remains as their obituary. Enormous groups and cultures perished to the last Red Indian. But, today, thirty million American Indians on our hemisphere testify to the strength of the certainty that, having been admitted through the gate and undergone their purgatory, they shall rise again.

John Collier, in *The Indians of the Americas.*

XI. TRAGEDY AND TRIUMPH

Throughout the Americas, the Red Men at the very outset of their contact with the European invaders proffered the hand of friendship.[16] Had it been accepted in good faith, there would have been no massacres by either of the two peoples. Historical records show that almost, if not always, the White Man was the aggressor; and he, not the Red Man, is responsible for what the White Man calls the Red Man's ruthlessness, which was the direct and naturally human result of the aggressiveness of the White Man. The Red Man had more than adequate justification for resenting the White Man's treatment of him; and if warfare is ever justifiable, it was when the Red Man went on the warpath against the White Man.

The Red Man saw his home, his ancestral domain and his hunting grounds being shamelessly stolen. His personal liberty was lost. The laws of the land did not protect him. Treaties promising him protection were unilaterally and cynically broken, and pledges and vows were disregarded. In a few generations the buffalo herds were destroyed, most of the mountain-sheep, moose, and elk were killed, and the wild ducks, geese, turkeys, and pigeons were decimated almost to extinction. The wild nut-bearing trees were felled; the wild berry bushes were uprooted; the forests were cut down; and the springs dried. Even the maize fields were taken away.

The Red Man's truly American art was either ignored or greedily exploited, and nothing which was culturally his was rightly valued. Because of his simple and unconventional way of living, and often merely on account of the sun-produced pigmentation of his skin, he was denied social equality.

Throughout the democracy of the United States, although born and bred and living there, in the land of his prehistoric ancestors, he was (prior to the enactment of the Citizenship Act of 1924), denied, like a minor or criminal, the rights of citizenship for more than three centuries. "As late as 1938, seven states still refused to let Indians go to the polls."[17] Religious freedom was frequently

[16]Cf. G. B. Grinnell, *The Indians of Today* (New York, 1906), pp. 173–75.
[17]Cf. H. L. Peterson, *American Indian Political Participation* in *The Annals of the American Academy of Political and Social Science* (Philadelphia, 1957), Vol. 311, p. 121.

denied to him. Revered beliefs which psychically he knew to be realizable were ridiculed. Although generally unsuccessfully, missionaries sought to eradicate his beliefs. The fixed policy of the government of which he was a ward was to annihilate him. For the Red Man of North America there remained no assurance of sustenance and not even of life.

In Mexico and South America, his two great empires (in some important respects more advanced, at that time, than the empires of the Old World) were pitilessly and wantonly destroyed and given over to pillage and massacre unparalleled in known history. After more than four centuries, the Red Men of Mexico and South America are but slowly recovering from the savagery of the Spanish Christians led by Cortez and Pizarro.

North of the Rio Grande, where his people had lived in freedom and in happiness for innumerable millenniums, the Red Man became an outcast and in some instances a starving pauper. Today his Christian despoilers call him " 'treacherous, vindictive, fiendish, murderous,' because, in his just and righteous indignation and wrath, he rose up and determined to slay all he could find of the hated white race."[18] Distorted and dishonest histories of the Red Men are taught in public schools to the children of the White Men and in Christian mission schools to children of the Red Men. Films and television continue the travesty of truth, and brotherliness is thwarted.

In the words of John Collier, in *The Indians of the Americas,* pages 307–8, "There was no method of destruction that was not used against them, and most of them coped with all the methods of destruction. Legal proscription, administrative proscription, military slaughter, enslavement, *encomienda,* forced labor, peonage, confiscation of nearly all lands, forced dividualization of residual lands, forced dispersal, forced mass-migration, forced religious conversions, religious persecutions which hunted down the social soul to its depths, and the propaganda of scorn; catastrophic depopulation, which mowed down the native leadership and the repositories of tradition, bribery of leadership, and

[18]Cf. G. W. James, "What the White Race May Learn From the Indian" (Chicago, 1908), p. 22; J. M. Oskison, *Tecumseh and His Times* (New York, 1938), pp. 118–19.

the intrusion of quisling governments by the exploiting powers."

True it is that not all Red Men were, or are now, paragons of human virtues, nor evolved beyond warfare, any more than their white brethren. On the whole, however, the Red Man in his dealings with his white despoilers has shown himself to be more trustworthy, less covetous, less thievish, and no more savage than they.

As has been wisely stressed by H. G. Barnett in *Indian Shakers,* when a people's indigenous way of life is disrupted, social and moral decay inevitably results. This is well illustrated in the instance of the Indians of the Puget Sound region, where, from 1840 onward, their traditional economics, native religious beliefs, and tribal organizations were under constant attack. Their shamanistic practices were outlawed; their institutions were sometimes forcibly suppressed and supplanted by those of the White Man; their children were educated to scoff at their ancestral heritage; and all the elements of their pre-Columbian culture were challenged and belittled.

In like manner, generally throughout North America as a whole, the Red Men, unable to adapt immediately to a superimposed and totally different way of life, and with their aboriginal and emotional controls upset, turned in their frustration to sensuous and selfish gratifications, although knowing them to be fleeting and unsatisfactory. Without understanding the underlying motivation, the government of the United States was appalled when, as a direct outcome of its own policy, its Indian wards, thus socially demoralized, resorted to "whisky, gambling, idleness, and general vice."[19]

For very good reasons, then, this volume has been written in sympathy with the Red Man's point of view. For *his* religious culture, and not the White Man's has been the essential objective of our research. He alone, and not his despoilers and belittlers, has the right to bear testimony.

The author confesses his astonishment when, as the research proceeded, he began to perceive that the pre-Columbian races of the Americas had seers and sages comparable to those of Asia's

---

[19]Cf. H. B. Barnett, *Indian Shakers,* Southern Illinois University Press (Carbondale, 1957), pp. 337–38.

most highly civilized peoples, and a method of going into retreat for meditation and psychic development comparable, in some measure, to that of Patanjali's yoga. This, along with the study of the Red Man's religious practices generally, led him to the conviction that only as the Red Man is known psychically can he be known rightly, and that therefore, the many efforts to understand him made by Occidental scholars—historians, ethnologists, archaeologists, and anthropologists generally—although laudable and quite worthwhile in themselves, especially in the interests of the advancement of scientific learning, are really subsidiary to the main issue.

Accordingly, readers of this book will have recognized that its approach to what has been called the "enigma of the Red Man" is not only markedly religious in essence, but is fundamentally psychic, although in treatment suggestive and far from exhaustive.

No race of men, not even the race that reveres the Great Rishis, has been more otherworldly in their life on this planet than our pre-Columbian Americans. Yet, even in the things of this world they have been masterful, as witnessed by their marvellous achievements in Mexico, Yucatan, and Peru.

Albeit socially and culturally fragmented, the Red Man has miraculously survived the Night. Inspired by an indomitable confidence in the future, vouchsafed to him in virtue of his psychic and prophetic insight, he has transcended the long dire centuries of his martyrdom. Now he ascends, as his forefathers have before him, one of the sacred High Places; and, reaching the summit, he stands erect and calm. Facing the East, he intones the ancient holy-song to the morning star and makes salutation to the Dawn. The kindling light of the New Day of his freedom gladdens his heart and enhaloes him as he sings and awaits the coming forth of the ever-triumphant Sun.

XII. THE AMERICAN RENAISSANCE

Frank Waters, notable for his American ethnological studies, in a letter dated December 27, 1957, to the late G. Warrington Bass, an explorer of the ruined cities of Yucatan, wrote:

"The Indians of all the Americas will arise. They will become federated and amalgamated. They will build a city, but the city will be spiritual, not physical."

"Such a truly American Renaissance is, even now, beginning in a submerged, invisible manner, on a rising level of consciousness."

Warrington Bass believed that all such visions of an American Renaissance are inspired, in at least some degree, by a "projection of Occult Truth from one of the old Mystery Centers of Mexico." He tells of having felt this projection while in Yucatan in the year 1928. "There is," he added, "evidence that the Indians north of the Rio Grande, now on the increase, may be sufficiently rejuvenated for the Work, in which the Supreme Chiefs and their helpers throughout the Americas will occupy white bodies as well as red bodies. Many of the helpers are already incarnate, some consciously and some unconsciously preparing the way. When the Solar System shall have progressed nearer to Aquarius,[20] and vibratory and psychic conditions have thereby become suitable, the others, too, will manifest themselves either in the flesh or on a plane whence their overshadowing influence will be perceptible on Earth."

The First Inter-American Conference on Indian Life, which had direct effect on this developing American Renaissance, was sponsored by John Collier, then the head of the United States Indian Bureau. It was convened in Patzcuaro, Michoacan, Mexico, in 1940. Apart from its importance ethnically, the Conference was also important historically, for it represented the first officially-directed recognition of the unique cultural heritage of the Indians of all the Americas. It tended to awaken them to the need of greater unity of inter-tribal action, and resulted in the establishment of a permanent Inter-American Indian Institute.

As John Collier stated, Indian group-life, as organized in its Indian societies, has outworn all the many destructions brought against it by the White Man. "Now, at last, the Indians' delaying action has changed in some countries, is changing in others, to a strategy of advance. The proscriptions are ended, or are being

[20]It is difficult to state with mathematical accuracy when the Aquarian Age (under the rule of Saturn and Uranus) will begin. The sun, by precession of the equinoxes, traverses the thirty degrees, into which each sign of the zodiac is divided, in approximately 2,150 years. Circa A.D. 1 has been computed as an approximate date of the beginning of the Piscean Age, which precedes the Aquarian Age. Accordingly, we are now in a transitional and preparatory period, the Piscean Age to end and the Aquarian Age to begin about the year 2,160 A.D. Cf. W. W. Reid, *Towards Aquarius* (London, n.d.), p. 108.

ended. The nations are accepting the Indians' societies as being unkillable and even indispensable. . . . These Indian social units will become federated within nations and over national boundaries. . . . With the advance of 'integral' education, including bilingual literacy, the realized mental potential and the social energy of the Indian societies, and their biological vigor, will increase by hundreds, even thousands of percent. . . . As the Indian societies move from their four-centuries-long delaying action into a confident and rejoicing advance, expressions along many lines of literature, of the arts, of religion, and of philosophy will come into being. The ancient-modern Indian affirmation of the deathless man-nature relationship will flow into poetry and symbolic art of cosmic intensity, tranquillity, and scope. The movement will be inward and outward at one and the same time—inward to the world-old springs, buried or never buried, which still flow because the societies have not died; outward to the world of events and affairs."[21]

Today, numerically, the pre-Columbian Americans constituting these Indian societies are dominant in Mexico, Central and South America; and north of the Rio Grande, they are no longer a diminishing, but a steadily increasing and, on the whole, an economically prosperous people.[22] Although their ancestral culture is in somewhat temporary eclipse, they are steadily advancing towards that time, foreseen by their seers, when there will be a restoration of it, purified and made additionally glorious by their long centuries of suffering and martyrdom. Once they regain their untrammeled freedom, they appear to be destined to outdistance the White Man in a Renaissance which will be truly American, born from their inmost being, and not essentially technological

[21]John Collier, *op. cit.,* pp. 308, 312–13.
[22]Now in the enjoyment of citizenship and freedom of movement and occupation after three hundred years of exploitation and martyrdom, the Red Men of the United States rejoice, like prisoners unexpectedly set free. Approximately fifty-six million acres of land, not including hundreds of thousands of acres of desert and mountain non-arable land, are in their legal possession. The greater part of this land was allotted to them because the White Men considered it almost wholly worthless, but, today, many portions of it have been proven to be extremely rich in oil, uranium, and other minerals. As for other lands, wrongfully taken away from them, these long-suffering Red Men have been, at last, awarded many millions of dollars. [Ed. nt.: See Addendum for current status. C.A.]

and utilitarian like the White Man's.[23] So it is of far-reaching importance that we, Americans of European lineage, try to attain right understanding of the Red Man's profound idealism and racial aspirations. It is the author's hope that to that end this suggestive rather than exhaustive treatise will in some measure contribute.

When the Light of the American Renaissance shall have illuminated all the Americas, the European Americans will come to recognize and value the virtues and spiritual significance of the pre-Columbian cultural heritage. The world, as a whole, will be enriched by its contribution to mankind's advancement.

Let all Americans of European lineage rejoice in this cultural rebirth soon to come. Let them greet their American brethren of pre-Columbian lineage with fraternal love, and assist them to grow strong in their Great New Age. Thereby will be neutralized, in at least some degree, the heavy karma created by the lamentable greed and unbrotherliness of the conquering Europeans throughout the Americas in past centuries. All Americans, of every ethnic group and faith, will, at last, be enabled to attain the at-one-ment of human brotherhood, becoming One Nation, indivisible and spiritually mighty.

And then shall the Sacred Fire be kindled as of yore, not only on Sacred Mount Cuchama, but on all of the Americas' Hallowed Heights.

[23]Soon after this had been written, I received a copy of "A Message to the North American Indians" by Herbert C. Holdridge, a retired Brigadier General of the United States Army, dated at Sherman Oaks, California, October 22, 1958, in which there is a foreseeing of an American Renaissance. The message very rightly advises the younger generation of the Indians who are glamorized "by the white man's material life, his television sets, indoor plumbing, automobiles, schools, juke-boxes, and *whiskey,*" not "to surrender to the white man's degenerate civilization."

ADDENDA

The Indian Renaissance
by Frank Waters

One can't deny the fundamental truth in Dr. Evans-Wentz' belief that an Indian or "American Renaissance" is under way. Yet it seems too open to general disbelief and rejection when it is not supported by literal fact. Hence these comments are being added to help explain the basis for his belief, and for the factual reality as we view it today.

Perhaps no other portion of his book gave Dr. Evans-Wentz so much trouble. He was wholly in accord with the high aspiration and political achievement of John Collier, Commissioner of the United States Bureau of Indian Affairs, who directed the First Inter-American Indian Conference convened at Patzcuaro, Michoacan, Mexico, in 1940. The Conference resulted in the establishment of an Inter-American Indian Institute to promote the cause of all Indian peoples. The Institute was to be ratified by all governments through treaty, under which they were to establish their own national institutes and to support, through quota payments, the parent Institute. These provisions were carried out by most of the nineteen member nations. The United States, however, as Collier reported later, breached the treaty by refusing to vote the funds. Eventually the Institute broke down as an effective organization, and the plight of Indians throughout the Americas became grievously worse, as will be recounted.

185

John Collier retired from federal service in 1945, serving for a short time as Advisor on Trusteeship to the American Delegation at the first session of the General Assembly of the United Nations. He then established in Washington, D.C., the Institute of Ethnic Affairs to ameliorate the condition of all dependent peoples throughout the world. It was not a success. Long a personal friend of mine, he retired from public life to live quietly in Taos, New Mexico, until his death in 1968.

During these years, he wrote two books, *The Indians of the Americas,* 1947, and *On the Gleaming Way,* 1949. Both reaffirmed his belief that the Western Hemisphere would turn to Indian societies for guidance in the future, "even if the nations regress in their Indian programs." Dr. Evans-Wentz subscribed completely to Collier's belief; and, as we have noted, quoted voluminously from Collier's books in his own present volume. It is a pity these two men never met; they were both great idealists, great humanitarians, and great Indianists.

By 1957 it was apparent that the Patzcuaro Conference of 1940 had not achieved the pan-American Indian Renaissance blueprinted by Collier. I so wrote Dr. Evans-Wentz, after reviewing a draft of his manuscript, saying there was no factual basis for his belief in it.

About the same time, however, he sent me, through George Bass, a booklet entitled *The Coming of the Great White Chief.* It described a secret, ancient city in the mountains of southern Mexico inhabited by white-skinned Chigarau Indians ruled by a Great White Chief, who prophesied the amalgamation of all Indians under his teachings. The amalgamation purportedly had begun at the First Inter-American Indian Conference in Patzcuaro where the Great White Chief had informed the delegates that the time had come to build a magnificent Indian capitol. Five quarries in Central America had been selected to provide white marble for the temple. Soon the transportation of the marble and the migration of tribes toward the north would begin. The tribes would cross the Rio Grande River and journey west toward a range of mountains on which only the morning sun would shine. There they would build the Great White City with its white marble temple.

The booklet, as I wrote Dr. Evans-Wentz and Mr. Bass, seemed to me too spurious to be taken seriously. The Great White Chief

had not appeared at the Patzcuaro Conference, which I had attended at the invitation of Mr. Collier. There was no record of an
ancient city inhabited by white-skinned Chigarau Indians in the
mountains of southern Mexico, which I had visited. The proposed
migration north to a site in the United States, together with the
transportation of tons of marble, I could not envision in view of
immigration restrictions, customs duties, unavailable land, and
other mundane problems.

Mr. Bass answered my letter fully on January 20, 1958.

In spite of crude inaccuracies and phony names [he wrote] I
believe the main theme of the booklet contains a revelation of
tremendous spiritual significance as it affects the future of the
American continent. Otherwise I would not have sent it to you or
the Doctor. . . . The whole implies a higher plane of consciousness. . . . The elevation of the "city," its size, its walls, the white
or light color of its buildings, and its gates, are but symbols of
spiritual conditions. . . . The mighty migration northward and the
building of the Temple indicates a flow of spiritual force in the
desired direction and the establishment of a New Spiritual Center
from the Old American Mystery Center in southern Mexico. And
this is the essence of the whole booklet.

White Marble is the symbol of Purity and Truth. The cutting of
separate and distinct sizes from the five great quarries indicates the
garnered Spiritual Truths from each age of civilization, ours being
the fifth and nearing its end in degenerative chaos. . . . The building
of the Temple of Truth and Justice denotes the ushering in of the
sixth age of civilization centered on the North American continent. . . .

Reference is made to the finding of a range of mountains where
only the morning sun shall shine. The "morning sun" is the
Spiritual Sun which is *always* shining in the "East" as perceived
by the Spiritual Eye in man. And the "range of mountains" refers
to the Spiritual Heights, progressive levels of consciousness. . . .

The migration indicates the preparation made on higher planes
ahead of time, viz: the Spiritual Impulse projected by the Supreme
Chiefs, and the reincarnation of souls of a highly evolved class who
have had important experiences in American Indian civilization
either remote or more recent. Reincarnation takes place as the
facilities and needs of the new race are developed on the material
plane. . . .

The moral and spiritual regeneration of the Whites seems to be
the most necessary thing at the present time. . . .

Mr. Bass sent a copy of his letter to Dr. Evans-Wentz, enclosing a note which read in part, "I can assure you that in sending you the booklet, I had no other thought than a spiritual interpretation. . . . There is no question of the present Indian remnants north of the Rio Grande rejuvenating sufficiently for the work. The Masters and their helpers will use White bodies to a large extent for their work. Many of the helpers are already here, some consciously and others unconsciously preparing the way. As the Solar System progresses into Aquarius, conditions and vibrations will be suitable for their manifestation in the flesh or at least on a much lower plane where their overshadowing influence may be felt. . . ."

Dr. Evans-Wentz agreed with this occult interpretation. At the same time he regarded my literal reading as "trustworthy." He accordingly revised his section of the manuscript, sending it to Mr. Bass saying, "I shall be glad to have you send a copy to Frank Waters, to adjust to his own liking, and to add as much as he wishes, explaining that my free editing is, for him, tentative. If there is no objection on your part and his part, I intend to incorporate the matter as an Appendix in the book. The subject is of vast importance, and is more or less an outgrowth of the booklet discussion. . . . I anticipate that Frank Waters will greatly improve the presentation. No one other than himself is better fitted to add to it."

Hence I rewrote his revised draft, which he in turn rewrote. It included my statement, which he has quoted, that the Indians of the Americas would indeed build a city, but that it would be spiritual, not physical; and that the Renaissance would take place on a rising level of consciousness.

This subject has been developed in my recent book *Mexico Mystique,* whose sub-title *The Coming Sixth Age of Consciousness* parallels Mr. Bass' "sixth age of civilization." The book recounts the ancient Mayas' myth that there had existed four previous worlds successively destroyed by catastrophes. Their present Fifth World, according to their precise mathematical and astronomical computations, had begun in 3113 B.C. and would be destroyed in 2011 A.D., being succeeded by a new Sixth World. These successive worlds seem to me dramatic allegories for the great stages in the evolution of man's expanding consciousness. If so, they warrant a close look at the fantastic prediction made by the Mayas a thousand years ago.

The Mayan date of 2011 A.D. corresponds approximately to the date of 2160 A.D. given in the footnote on page 181 of the present book as the approximate ending of our present Piscean Age and the beginning of the Aquarian Age. It has still greater significance. For as the 2160-year Age of Pisces is the twelfth and last age of the zodiacal cycle, it marks also the end of the present great Precessional cycle of 25,160 years.

The approaching first age in the new Precessional cycle is that of Aquarius. Its astrological sign is the Water Bearer. As water is believed to be a symbol of the unconscious, this betokens another stage in man's continuous psychological development, in which he will add to his conscious, rational knowledge the truths hidden in the unconscious. Its advent seems to be already reflected in our recent interest in modern depth psychology, in ancient myths, and in the religious philosophies of the East and Indian America.

So we can't sell short too hastily the booklet of *The Coming of the Great White Chief.* For all its errors of fact, it reasserted a common myth born from the unconscious of all Indian America: the return of the Great White God to his people; the rebirth of their ancient culture after centuries of submergence; and the beginning of a new era of brotherhood with all mankind. How dear the belief, and how stubbornly it has persisted! From the Aztecs of Mexico, who believed the arrival of the Spanish conqueror Cortés was the return of the Great White God, Quetzalcoatl, to the present Hopis in Arizona who still nurture the prophecy that soon their Lost White Brother, Pahána, will return from the land of the rising sun to initiate an era when men of all races will be united.

The myth, for all its tribal variations, is the same. It is the unconscious projection of Indian America's longing for fulfillment and brotherhood with all races. It is the unfulfilled dream of all humanity. And it is the essence of Dr. Evans-Wentz' present book.

So much for mytho-religious tradition which wells from man's deep unconscious. Attuned to this pole of our dual nature, Dr. Evans-Wentz and Mr. Bass readily discerned the esoteric meaning below the literal surface of the disputed booklet. Most of us are attuned to the other pole, our rational consciousness, which relates us to the daily aspects of worldly life. The reconciliation of these two opposite polarities is, as Jung states, mankind's task for the future.

The difficulty is illustrated by the grievous problems confronting the Indians throughout the Americas. The picture has changed considerably since the regenerative reforms blueprinted by John Collier. The Pan-Indian movement is still a nebulous ideal. Throughout almost all countries the plight of the Indian populations has reached a new low.

In Brazil, the Amazon River basin of 1.5 million square miles had been the homeland of indigenous tribes numbering about one million Indians when Europeans arrived in 1500. There are now scarcely 140,000, and eighty-seven tribes have been obliterated. Their decimation is continuing.

In 1978 an eight-nation multilateral accord, the Amazon Pact, was reached to coordinate economic development of the immense Amazon basin. The network of 14,000 kilometers of highways being constructed includes the 5,000 kilometer Trans-Amazonian Highway bisecting more than half of the 171 tribal areas; the 4,000 kilometer Northern Perimeter Highway cutting through the homeland of the Yamomano tribe in Brazil and Venezuela; and the Santarem-Cuiaba Highway. These highways are opening up the area to multinational corporations like Westinghouse, General Motors, and the World Bank, exploiting the vast ore deposits of iron, aluminum, manganese, tin, and copper, and clearing millions of hectares of rain forest for grazing cattle to supply cheap beef to the United States. In the wake of the highways have come epidemics of measles, influenza, and venereal diseases brought by construction workers, decimating villages of the Yamomano and the Xingu in Mato Grosso. They have been accompanied by documented methods of genocide including massacre by armed forces, poison, germ warfare, and aerial dropping of napalm bombs. The National Indian Foundation of Brazil, FUNAI, asserting that "The Indian cannot be allowed to impede development," exercises the right to lease Indian lands for development.

Similarly in the Amazon basin in Colombia, the lands of its 70,000 Indians are being taken over by non-Indians.

In Paraguay, the preponderant population of Ache and Guarani Indians is denied the right to speak their own language, to sing their own songs, and to observe their religious rites.

Uraguay has been called the "torture chamber of South America" because of the military forces' persecution of the Indian population.

Half of the Andean population of 13.5 million people are Indians. In Peru the Agrarian Reform Law of 1969 prohibits their calling themselves "Indios." They must identify themselves as "Campesinos" or farmers.

Of Bolivia's population of five million, about four million are Indians suffering genocide and ethnocide under military dictatorship.

In Guatemala, it is estimated that only one percent of its six million population owns eighty percent of the land. The majority of the people are Indians, virtually slaves of the Ladino landholders, and whose average pay is about eighty cents a day.

In Chile the rights of its Mapucha Indians have suffered continuous repression and violation since the coup of the Military Junta in 1973.

And the continuing revolution in El Salvador is too well known for comment here.

There is no need to document these and other anti-Indian measures perpetuated by national governments backed by military aid from the United States and economic support from multinational corporations. They were presented by 125 Indian delegates during a Human Rights Conference in Geneva, Switzerland, in September 1977, held by Non-Governmental Organizations to hear documentation on "Discrimination Against the Indigenous Peoples of the Americas."

The Indian situation in the United States presents a confused picture of contrasts. On the negative side are the Indian substandard levels of life compared to other groups in the country. Indians have the highest infant-mortality rate, the highest school dropout rate, and the highest unemployment; and the lowest percapita income, and lowest life expectancy. Some steps have been taken to raise the levels of Indian housing, health, and education. Yet Congress has cut appropriations for recent Indian programs in health, education, social welfare, and economic development. Bills

192 | *Cuchama and Sacred Mountains*

have been introduced in the House of Representatives to abrogate all Indian treaties, to abrogate all general Indian jurisdiction, and to limit water rights on Indian land. The industrialization of some reservations is being accomplished by the federal government's leasing of lands for coal strip-mining, a highly publicized example being the "Rape of Black Mesa," sacred to the Navajos and Hopis. Lease of this Indian-owned land to private power interests was made by the Department of the Interior through the legal consent of the Tribal Councils of both tribes, but without the general knowledge of their people.

Most tribes consider these Tribal Councils as puppet local governing bodies under the strict control of the Bureau of Indian Affairs. The system is a major bone of contention. Resentment against it has given rise to the formation of the militant American Indian Movement, resulting in the occupation of Alcatraz in 1968, followed in 1972 by the AIM's "Trail of Broken Treaties" caravan to Washington, D.C. The latter began as a peaceful presentation of Indian rights to the federal government and ended in the demonstrators' forceful occupation of the BIA headquarters building. In 1973 occurred the bloody, tragic, and second confrontation at historic Wounded Knee, South Dakota. And this was followed in 1978 by the "Longest Walk" of Indian representatives from California to Washington, D.C., to present again their grievances to the Congress. These events, with many others, clearly indicate the still grievous imbalance between Indians and Whites.

On the positive side of the ledger, Congress in 1946 established the Indian Claims Commission, and millions of dollars have been awarded to many Indian tribes in reparation for lands unjustly taken from them. The Alaska Native Claims Settlement Act of 1971 provided for a cash settlement of $962.5 million to be paid over a period of years, plus forty million acres of federally owned land, to the Native Americans of Alaska. Another promising step was the establishment of an American Indian Policy Review Commission, which recommended among other things a complete restructuring of the controversial Bureau of Indian Affairs. Such legislative measures reflect the growing pride of Indians in their natural heritage, and their insistence on their sovereign rights. They also are accompanied by our own recent interest in Indian culture and religion after a century or more of neglect.

All these contradictions and contrasts indicate the still grievous imbalance between Indians and Whites throughout the Americas. Their conflict is rooted in their inherently different views of nature and man. It has resulted in the tragic dominance of materialistic Western civilization over naturalistic Indian society, to the detriment of both. The political, social, and economic balance between them cannot be fully restored until their ideological differences are reconciled on a deeper level.

This reconciliation will take a long time, but it will inexorably take place in compliance with the spiritual laws governing the evolution of all life throughout the universe. Then will be achieved not only the American Renaissance envisioned in the present book, but also the unity of the East and the West—that goal toward which Dr. Evans-Wentz devoted his life and his work.

ADDENDA

Editorial Commentary
by Charles L. Adams

Dr. Evans-Wentz included in his manuscript the following additional acknowledgments:

I am particularly indebted to certain of the authors and publishers whose books have been of special assistance, for the much appreciated permission to quote, in some instances rather copiously, from the books, as follows:

To Mr. John Collier, author of *The Indians of the Americas,* published by W. W. Norton and Company, New York, in 1947, and by The New American Library of World Literature, Inc., New York, in 1948;

To Random House, Inc., New York, publishers of the *History of the Conquest of Mexico* and *History of the Conquest of Peru,* published in 1847, by William H. Prescott, which has been of paramount importance;

To Mr. Paul Burlin, executor of the estate of Natalie Curtis Burlin, author of *The Indians' Book,* published in 1907, by Harper and Brothers, New York and London, which has been of unique value in the writing of our own book;

To Mrs. Elaine Gasdale Eastman, widow of Charles A. Eastman, Ohiyesa, author of *The Soul of the Indian,* published in 1911, by Houghton-Mifflin Company, Boston and New York, which was indispensable in our presentation of the religion of the Indian;

To Mr. Frank Waters for the unlimited use of his *Masked Gods,* published in 1950, by the University of New Mexico Press, Albuquerque [in 1968, by The Swallow Press, Chicago];

To Houghton-Mifflin Company, Boston, for permission to quote from E. R. Embree's *Indians of the Americas,* published in 1939;

To William Morrow and Company, Inc., New York, for permission to quote from *Black Elk Speaks,* by John G. Neihardt, in accordance with the copyright notice as it appears in the book, published in 1932;

To Alfred A. Knopf Incorporated, New York, for permission to quote from *Dancing Gods,* by Erna Fergusson, published in 1931;

To the California Book Company, Ltd., Berkeley, California, for permission to quote from A. L. Kroeber's *Handbook of the Indians of California,* published in 1953;

To the Smithsonian Institution, Bureau of American Ethnology, Washington, D.C., for permission to quote from Alice C. Fletcher's *The Hako: A Pawnee Ceremony,* 22nd Annual Report, Bureau of Ethnology, Part II (1904), page 335; and from John P. Harrington's *A New Original Version of Boscana's Historical Account of the San Juan Capistrano Indians of Southern California* (City of Washington, 1934), Smithsonian Miscellaneous Collection, Vol. 92, no. 4;

To Mrs. Ruth Verrill for permission to quote from *The Real Americans,* by her husband, the late Mr. A. Hyatt Verrill, and published in 1954 by G. P. Putnam's Sons, New York; and, also, for the assistance afforded by *The American Indian,* by the same author and published in 1927 by D. Appleton and Company, New York and London;

To D. G. Brinton's *Myths of the New World,* published in Philadelphia, in 1905, by what is now the David McKay Company, Inc., New York.

In the shaping of Part II, I am indebted:

To Dr. D. L. Phelps, of the West China Union University, for the inspiration afforded by his *Omei Illustrated Guide Book,* published at Changtu, Szechwan, in 1936, and for the quotations made therefrom;

To Dr. Ferdinand C. Lane for the geographical guidance of his *The Story of Mountains,* published by Doubleday and Company, Inc., at Garden City, N.Y., in 1950;

To T. R. Tsunoda, W. T. de Bary and D. Keene for aid rendered by their *Sources of Japanese Tradition,* in No. LIV of *Records of Civilization,* published by the Columbia University Press, New York, in 1958;

To A. S. Barnes and Company, Inc., New York, for permission to quote from *The Rhythm of the Redman,* by Julia M. Buttree, published in 1930.

Mention should also be made of those whose interest and support have made publication possible: Special gratitude is expressed to Patricia Palmer, Manuscript Librarian, The Stanford University Libraries, for continued "above-and-beyond-the-call-of-duty" performance; to Mr. Florian J. Shasky, Chief, Department of Special Collections, The Stanford University Libraries, who, perceiving the value of this manuscript and protecting it, played a large part in its ultimate publication; and a very special word of thanks to Mr. Robert P. Blanchard, whose volunteer contributions as unofficial "assistant editor" have constituted months of intellectual and moral support.

To these and to the countless others who have assisted, and especially to Frank Waters, my gratitude for this opportunity to work with greatness.